Game of My Life

SAN FRANCISCO 49ERS

MEMORABLE STORIES OF 49ERS FOOTBALL

Dennis Georgatos

SportsPublishingLLC.com

ISBN 13: 978-1-59670-118-2

Publishers: Peter L. Bannon and Joseph J. Bannon Sr.
Senior managing editor: Susan M. Moyer
Acquisitions editor: John Humenik
Developmental editor: Jennine Crucet
Art director: Dustin J. Hubbart
Dust jacket design: Joseph Brumleve
Interior design: Kathryn R. Holleman
Photo editor: Erin Linden-Levy

Sports Publishing L.L.C.
804 North Neil Street
Champaign, IL 61820
Phone: 1-877-424-2665
Fax: 217-363-2073
SportsPublishingLLC.com

Printed in the United States of America

Library of Congress Cataloging-in-Publication Data

Georgatos, Dennis.
  Game of my life. San Francisco 49ers : memorable stories of 49ers football
/ Dennis Georgatos.
     p. cm.
  ISBN 978-1-59670-118-2 (hard cover : alk. paper)
  1. San Francisco 49ers (Football team)--History. I. Title.

GV956.S3G44 2007
796.332'640979461--dc22
                              2007032785

THIS BOOK IS FOR MOM AND DAD

CONTENTS

INTRODUCTION

Stopping to smell the roses was something we never did in my 11 years with the San Francisco 49ers. Sure, we enjoyed and celebrated important regular season victories, playoff wins, and Super Bowl titles, but never for more than a fleeting moment, because it had been drilled into us that sitting on our laurels was no way to get another championship.

That drive, that hunger to always do our best and be our best, as players and as a team, was a trait instilled in us by Hall of Fame coach Bill Walsh. He was the force and inspiration behind the 49ers' rise to the top and our unrivaled 20-year run of success. And it was his relentless cajoling at practice and his high expectations for our team and us as individuals that brought out the best in all of us.

In *Game of My Life: San Francisco 49ers,* Dennis Georgatos gives players from throughout the team's history and Coach Walsh a chance to stop and reflect on pivotal moments in their careers.

For my teammate, linebacker Gary Plummer, it was a redeeming hit after missing a tackle. For my onetime roommate, Steve Young, who weathered intense scrutiny and criticism in trying to live up to Joe Montana's legacy, it was the exhilaration, relief, and calm that came in a Super Bowl triumph. For Bryant Young, it was his return from a horrific leg injury, and for Garrison Hearst, it was his transformation of a cloud-of-dust play into the longest run in team history. Coach Walsh recalls the drive that culminated in "The Catch," and quarterback John Brodie remembers coming off the bench in a rare relief appearance to pull out a crucial victory. Frank Gore, the "youngest" 49er (in the book anyway), details coming back from a concussion with a record-setting performance.

Those are a few of the stories. There are more. I've had the good fortune to see many of them from a unique perspective, watching the 49ers from afar as a fan and up close as a player.

I was born and raised in the San Francisco Bay Area, played football locally at the University of Santa Clara, and had the opportunity to play professionally for my hometown team.

John Brodie was the first 49er that I can remember. There was nothing like John dropping back and letting loose with a pass downfield to Gene Washington. When I was a teenager, my grandfathers would tell me about the good old days, when the 49ers played at Kezar Stadium and Joe "The Jet" Perry and R.C. "Alley Oop" Owens captivated the team's followers with their play.

It had sure seemed like a long time since the 49ers had been on top, and then all of the sudden, here came Dwight Hicks and his Hot Licks—the greatest group of young defensive backs in the history of the game, along with some guy named Joe, to spark the 49ers to a huge Super Bowl season in 1981. It was just amazing. Even more amazing to me was that six years later, I was in the huddle with many of those same Bay Area heroes. I consider myself a very lucky man to have played with some of the best players to ever put on a helmet.

It's hard for me to isolate on one most memorable story. The whole experience is something I treasure. But there were moments that stood out as being formative in my career, just like those moments related with passion, exuberance, and grace by my kinsmen in the pages of this book.

I became the starting tight end in my third season with the 49ers in 1989. About a month into the season, I learned an enduring lesson about the power of teamwork in the face of adversity. We were on the road in Philadelphia, under the gun from Buddy Ryan's "46" defense. We were confronted by a pass rush unlike any we had seen in terms of its ferocity. It seemed every time I went out on a pass route, I turned around to see Joe Montana on his back.

As bad as it was, we never let it get to where there was just a complete breakdown in our play. We stuck with the 49er way. We made adjustments. Joe began to beat their blitz, and the next thing you know, he threw fourth-quarter touchdown passes, starting with John Taylor's 70-yard catch-and-run. I ran a seam route, broke into the open in the middle of the field, and Joe hit me with a 24-yard scoring pass, his third of the quarter and the one that put us in front to stay. I sprinted into the end zone with the ball to the most pleasant sound that you can hear on the road—deafening silence!

Beyond the games, though, the relationships with teammates, coaches, staff, and of course, Eddie DeBartolo, are what mattered to me most. And what we all accomplished together will be branded in my mind forever.

I also know that my teammates and 49ers of the past and present would want me to relay how important our fans were to all of us. I'll never forget the roar of the 49er Faithful. It was magic, and that helped us all pull off our own brand of magic.

—BRENT JONES
DANVILLE, CALIFORNIA
JULY 24, 2007

Chapter 1

R.C. OWENS

Elgin Baylor can't say R.C. Owens wasn't looking out for him. In 1954-55, the two were friends and basketball teammates at the College of Idaho. Owens, a two-sport star, also played football at the school. Baylor wanted to do the same thing.

"One day, after the season, [Baylor] pulled me aside and said, 'R, I'm going to go out for the football team,'" Owens recalls. "I told him, 'That would be the worst mistake you ever made. You're the only one I know who can play and hang in the air like you do. Nobody else is doing that. Why play something you've never played before in your life?' He was just an amazing basketball player. No one at the time played basketball like him. He was ahead of his time."

Baylor never did go out for football. The 6-foot-5 forward heeded Owens' cautionary advice and continued his pursuit of basketball, transferring to Seattle University before taking his remarkable shooting and dazzling moves to the NBA. In 14 years with the Lakers in Minneapolis and Los Angeles, Baylor won rookie of the year honors, was named to the All-Star team 11 times, and was inducted into the Basketball Hall of Fame in 1977.

The 6-foot-3 Owens was a pretty good basketball player in his own right, using his tremendous leaping ability to average 20 points and 19.8 rebounds per game. His 2,142 career rebounds remains the record at the school, now known as Albertson College of Idaho. He even played a

1

season for the top amateur basketball team in the country at the time, the Buchan Bakers of Seattle.

But football was where Owens made his mark, though his basketball jumping and ball-handling skills inspired the "Alley Oop" plays that Owens and quarterback Y.A. Tittle made famous during their years with the 49ers.

Named a little All-America end during his career at College of Idaho, Owens was a 14th-round pick of the 49ers in 1956. Owens played A.A.U. basketball with the Bakers before committing to the 49ers the next summer. He arrived in training camp as a long shot to make a team already loaded at receiver with Clyde Conner, Gordy Soltau, Hugh McElhenny, and Billy Wilson all in the mix.

But Owens snagged three passes for 109 yards in an exhibition game against the Chicago Cardinals to cement a roster spot. He also foreshadowed his trademark leaping catch when he corralled a desperate pass from Tittle in the end zone by jumping over a gaggle of defenders for the ball.

"Back in the day, guys weren't jumping," Owens says. "I was blessed to be a jumper on the court. That's what gave me that leaping ability on the football field." Tittle sought out Owens after the game and thanked him for turning his high, wobbly pass into a touchdown. "I can do it every time," Owens gushed.

Though it would be a couple more weeks before their accidental connection would be refined and put into the 49ers playbook, the seeds for the "Alley-Oop" had been planted. And the bitter aftermath of the 49ers' season-opening loss to those same Chicago Cardinals two weeks later would bring them to fruition.

The Cardinals had come into the season opener all fired up after 49ers Coach Frankie Albert had said in the days leading up to the game that his team should beat the "weaker" Cardinals.

Instead, the Cardinals scored a 20-10 upset, and a chagrined Albert and his staff responded by leading the players through intensified practices before the next game against the 49ers' biggest rival, the Los Angeles Rams.

During the team's Tuesday workout at their Redwood City practice site, the 49ers offense stepped into the role of the Rams offense to help

R.C. Owens *San Francisco 49ers archives*

their defense prepare for the deep passing game favored by Los Angeles' quarterback Norm Van Brocklin.

But Y.A. Tittle didn't like throwing interceptions, even when he was simulating the opposing quarterback. So when the 49ers defensive backs blanketed the scout team receivers on the vertical routes, he'd throw the ball somewhere else.

Tittle's reluctance exasperated offensive assistant Red Hickey. "Look, how are we going to get any practice on those pass routes if you don't throw it?" Hickey told Tittle. "All I want you to do is get the ball downfield so they can have some feel for the pass routes."

Tittle reluctantly complied, lofting the ball downfield to a well-covered Owens, who jumped over two defenders to make the catch. "Gosh, darn," Tittle said.

They lined up for another play. Owens caught it again.

After connecting on a third consecutive downfield pass, Tittle piped up and said, "Hey, Coach, we ought to put that play in on Sunday."

Hickey and Albert, who had also witnessed Owens winning the "jump-ball" with 49ers defenders, agreed but also wondered what they should call the play.

In his 1960 book, *San Francisco 49ers*, the team's public relations director, Dan McGuire, said Hickey blurted out the suggestion that it be called the "Alley-Oop." Owens says he heard someone suggest "Alley-Oop" from a group that included Hickey, Albert, Tittle, and fellow quarterback John Brodie. But to this day, Owens says he's not sure which one came up with the name.

For the rest of the week, though, Tittle and Owens spent a few minutes a day practicing the high, arching pass and the leaping catch. Tittle began putting a "wobble" in his arching throws—at Owens' urging—because the receiver said that made them easier to catch.

Their collaboration would pay immediate dividends against the Rams, who were the foil in the 49ers' unveiling of the "Alley-Oop" before a sellout crowd of 59,637 at Kezar Stadium. Setting aside any embarrassment over fluttering his throws, Tittle went to the "blooper" pass to Owens twice. On both occasions, they resulted in touchdowns.

With less than a minute left before halftime, Tittle lofted the ball some 40 yards downfield to Owens, who outjumped Don Burroughs in the end zone for the score.

The Rams surged back in front 20-16 on Van Brocklin's 70-yard touchdown pass to Leon Clarke and a couple field goals, but the 49ers again turned to the Alley-Oop. With the 49ers at the Rams' 11 with little more than three minutes, Tittle told Owens to head for the goal line. "We'll go for the Alley-Oop," Tittle told him in the huddle.

Owens ran to the goal line and turned around in anticipation of Tittle's pass. Jesse Castete was right beside him, but Owens timed his leap perfectly and came up with another scoring catch that put the 49ers in front, and they hung on for their first win of the 1957 season.

It was a scene that would be repeated over the course of the season in a series of thrilling sequences. Tittle and Owens teamed up for the deciding scores in three of the team's eight regular-season wins (as part of a 12-game season).

And in terms of significance in the standings and their standing among their peers in the league, no game captured the drama and impact of the Alley-Oop like the 49ers' first meeting of the year with the Detroit Lions.

GAME OF MY LIFE
BY R.C. OWENS
NOVEMBER 3, 1957—SAN FRANCISCO, CALIFORNIA

We had plenty of cliffhangers in 1957 and there was tragedy that went with some of those last-second wins. About five people had heart attacks during the season watching us. One of them was our owner, Tony Morabito, who had a fatal heart attack the week before when we played Chicago at Kezar Stadium.

But there we were, a week later, with another game to play. And it was a big game at home, against a big rival, the Detroit Lions.

We were out to prove that, after seven years in the league without making it to the postseason, San Francisco was right there with the elite teams of the NFL. Since losing our opener, we had won four straight, including coming back to beat the Monsters of the Midway when Billy Wilson caught a last-second touchdown pass against the Bears.

We were trying to get a victory against Detroit so we could stay one game ahead of the Lions, but we knew it wasn't going to be easy.

The Lions had a great defensive team, especially in the secondary, where they had "Chris' Crew." That was Jack Christiansen, who would later become the 49ers coach, and Yale Larry, Jim David, and Gary Lowe. They had some monsters up front and great, great linebackers. Plus they had a great offensive team led by the great Bobby Layne and backed up by another great quarterback, Tobin Rote. Those guys were wonders, really wonders.

We spent the night before the game at the Villa Hotel in San Mateo. The next morning, on the bus on the way to the stadium, our coach, Frankie Albert, was giving us the pitch to beat them. What he said isn't printable, but we sure got his message.

By the time we walked into the locker room at Kezar, Chico Norton, our equipment manager, had all of our gear where it was supposed to be, neatly tucked in the lockers. We were putting on our uniforms, getting ready, and everybody had their ritual. Some guys, like Joe Perry, threw up before every game. Some guys had to go to a corner and sleep for a while. Everybody seemed to have that touch of football madness, if you will.

The next thing, we would be waiting for Visco Grgich. He'd been on the original 1946 49ers team. He was retired from playing, but every Sunday he'd come in, and he had this routine where he'd hit the locker room walls with a forearm smash. Frankie Albert would start talking about doing some ass-kicking. And Visco would say, "Darn right!"

Visco just had this ritual. He'd say, "We've got to go out today, guys, and we've got to take it to 'em." And then he'd say, "This is how you do it, like this." He'd move his shoulder in a blocking position and run up against the wall and hit it. Right into the wall. And recoil and hit it again. And again and again. "Until that sucker is on his knees," he'd tell us. Then Visco would say, "That's how you play football in the NFL. That's 49ers football."

We were all in awe of what he was doing. I would wonder, "Is something wrong with that guy?" He was hot. He was mad. And we were all fired up. Those moments were really meaningful to me.

Kickoff was at 1 p.m. and the stadium was sold out. It was a perfect sunny day. And there were the seagulls. When the teams were on one end, the seagulls were on the other, and when we were at midfield, they would be flying around us. They were watching a good game, I'll tell you that.

We had taken a 28-10 lead about a minute into the fourth quarter on a short touchdown run by Gene Babb. But then Tobin Rote got hot. He threw three touchdown passes—two of them after we committed turnovers—and with a little more than a minute left, the Lions took a 31-28 lead.

We got the ball back. Y.A. Tittle was talking in the huddle during the last drive. We were saying, "We can do it, Colonel." That was one of Y.A.'s nicknames. We'd tell him, "You've got to lead us to the Promised Land, Colonel."

Y.A. told us, "We're not here to lose this game." And then the last thing he'd say before breaking the huddle was to his center: "All right, put that ball in there."

We made a few plays and we had gotten to the Lions 41, but now there were only a few seconds left. It was second-and-2 and he called "West Four right," which was another name for our "Alley-Oop" play. Y.A. believed in it and I was comfortable making the jump to make the catch. The thing was, I was going to have to get down field.

I'd caught a couple of Alley-Oops earlier in the season and two guys were on me automatically. The corner, Jim David, was on me, and the safety, Jack Christiansen, was coming across the field to help.

I raced down the field and the three of us were all right there. Y.A. had let fly with a high arching pass. I went up on my left foot and turned my body toward the ball above those two guys. My elbows ended up above their shoulders, so they really couldn't get off the ground. I jumped up, like I was going in for a slam dunk in basketball, and came up with the catch with a few seconds to spare. Both defenders were at my feet when I came down with the ball in the end zone. They were both pounding the ground in frustration. I remember some of my teammates ran down to congratulate me. They circled me in the end zone. They were happy. I was happy. I've had some great moments in football, but that feeling at that moment in that game was unimaginable.

The win over Detroit left the 49ers at 5-1 with a one-game lead halfway through the season. They lost their next three, all on the road, but closed with three consecutive wins to tie Detroit for the Western Conference title. That forced a playoff, marking the 49ers' first postseason appearance since joining the National Football League in 1950.

Fittingly, the first postseason touchdown scored by the 49ers came on a 34-yard Alley-Oop pass from Tittle to Owens. By halftime, the 49ers extended their lead to 24-7, and on the first play of the second half, Hugh McElhenny broke loose for a 71-yard gain to Detroit's 9-yard line.

But the Lions' defense dug in and limited the 49ers to a field goal. The 49ers still led 27-7 but their hold on the Lions—and the game—started to crumble.

"We didn't want to blow it after having such a great year, but it just seemed like someone had the let the air out of our sails," Owens says. "It seemed like we were just going through the motions and we just were not making clean blocks and not catching or throwing the ball well. We just couldn't put it away."

After getting to their first NFL playoff with a series of last-minute comebacks, the 49ers fell victim to one when the Lions rallied for a 31-27 win. The Lions scored the game's final 24 points, denying the 49ers' bid to advance to their first NFL championship game. Thirteen years would pass before the 49ers returned to the postseason under Dick Nolan, who won three straight division titles from 1970-72.

Owens played four more years with the 49ers, becoming the first player in team history to surpass 1,000 yards receiving in 1961, his final season with the 49ers, when he caught a career-best 55 passes for 1,032 yards. He had played out his option that season—one of the first veteran free agents to do so—and moved to Baltimore, where he played for two years. He spent 1964, his final season, playing for the New York Giants.

Johnny Unitas was Owens' quarterback in Baltimore, but aside from a few "Alley-Oop" passes in practice for kicks, the Hall of Famer never threw the high, arching throws to his new wide receiver in a game.

Owens still managed to showcase his tremendous leaping ability. In 1962, Owens became the only player in NFL history to block a field goal from a standing jump under the goal post. At the time, the goal post was anchored in the center of the field squarely on the goal line. When Washington's Bob Khayat sent a line-drive attempt toward the goal post, Owens jumped up, and with his hand above the cross bar, swatted the kick away.

Owens said he actually got the idea to try to block field goals from a standing jump while he was with the 49ers. During a 1961 practice, the 49ers' kicker, Tommy Davis, asked Owens to shag some balls for him.

"I'd stand there in front of the goal post, chase the balls down for him and throw them back," Owens said. "One of his kicks was a line drive and I jumped up and knocked it down."

Offensive assistant Red Hickey happened to be nearby and saw Owens block the field goal. "Hey, R.C., I'm going to put you in a game to do that," Hickey told Owens.

Owens said he twice retreated to the goal line in games that season for the 49ers to try to knock down field goal tries, but both attempts sailed wide and there was no need to try to swat them. But when he got to Baltimore, Owens demonstrated his field-goal blocking ability for Colts coach Weeb Eubank, who began sending him in if the field goal attempt was 40 yards or longer.

When he knocked down Khayat's attempt, Owens chased down the live ball and headed up field. "The stadium was going wild," Owens said. "I advanced it as far as I could. There was a guy chasing me—Big Ben Davidson. He and another guy brought me down along the sideline."

Don't look for Owens' field-goal blocking feat to be repeated; NFL rules no longer allow it. "A couple years later, the NFL moved the goal post from the goal line to the back of the end zone and you really couldn't block them anymore because you weren't allowed to stand in the end zone," said Owens, who still has the ball from his block.

During Owens' final season of play in New York, he was reunited with Y.A. Tittle, who had been dealt to the Giants by the 49ers in 1961. And he was on the field for the searing hit on Tittle by Pittsburgh's John Baker. The devastating hit was frozen in time by a photograph showing a helmetless, shaken Tittle on his knees, with a trickle of blood coming from his ear.

"I could see it all the way," said Owens, who had turned around after running 20 yards downfield on his pass route. "I could see Lane Howell using the 'lookout block.' He whiffed and then it was, 'LOOKOUT!'

"It was like somebody being hit with a crow bar across his neck. He slumped down to both knees. No players on the field had moved. They were all in shock. I circled right on back. I was saying 'Colonel, are you all right?' He was bleeding and he was telling me he was all right. But I knew we had to get the trainers out there. He was still on his knees, so you knew he was in shock. He was really clobbered. He didn't even remember I was out there. Years later, he realized I was there when I showed him a picture. He sent me a note with words to the effect of 'Thanks for being there.'"

Tittle and Owens went out together, both retiring after the 1964 season. Tittle returned to the San Francisco Bay area to run his insurance agency. Owens, a native of Shreveport, Louisiana, who was raised in Santa Monica, began working full time as a national public relations representative for the J.C. Penney Company. He also spent time working for the Department of Health, Education, and Welfare as a contract compliance officer.

But Owens longed for a return to football, and in 1979, newly hired 49ers coach Bill Walsh re-opened the door to the game when he brought him in as assistant director of training camp. Owens ran the team's training camp for years. Later, Owens also worked as Walsh's administrative assistant and became the 49ers' alumni coordinator.

Relations between the team and its former players had been just about broken by the bitter reign of Joe Thomas. The first general manager hired by the DeBartolo family after their 1977 purchase of the club, Thomas threw out game books, photographs, and other memorabilia in an overzealous and misguided attempt to make a clean break from the 49ers' past failures. His actions infuriated and alienated alumni players and staff. Some employees literally pulled pictures and other mementos from the trash in a bid to save pieces of 49ers history.

Walsh, a student of the game who cherished the 49ers' history and the players who forged it, put Owens in charge of patching up the team's relationship with its former players and helping to restore its links to the past.

"That was a real focal point for me from the beginning because every team has a lot of history," said Owens. "We've had great coaches. We've had so many outstanding players and administrators and owners that helped this organization become what it is. I just thought it was so important to recognize that and carry it on."

In his 22 years as alumni coordinator, former players became vital parts of the team's community outreach programs. He organized numerous picnics, dinners, and trips for former players, and the 49ers became the first team to have an annual alumni day where former players were re-introduced to fans during halftime of a particular game. Just as Owens' accomplishments on the field left a lasting impact, so did his work in fostering the team's ties to its own history.

When Owens retired in 2001, he recalled a conversation he had with Walsh 20 years earlier. Both talked about finding a way to pay tribute to the team's long-serving players and award winners at the club's Santa Clara headquarters. The team's equipment manager, Chico Norton, who passed away in 1995, had overheard them. Norton told them that in defiance of Thomas' "throw-out-the-past" edict, he had secretly retrieved dozens of pictures and plaques from the trash and saved them at home.

"A lot of those pictures that we have on the 10-year wall and for Len Eshmont winners, they were in a garbage bin at Redwood City," Owens said. "There were other things that didn't get recovered, but at least those pictures are on display.

"Bill's vision was we needed alumni support and we were going to make those guys feel they helped build the future of the 49ers. And seeing that whole marriage between the players and the organization evolving again, that was sweet."

Chapter 2

JOE PERRY

Hall of Fame fullback Joe Perry always played with uncommon speed and power. John Woudenberg, a 49ers tackle, saw those qualities early on while moonlighting as an assistant coach for the Hellcats, a military service team attached to Naval Air Station Alameda, located across the bay from San Francisco.

Perry was finishing out his World War II-era Navy enlistment in 1947, splitting time between helping to maintain warships and starring on a service team that wreaked havoc with the local college junior varsity squads, including those from Stanford and Cal.

At 6-foot-0, 210 pounds, Perry had a sprinter's speed but ran with the finesse of a battering ram. There were times he was simply unstoppable.

"I was more power than evasive, but I had quite a bit of evasiveness that people didn't consider," said Perry, whose 9,723 career rushing yards were second only to fellow Hall of Famer Jim Brown when he retired in 1963. "I could move to the side to sidestep you before you realized anything. I never depended on power all the time, but I utilized the power I had. I had a lot of drive in my legs and I could run over people. I don't think they thought I could. I looked small but I ran big and I fooled a lot of guys."

Woudenberg wasn't fooled. Indeed, he was so impressed that he urged 49ers owner Anthony Morabito to come see Perry play and to consider signing him. Perry didn't disappoint.

As Morabito watched a Hellcats game, Perry carried the ball four times. He scored a touchdown each time, and his shortest run of the day was 55 yards. Morabito could barely contain himself, but just to be sure, he scouted Perry one more time. He returned a week later and watched as Perry nearly duplicated the effort from the week before.

Afterward, Morabito introduced himself to Perry and told him he wanted him to play for the 49ers, then members of the All-America Football Conference, which would be merged into the NFL in 1950.

Perry was torn at first. He still harbored ambitions of becoming an electrical engineer, and with his Navy enlistment almost up, the universities of Oregon, Washington, and Nevada, as well as Columbia of the Ivy League, had offered him scholarships.

But he also had a wife and young child to consider, and pro football offered a way to provide for them. The more Perry spoke with Morabito about his future, his playing potential, and what the game could offer him as a livelihood, the better they got along. In the end, the decision was easy for Perry. He concluded Morabito was the kind of person he wanted to work for and at least he could start making some money right away to start taking care of his growing family. The two sealed the deal with a handshake.

"That's how I started playing for the 49ers, with a handshake, not a contract," Perry said. "That's the way we did it for nine years." It was emblematic of the strong and very close relationship that developed between Morabito and Perry, who was the first black player to play for the 49ers.

Integration of American professional sports was still in its infancy when Perry joined the 49ers in 1948. Jackie Robinson broke major league baseball's color line the year before when he was signed by the Brooklyn Dodgers. Two other former UCLA players, running back Kenny Washington and split end Woody Strode, became the first black players in the NFL's modern era when they were signed by the Los Angeles Rams in 1946. In that same year, the Cleveland Browns of the All-America Conference signed guard Bill Willis and running back Marion Motley.

Though Perry was generally welcomed by his 49ers teammates, Morabito was keenly aware of the abuse he could face as part of the vanguard of black players breaking down color barriers throughout

Joe Perry *San Francisco 49ers archives*

sports. The 49ers owner told Perry he had to be stoic in dealing with what came his way.

"Not only are you going to get it physically out on the field, but you're going to hear language that you're not going to care for," said Morabito, according to Perry's recollection. "But you know, you're going to have to ride with it. You're going to have to bite the bullet."

Perry told Morabito he would abide by his wishes. "I've been called everything but a child of God," Perry said he told Morabito. "But you can't hurt me by calling me a name. You just make me come back at you that much harder.

"That's what used to happen all the time in games," added Perry. "A guy would say, 'You'd better not come back through here, you n-----!' I said, 'I'll be right back,' and I'd come back that much harder. That's the way I played. That's how I dealt with it. For years it went that way and we never had a problem. But a season never went by without hearing racial slurs tossed my way. I could care less what you called me. But you had to put the leather on me to stop me."

That was evident from the first game that Perry, who was nicknamed "The Jet" for the explosive burst out of his stance, ever played with the 49ers.

The 49ers opened the 1948 season against the Buffalo Bills. Their owner, Jim Breuil, had been critical of Morabito for signing a black player. He renewed his criticism as they watched the game together, saying Morabito's hiring of Perry "makes it tough on all of us who don't sign a Negro."

"Why did you do it, Tony?" Breuil asked.

About that time, quarterback Frankie Albert tossed the ball to Perry on a pitchout and the bruising speedster took it 58 yards for a touchdown on his first play as a 49er.

"That's why," Morabito told Breuil as Perry went the distance.

"It was a 38-pitch off a 34-trap fake," said Perry. "They just had no idea the speed I had, and I went for a touchdown the first time I touched the ball in pro football. From there, it just kind of blossomed."

Perry averaged 7.1 yards per carry, scored 18 rushing touchdowns, and ran for 1,379 yards in his two seasons with the 49ers while they were in the All-America Football Conference.

He rushed for 1,018 yards in 1953, becoming the first 49er to achieve that milestone. He was the leading figure in the first season of the

"Million Dollar Backfield," coming back in 1954 to run for 1,049. It was the first time a player had successive 1,000-yard rushing seasons in NFL history.

Perry, John Henry Johnson, Hugh McElhenny, and quarterback Y.A. Tittle made up the flashy foursome, considered by some to be the greatest backfield ever put together. They were known for their sensational and productive play, though that did not necessarily translate to team success. The 49ers had only one winning season while the "Million Dollar Backfield" was intact, going 7-4-1 in 1954. The star-studded backfield unit was broken up after the 1956 season with the trade of Johnson to the Detroit Lions.

A year later, the 49ers drove toward their first NFL postseason appearance, fueled by four victories early in the season that relied on last-ditch scores.

The third game in that sequence of cliffhangers was against the Chicago Bears at Kezar Stadium. The 49ers beat the Bears at Chicago two weeks earlier when Y.A. Tittle threw a late scoring pass to R.C. Owens, who caught the ball on his knees after being cut down by Bears defenders.

Team owner Anthony Morabito watched the rematch with the Bears at Kezar Stadium from his guest box with his wife, Josephine, and brother, co-owner Vic Morabito. During the second quarter, he was stricken by a massive heart attack just after the 49ers had pulled to 14-7 and kicked off to the Bears. Doctors began tending to him almost immediately and Father Bill McGuire, who was also at the game, was summoned to Morabito's side to give him final absolution.

"Thank you, Father," Morabito said, uttering his last words.

Morabito suffered a heart attack five years earlier and doctors advised him then to sell the team to lessen the pressures that came with involvement in such a roller-coaster enterprise. But Morabito wouldn't think of getting out of the football business.

"What the hell," he once said, "If I'm going to die, I might as well die at a football game."

Morabito's unwavering passion for the game was one of the qualities that endeared him to his players and engendered their strong feelings for him in return.

When word swept through the 49ers sideline that Morabito had suffered a heart attack, the concern among the players was palpable. The concern turned to grief midway through the third quarter when team physician Dr. Bill O'Grady brought word back that Morabito had been pronounced dead at the hospital.

"There was a moment of stunned silence, then the bench became a madhouse of crying, shouting players," wrote Dan McGuire in his book *San Francisco 49ers*, which detailed the team's first 12 years.

Perry, too, was shaken by the loss of Morabito. His first thought was to get in the game as a tribute to Morabito. Knee problems had limited his playing time during the first month of the season and Gene Babb started in his place against the Bears. But Perry approached coach Frankie Albert on the sideline and pleaded with him to let him play.

Perry doesn't remember whether he got a yes or no from Albert. All he knows is he got in the game when he had to, and he looks back on his four-carry effort as the most meaningful of his career.

GAME OF MY LIFE
BY JOE PERRY
OCTOBER 27, 1957—SAN FRANCISCO, CALIFORNIA

We always seemed to have trouble with the Chicago Bears, and the way the game started, it seemed like it would be no different because we were down 14-0 in the first quarter. We were playing like a bunch of deadbeats. They were just kicking the hell out of us.

Finally, we started to get on track a little bit. We got a drive going and we scored a touchdown.

All of a sudden, some of the players standing on the sideline noticed a commotion around Tony's guest box. We weren't sure what was going on until Coach Albert told us at halftime that Tony had been stricken by a heart attack and things looked grim. There was almost complete silence in the locker room.

Sometime in the third quarter, we got word on the sideline that Tony had died. It was like someone just told me that my father had died. That's how close we were. It was like a father-son relationship.

But our whole team was affected. Tony loved all his players and his players loved him back. With Tony, I never even drew up a contract. I signed a blank one and he filled out the rest. I never knew what I was making until I got my paycheck. I never even worried about it, and the reason I didn't worry about it was the kind of guy he was. He looked you right in the eye when he talked to you. He was honest, and he was fair.

That season, I'd been struggling with injuries. I really hadn't been playing that much. But we were all caught up in an emotional wave when we learned Tony had died. There was a lot of crying on the sideline and a lot of headshaking, just disbelief, shock.

But there was also kind of a groundswell of emotion among all of us to just win the game, win the game for Tony. At that point, there were really only two things we could do for Tony: pray for him and play for him.

I wanted to go play for Tony, too, so I pleaded with the coach, Frankie Albert, to let me go in. I think Frankie knew nothing was going to stop me, not him and certainly not any aches and pains in my legs. I still don't know whether Frankie put me back on the field or not, but I played pretty much the rest of the game.

We pulled to within 17-14 when Bill Herchman, one of our defensive tackles, returned an interception for a touchdown. Our other tackle, Leo Nomellini, who was on the field crying as he played, had broken through on a pass rush and forced an errant throw by Brown that Herchman was there to swipe.

Another interception, this one by Dickie Moegle, set us up for the go-ahead score. I had my longest run of the day on that drive, an 8-yarder, and Y.A. Tittle finished off the drive off with an 11-yard touchdown pass to Billy Wilson to put us in front.

We had to hold on for the win, though. The Bears mounted one more threat, but Moegle turned them away with a goal-line interception. It was his third interception of the day, and we ran out the clock for the victory.

I had other games where I ran for a lot more yards. There were other seasons where we won more games and maybe reached more goals, both as an individual and as a team. But for me, this is the game I look back on the most, because it reminds me of my friend who just happened to be my boss.

I loved him and I have no qualms about saying that. We did a lot of things together. We were pals who could talk about anything. There were never any secrets between us. That's the way it went between us. Honestly, I never knew any player, or really anybody, who was that close to an owner. I mean, owners just didn't chum around with the players. But here's a black ballplayer and a white Italian-American owner and we were out and about, on the town like two peas in a pod. The day we met, the first thing he told me was, "Don't call me Mr. Morabito. Call me Tony." I said, "OK." From then on we were inseparable, until the day he had that fatal heart attack. Things like that aren't supposed to happen, but they did, and my life was never the same. I think I was the luckiest S.O.B in the world. Either that, or somebody up above was looking down on me.

Anthony Morabito, the lumberman turned founding owner of the 49ers, was 47 when he died. He was responsible for bringing San Francisco its first major professional sports franchise and the 49ers today remain a thriving NFL team.

Perry played three more years with the 49ers before being traded to the Baltimore Colts after a falling out with then coach Red Hickey. He returned to the 49ers to play his final season in 1963 at the urging of Vic Morabito, who convinced Perry he should finish his career where he started.

He played 16 seasons of professional football, the most ever by a running back. Marcus Allen is the only other running back to play pro football that long, playing 16 NFL seasons to match Perry's feat.

Perry's links to the Morabito family remained strong throughout his life. His loyalty to the family was the principal reason he turned down an offer to join the Pittsburgh Steelers in favor of returning to the 49ers. When he was inducted into the Pro Football Hall of Fame in Canton, Ohio, in 1969, Tony Morabito's widow and former 49ers owner Josephine Morabito presented him. And hanging in the den of his Arizona home is a portrait of Anthony Morabito that he acquired soon after the 49ers owner died.

"Wherever I've been, that painting has always gone with me," Perry said. "You've got to understand that Tony and I were like father and son from the get-go. But that's the way he treated all his players.

"If anyone degraded his players, it was like they were degrading his family. Those were fighting words for him. And that's why we gave our all for him."

Chapter 3

DICK MOEGLE

While running free down the sideline with the end zone in sight, the biggest concern that raced through Rice University halfback Dick Moegle's mind was keeping his distance from the sideline.

"I wanted to be doggone sure I didn't kick up any chalk and get called for stepping out of bounds, because no one was going to catch me," Moegle said. "I was being sure to stay two or three feet away from the sideline."

Not far enough, though, to steer clear of one of the strangest, craziest, and most unexpected moments in college football history.

Moegle, later to become a first-round draft choice of the 49ers, was flying down the field toward a certain touchdown that would extend underdog Rice's lead over mighty Alabama in the 1954 Cotton Bowl. He had taken the handoff at the 5-yard line, swept around right end, and sprinted past Alabama defenders that included safety and quarterback Bart Starr.

As he approached midfield, Moegle looked over his shoulder and saw a lone Alabama player trying to close on him but not really gaining ground.

The danger, it turned out, was gathering steam right in front of him. But Moegle didn't see Alabama fullback Tommy Lewis come charging off the bench—without his helmet—until the last moment.

"I just caught sight of this guy crouching down and I remember thinking, 'Why is he coming out on the field now to get his head gear?'"

Moegle said. "It was only at the last instant that I realized he was going after me. I was able to take only one step to my left to try to avoid him but he squared up and really cracked me a good one with a cross-body block tackle, and down I went."

Moegle wasn't the only one shocked by the out-of-nowhere tackle. It stunned a Cotton Bowl crowd of 75,000, along with millions of television viewers.

Lewis, too, was mortified over his own actions. Moegle says Lewis apologized to him on the spot and again at halftime.

"I had gotten up quickly and was jogging off the field," Moegle recalled. "He comes up and puts his arm around me and he's crying, 'I'm so sorry, man. I don't know what the heck got into me.' Then he got into the dressing room and apologized again, to me and to the team. All I know is you had to be pretty goofy to do something like that."

Lewis knocked Moegle down at around the Alabama 40-yard line. Referee Cliff Shaw ruled Moegle would have scored but for the illegal hit, and awarded him a 95-yard touchdown run.

The score was the longest of three touchdown runs that Moegle, a 19-year-old junior, had as part of a Cotton Bowl-record 265-yard rushing performance. His effort powered Rice's 28-6 Cotton Bowl victory and raised his profile with pro scouts heading into his senior season.

He finished his college career with a flourish, ranking fourth in the country with 905 yards rushing. He averaged 6.2 yards per carry and showed his versatility by leading the nation in punt returns with 15 for 293 yards, including a 91-yarder in his final game against Baylor.

Also a standout defensive back, Moegle had three interceptions in a 1953 game against Baylor, tying him with seven others for the school record. He solidified his defensive credentials at the Hula Bowl in Honolulu, when he shut down Los Angeles Rams wide receiver Elroy "Crazy Legs" Hirsch in a game pitting college all-stars against a collection of pros.

"He didn't catch a pass on me," Moegle said. "They put that out on AP, and I remember people were saying, 'Who is this guy?'"

The 49ers decided to find out the answer to that question for themselves. They used their first-round pick on Moegle, making him the 10th player selected overall in the 1955 NFL draft.

Dick Moegle finished his career with the Dallas Cowboys after playing from 1955-59 for the 49ers. *Photo courtesy of the Dallas Cowboys*

Moegle's ability to play different positions gave the 49ers some flexibility in determining his role with the team. At the time, the 49ers already had the "Million Dollar Backfield," made up of quarterback Y.A. Tittle, fullback Joe Perry, and running backs John Henry Johnson and Hugh McElhenny, all of whom ended up in the Hall of Fame.

But they were also a team in transition. Buck Shaw, the 49ers coach for the first nine years of the team's existence, had been fired by owner Anthony Morabito. Morabito believed one of the reasons a championship had eluded the 49ers was Shaw's easy-going manner with players, and he decided to replace him with Red Strader, who was known as a strict disciplinarian.

Moegle says he sensed the change left many of the veteran players demoralized. But he concerned himself with finding his niche and with gaining the respect of his teammates with his play.

The 49ers told Moegle they expected him to spend most of his time in the secondary, but he should also be ready play as a running back and a return man.

"When I got drafted, they said, 'Do you care where we play you?'" Moegle said. "'We're not doing good defensively. We need a good strong safety.' I said, 'It doesn't make any difference to me. If you pay me, I'll play it.'"

Against the Detroit Lions a month into his first season, he had a chance to do a little bit of everything for the 49ers. At the time, the Lions were one of the NFL's elite teams. They were coming off a Western Conference championship and had won the league championship in 1953.

Though the start of the game included one of his lowest moments as a rookie, Moegle bounced back to contribute in a big way on offense, defense, and special teams, enough to look back on his performance as the game of his life.

GAME OF MY LIFE
BY DICK MOEGLE
OCTOBER 16, 1955—DETROIT, MICHIGAN

This might sound real funny, but I was kind of the Deion Sanders of my day. I could play anywhere—offense, defense, and special teams. And I did a little bit of everything, just like him.

That's kind of what I was doing for the 49ers. I was the safetyman for kickoffs and sometimes for punts. I played defensive back, and with Hugh McElhenny fighting a foot injury for much of the 1955 season, I was getting time at halfback as well.

We were in the middle of an Eastern road swing. We flew around on propeller planes. We'd be away from home for three weeks sometimes. We'd play at Chicago or Detroit and then swing over to play at Green Bay. With the weather, it could get pretty brutal. That was a tough gig, winning on the road, I'll tell you.

No place was tougher than Detroit. That was a tough team and they had a tough crowd behind them. People threw bottles out of the stands at visiting teams and booed them to high heaven. It was a rough atmosphere.

Coming in to play Detroit, we had lost two of our first three games, but we were coming off a win at Chicago. The Lions were a terrific team. They had Bobby Layne at quarterback and Doak Walker at running back. Walker was a Heisman Trophy winner, a fellow Texan, and a friend, someone I looked up to. Layne was an All-American. The year before, they had helped the Lions to the conference championship after taking them to an NFL title in 1953.

It was overcast and pretty cool, but not real cold, on game day. There were rain showers right up to the kickoff. We were playing on a combination football-baseball field. It was hard. It was not a great field at all. But back then, none of them were.

We won the pregame coin toss and elected to receive. I went back to receive the opening kickoff. I caught the ball and started running to get behind the wedge. One of the linemen got hit and knocked back into me. At the same time, I got hit by a Detroit player and the ball squirted up in the air. It got kicked around for a while but the Lions recovered it at our 15-yard line. They needed only a few plays to go in for the touchdown. I felt terrible and it seemed like everyone was looking at me. I could feel my teammates' eyes on me. I could see them thinking, "Yeah, rookie, All-America, huh. No. 1 draft choice, huh." They were probably thinking they got a real dud in me. So the Lions kicked off to me again. I ran up behind the wedge, saw an opening to my right, and went down the sideline in front of the benches for both teams—they were on the same side—and my friend, Doak Walker, finally knocked me out of bounds. I'd gone 61 yards down to the Detroit 31-yard line.

We fumbled the ball back to Detroit, but I felt like I'd done something right at least.

A little while later, the Lions started a drive and Layne passed to Dorne Dibble. I cut in front of him and intercepted it, took it back a few yards, and suddenly we were sitting on the Lions' 27-yard line. Gordy Soltau came on to try a field goal but it was blocked. At least we had stopped one of their drives, though.

Still, by late in the third quarter, Detroit had scored its third touchdown and we were down 24-6.

I got loose on the kickoff return and went to midfield. A couple plays later, I was playing offense and caught a 25-yard pass to the Lions' 10. After a couple of incompletions, we tried running it in, and I was able to turn the corner on a sweep and squeeze into the end zone for a touchdown.

On the very next series, my fellow safety, Rex Berry, intercepted Detroit backup quarterback Harry Gilmer's pass and returned it 44 yards for a touchdown, pulling us to within 24-20.

We stopped the Lions and put one more drive together and we scored from the 5-yard line on a broken play on fourth down. Y.A. Tittle fumbled the snap but managed to pick it up. With three guys hanging on him, he pitched it to Joe Perry, and Perry scooted around left end for the touchdown that put us on top.

Detroit got the ball one more time, but we made sure they didn't go anywhere.

That game was a doozy, very exciting. I was in awe of the whole thing. I consider it the best game I ever played as a pro. Because after a bad start, I did everything I could do and I did it right, and we ended up beating a championship-caliber team. It said a lot about us as a team, and it told me a lot about myself and the things I was capable of as a player. When I got in a pinch or found myself in a tough spot in a game, I could always look back on that Detroit game and draw strength from knowing I'd worked my way out of a pickle before.

Moegle came out of that game with 251 all-purpose yards, putting up numbers in four different categories topped by 150 yards on five kick returns. He also caught two passes for 78 yards, rushed four times for 16 yards and a touchdown, and had seven yards on his interception return.

He finished his rookie season as the 49ers' leader in interceptions (6), yards per rush (5.73), rushing touchdowns (5), and kickoff return average (24.90).

"When I think about it, that was a pretty doggone big feather to have in your cap," Moegle said.

Moegle went on to become the first 49ers player to lead the team in interceptions in three consecutive seasons, totaling 20 interceptions in that span. And he played a major role in one of the 49ers' most dramatic victories in 1957 when they came back to beat the Chicago Bears after learning owner Anthony Morabito had collapsed and died of a heart attack while watching the game at Kezar Stadium.

Moegle matched a team record with a career-high three interceptions against the Bears. He returned the second 40 yards to set up the go-ahead touchdown. His third interception was a goal-line theft in the final seconds, preserving a victory that helped the 49ers reach the postseason for the first time since joining the NFL in 1950.

In 1958, Moegle suffered a knee injury in the fourth game and missed the rest of the season. When Moegle came back in 1959, he had a new coach, Red Hickey, who was hired in place of Frankie Albert.

But Moegle and Hickey didn't get along, and before the 1960 season, Moegle asked team owner Vic Morabito to trade him. Morabito obliged, sending Moegle to Pittsburgh in exchange for the Steelers' No. 1 draft pick in 1961. The 49ers used the selection to draft cornerback Jimmy Johnson, who was inducted into the pro football Hall of Fame after his standout 16-year career with the 49ers.

Moegle was miserable in Pittsburgh and played just one season for the Steelers.

"It was the worst experience of my life," he said. "The year I was there they had the worst winter in 30 years. It was so cold. I got strep throat. Nothing against the city of Pittsburgh, but I was miserable."

Dallas coach Tom Landry acquired Moegle as a player-coach in a trade with Pittsburgh before the start of the 1961 season. Midway through the season, Moegle broke a bone in his foot. He got through the last eight games by taking pain-killing injections in the foot.

"The needle looked like a pencil. They had to hold me down while they shot that thing in there," Moegle said. "After the season, in February, they operated. They cut my foot open from the toe to the middle of the foot and I was on the mend again."

Moegle went back to training camp with the Cowboys but sensed his football playing days were coming to a close.

"My foot was still bad," he said. "I could run but I just couldn't run good enough. I told Coach Landry, 'That's it for me, Tom. I can't do it any more. I'm going home.'"

After his playing days, Moegle settled in Houston with his family. He worked as a football broadcaster and ran two hotels for more than 30 years.

And his football career seems to have come full circle, because to this day he continues to be asked about his Cotton Bowl encounter with Alabama's "12th man" tackler.

"Pretty much every day since it happened more than 50 years ago, somebody has asked me about it," Moegle said.

The Alabama fullback, Tommy Lewis, who barreled into Moegle as he sprinted toward a touchdown for Rice University in the Cotton Bowl, is filled with regret over the episode.

"If I could take anything back in my life," Lewis told Don Wade in the book *Always Alabama*, "…it would be that play because it just won't ever go away."

Not for Lewis, and not for Moegle.

"It's something I'll probably always be dealing with," Moegle said.

Chapter 4

GORDY SOLTAU

Gordy Soltau laid the foundation for his career with the 49ers as a youth in Duluth, Minnesota, passionately pursuing an eclectic mix of sports. It was almost as if Soltau was trying to cram every conceivable experience in as many sports as he could. With his neighborhood friends, he played sandlot football on the shores of Lake Superior. He played baseball, basketball, and ice hockey, and also went skiing. He couldn't seem to get enough of sports. At Duluth Central High School, he starred in basketball, track and field, and skiing in addition to football.

But it was far from just fun and games for Soltau. He came of age in the midst of World War II. "I was a senior in high school and the war had been going on for a couple years," Soltau said. "As soon as we graduated, we had to go into the service."

Soltau enlisted in the Navy in June 1943 and gravitated toward a still emerging military specialty dealing with underwater demolition. He became part of the Navy's first class of "Frogmen," and was later detailed, along with some other divers, to the Office of Strategic Services, or OSS, the forerunner of the CIA.

"We trained in Florida at Ft. Pierce and went to California to train at Camp Pendleton," Soltau said, recalling some of the training swims were up to five miles long. "Then they sent a bunch of us to get ready for the invasion of Europe, but the mission was called off right at the last minute," Soltau said.

Soltau was part of an eight-man unit that had planned to sabotage German submarine pens on the west coast of Nazi-occupied France in conjunction with D-Day. They had spent six months in England training for the mission on a river that had some similar geographic points as their target.

The German submarines, or U-boats, had been wreaking havoc on Allied shipping, and their base in France was so well situated and so strongly constructed that aerial bombardment had been ineffective. The OSS hoped to have its underwater demolition crew attach timed explosives as the German submarines were returning to their base and then detonate the explosives after the U-boats docked inside their pen.

"We had it pretty well worked out," Soltau said. "We had all trained hard and we were prepared to go in there and blow it up."

Apparently, concerns about the ability to pack enough explosives to significantly damage the pens figured in the decision to scrub the mission. The operation also had the aura of a suicide mission because there was no specific plan for the men's escape.

"It was a very risky program to start with and there was no plan to get us out," Soltau said. "We would be on our own in France once we completed the mission and hopefully, D-Day operations would take care of the Germans. We were a little dubious of that. Fortunately for us, it never happened."

Instead, Soltau said, he and the others in his unit were sent to Nassau, in the Bahamas, for additional training before heading to the China-Burma-India theater to join the fight against the Japanese.

They were headquartered in Ceylon for nearly a year and conducted sabotage and rescue operations up and down the Malaysian peninsula, getting around on a British frigate and going ashore on motor-driven rafts. Much of their work involved checking the welfare of OSS radio operators who were behind enemy lines gathering intelligence on the movement of Japanese warships and troops.

"They were involved in very risky business because the Japanese were everywhere," Soltau said. "Some got caught and were never heard from again. We did manage to get some of them out without injury, and in the process, knocked out some Japanese outposts. But we were very lucky, very fortunate. At times, we got shot at a lot, but we never got captured."

Gordy Soltau *San Francisco 49ers archives*

Through it all, though, football wasn't totally out of the picture for Soltau. One of his superiors, Jim Camp, had played in college and a couple years in the pro ranks.

"I used to bug him all the time about playing football at a higher level," Soltau said. "I thought about it a lot while I was in the service, and one of the things in my favor in returning to football after a long absence was the kind of work we were doing. It required we stay in top shape."

After the war ended, Soltau went home and like so many other veterans, resumed his education. Soltau enrolled at the University of Minnesota and, just as he did in high school, took up a range of sports. He tried out for the football team and went on from there to play everything from basketball and ice hockey in the winter to baseball in the spring.

Though he became a highly regarded pitcher, it was football where Soltau showed the greatest promise. He played four years in college under coach Bernie Bierman, developing into a reliable place-kicker, a hard-hitter on defense and special teams, and a shifty, sure-handed receiver. Soltau's teammates included defensive tackle Leo Nomellini, who went on to a Hall of Fame career with the 49ers, and Bud Grant, a fellow wide receiver who went on to become coach of the Minnesota Vikings, taking them to four Super Bowls.

Both Soltau and Grant became all-conference selections. Soltau played in the Hula Bowl, the East-West Shrine game, and for the College All-Stars team that beat the NFL champion Philadelphia Eagles 17-7 in a 1950 exhibition.

The Green Bay Packers had made Soltau their third-round pick in that same year. But it proved to be only a starting point for Soltau in his NFL career, and a short one at that.

"We had played the All-Star game at Soldier Field in Chicago," Soltau said. "I spent a couple more days there, packed up my things in the car, and drove to Green Bay to report to the Packers training camp. I didn't know it at the time, but they had already traded me to Cleveland. I didn't even stay there. I got back in the car and drove right to Bowling Green, where the Browns were training."

Soltau was there for little more than two weeks before he was on the move again. Browns coach Paul Brown told Soltau he could make the team but probably would see very little, if any, playing time because Lou

Groza was ahead of him as Cleveland's place kicker and the Browns had a strong tandem at wide receiver in Dante Lavelli and Mac Speedie.

"If you go to San Francisco," Brown told Soltau, "you'll be a regular from the day you arrive." Soltau accepted the advice from Paul Brown, who was a friend of 49ers coach Buck Shaw from the time the teams were rivals in the All-America Conference. Both the 49ers and Browns were playing their first NFL season in 1950 after elements of the All-America Conference merged with the NFL.

Soltau packed his bags once again, jumped in the car, and headed for San Francisco. "I drove there in four days. It was kind of a crazy drive but I made it," Soltau said.

The 49ers were in the market for a place kicker and wide receiver, and Shaw was happy to acquire Soltau because he could help them out in both areas. Soltau took over the place-kicking chores after the 49ers released Joe "Little Toe" Vetrano in training camp.

For the first couple of seasons, Soltau also played both ways, seeing time at defensive end as well as wide receiver. By his third year with the team, he was kicking and playing offense exclusively.

One game in particular, in Soltau's second season with the 49ers, epitomized his dual capabilities as a receiver and a kicker. In a 1951 game against the Rams, Soltau accounted for 26 of the 49ers' 44 points. He caught three touchdown passes from two different quarterbacks, converted a field goal, and kicked five extra points. It was a milestone performance for the 49ers' young receiver in a milestone win for one of the NFL's youngest franchises, going into the books as the first victory in their long, intense rivalry with the Rams.

GAME OF MY LIFE
BY GORDY SOLTAU
OCTOBER 28, 1951—SAN FRANCISCO, CALIFORNIA

The 1951 game against the Rams was a big one for us. You had the 49ers and the Rams, the two teams in California, and it was sort of a natural that there would be a rivalry. In 1950, when the 49ers went into NFL, we played the Rams a couple of times and they beat the tar out of us. But we were building up a lot of steam against the Rams in 1951. They came to Kezar and we had a full house. Everybody expected a great game.

The Rams had a sensational team: Bob Waterfield and Norm Van Brocklin, two great quarterbacks. They had these bruising fullbacks, "Deacon" Dan Towler, Tank Younger, and Dick Hoener. They had great receivers, Elroy "Crazylegs" Hirsch and Tommy Fears. Their defense was solid.

The year before, they reached the NFL championship but lost to Cleveland. They were heading back to the title game in 1951 but they had to play us first.

It was a beautiful day for football, sunny, one of San Francisco's finest days, but there were still a few seagulls flying around Kezar. We started out running the ball, and we were running it very well. Joe Perry was carrying the load. Frankie Albert was the starting quarterback. But in those days, they might have Frankie Albert throw the first few passes and then Y.A. Tittle would come in and throw a few passes, like a platoon system.

But I remember Frankie was particularly sharp that day. He threw a nice pass to me in our first series and it went for about 40 yards. It set up our first score; I wound up kicking a field goal. I caught a couple more touchdown passes, one from Albert and the other from Tittle, in the second quarter. And by halftime, we were leading 38-10.

Our defense was doing well. I remember one of our linebackers, Hardy Brown, was particularly devastating in that game. He had one shot where he just leveled Glenn Davis, and I think that was basically the hit that led him to cut short his career. I remembered Davis mostly from his days at Army when he was "Mr. Outside" to Doc Blanchard's "Mr. Inside." They had both won the Heisman Trophy. Davis was just a great athlete and a wonderful person. But he retired after the 1951 season, only his second in the NFL. I was sorry to hear that he passed away in 2005.

That day, Hardy just lowered his shoulder and hit him. Davis was coming across the middle and he was looking back for the ball. Hardy just caught him square. He was down on the ground for some time and had to be carried off the field.

The Rams were the league's No. 1 offense in 1950 and 1951 and they still had plenty of firepower after losing Davis. But we just kept mixing it, running and passing, and our defense played a great game. Leo Nomellini blocked a punt by Norm Van Brocklin and recovered it in the end zone for a touchdown. And Waterfield and Van Brocklin were intercepted six times.

That helped us build up a big enough score that they weren't able to catch us. I got another touchdown late in the game, and I guess that made a good game for me even better. It was exciting to have a game where I kicked a field goal, caught three touchdowns, and had five extra points. My sixth PAT got blocked after Tittle fumbled the hold.

But better still, though, it was a great game for the 49ers. That was the first time we had beaten the Rams. They went on to win the NFL championship that year and by beating them, that game told us a lot about ourselves. We finished with our first winning season in the NFL and that was a watershed for us because we came into the league from the All-America Conference and we had to prove ourselves against the NFL's old guard. With that win, I think we emphatically showed that we could play with anybody and were capable of beating the best the NFL had to offer.

Soltau finished with six catches for 132 yards, and half of his receptions went for touchdowns, with the longest covering 48 yards. He added a field goal and five conversions to account for a team-record 26 points.

Soltau's performance stood as the 49ers' single-game scoring record for the next 39 years, and it took an extraordinary effort by Jerry Rice to eclipse it. In a 1990 game against Atlanta, Rice caught five touchdown passes, beating Falcons defensive back Charles Dimry in each instance to move ahead of Soltau in the 49ers' record book.

Soltau played for the 49ers from 1950-58, leading the team in scoring in each of his nine seasons. He led the NFL in scoring in 1952 and 1953 when he scored 94 points and a career-high 114 points. He helped the 49ers to five winning seasons during his tenure and went to the Pro Bowl three times, including after a 1952 season that was highlighted by a 10-catch, 196-yard game against the New York Giants.

Soltau also figured prominently in the 49ers' first season sweep of the Rams. He kicked a game-winning field goal in the first meeting and caught a 17-yard touchdown in the final minute of the second during a 9-3 campaign in 1953. The win total was the most in a season during the club's first 20 years in the NFL, but the 49ers were denied their first playoff berth, finishing a game behind conference champion Detroit.

"We were a little short-handed on defense most of the time," Soltau said. "Buck Shaw [the 49ers' coach during the first nine years of their existence] was an excellent offensive coach, and his drafting and trading was more directed toward the offense. We tended to get outmanned on defense. We could score 30 points on almost anybody but we couldn't stop them."

That was evident in 1957, when the 49ers made their first NFL postseason appearance in a playoff to break a first-place tie with Detroit in the Western Conference.

After a Soltau field goal early in the third quarter, the 49ers extended their lead over the Lions to 27-7. But the Lions scored the next 24 points against an injury-weakened 49ers defense to advance to the championship game, where they routed Cleveland.

"There were a couple of games early in the season we should have won and we would never have been put in the position of playing Detroit in a playoff," Soltau said. "But Detroit was a lot like us. They had a lot of good players and good coaches. They played well and they beat us. But losing like we did, that never goes away. When you lose a championship, that sticks with you forever."

Soltau played only one more season and he was largely limited to kicking field goals during the 1958 season. Frankie Albert was fired as the 49ers coach following a 6-6 campaign and Soltau, who figured he wouldn't get much of a chance to play under new coach Red Hickey, opted to retire.

For a time, Soltau considered joining the CIA, a descendant of the World War II-era OSS that Soltau had been a part of during World War II.

"I had a lot of friends who stayed with the OSS and later came under the CIA when there was an agency transition." Soltau said. "I even signed up and went through the background check and had received my clearance. I was approved for the job. But that was when I was finishing my football career and I had a very good job lined up as a broadcast analyst for CBS television. We were pretty much settled in Palo Alto and my wife and I had started a family. We decided to stay put."

Soltau continues to reside in the San Francisco Bay area and maintains his ties with the 49ers through various alumni activities.

"We always had such great support. The way the crowds were, the way they backed us, it felt like to me I was still playing in college," Soltau said. "San Francisco was just a great place to play."

Chapter 5

DAVE PARKS

Less than a month into the 49ers' 1963 season, Red Hickey had had enough. With the 49ers at 0-3 and no better than mediocre in four previous seasons under Hickey, he abruptly quit as the team's coach. Jack Christiansen was hired to replace him.

The coaching change was part of a 2-12 campaign that produced a dubious distinction: fewest wins in a season in the 49ers' history. The silver lining to the lousy finish was the 49ers had the No. 1 pick in the 1964 NFL draft and they zeroed in on Dave Parks, an All-America wide receiver from Texas Tech.

"He was No. 1 on almost everybody's list," said Lou Spadia, the 49ers general manager at the time. "We knew he was a fine football player, and that's what we were looking for. He was big, strong, and fast. When he'd get out front, no one could catch him because he'd run as fast as he had to."

Parks recalled the 49ers were so intent on drafting him—and so fearful that a team from the rival AFL would lure him away—that Spadia traveled to Dallas, Texas, to hang around with him in the days before the draft. After the 49ers made Parks the No. 1 pick, Spadia accompanied Parks to his home in Abilene and refused to leave until he got Parks' signature on a contract.

"It was a three-year deal that, with bonuses and stuff, was worth a little over $100,000," Parks said.

Parks gave the 49ers their money's worth—and then some. He became a starter as a rookie and gave an immediate lift to a struggling offense while becoming John Brodie's go-to receiver. He had 36 receptions for 703 yards, averaging a team-high 19.5 yards. His eight receiving touchdowns remain the most ever by a rookie in team history.

The next year, Parks got even better. To this day, he credits Brodie's influence.

"Offensively, I think there was something John and I had," Parks said. "We just made things happen. They would flat out try to take me away and they were never able to do it because John wouldn't let them.

"It got to the point where John knew exactly where I'd be. He put so many balls in the air on faith, where he was just counting on me to be there and for the line to hold up. That took a ton of guts. We made it work."

Two years after their last-place finish, the 49ers improved to fourth in the NFL's Western Division and led the league in total offense and scoring. Parks was a big part of the equation, finishing with a league-leading 80 receptions for 1,344 yards and 12 touchdowns.

The Brodie-Parks connection reached a pinnacle in a narrow loss at Baltimore. Parks finished with a team-record 231 yards receiving on nine receptions. Three of his catches went for touchdowns—all of them were 45 yards or longer—but it was the one that got away that Parks remembers the most.

GAME OF MY LIFE
BY DAVE PARKS
OCTOBER 3, 1965—BALTIMORE, MARYLAND

The Baltimore Colts were a strong team. They had an excellent defense and a great offense. They had Johnny Unitas at quarterback, and for us, it was one of those things where we knew we were going to have to get down the field and score.

Personnel-wise, we had talent. We struggled at times to stop people but we had a lot of confidence in our offense. As for me, I had a tough match up with Baltimore defensive back Lenny Lyles.

Lenny really woke me up a year before when I was a rookie. He clipped me, took a shot at me, trying to get my attention, trying to

Dave Parks *San Francisco 49ers archives*

intimidate me. He didn't intimidate me but he got my attention. I went after him every chance I could after that, but he kind of took me out of my game.

Whenever we played each other after that, we'd pop each other pretty good on the first play of the game. It was like we were saying to each other, "Hey, remember me?" Over the years, I think it became a sign of a mutual respect. But certainly, I got fired up when I faced him and when we played the Colts, and that Sunday was no different.

I know John Brodie, our quarterback, also had a running battle with their great linebacker, Don Shinnick. He just didn't like him. Shinnick was like a crazy man, running all over the place before the snap. He was always trying to fool John or get the jump on him. Shinnick was an excellent player and he gave John fits. I never saw any other player get under John's skin like Shinnick did. I know that John wanted to win that game bad and so did I.

One other thing was I always liked playing the better teams because it seemed like John would use me more.

The game didn't start out well for us. We fell behind 17-0 but then we started to get on track. I got behind the Baltimore secondary and John threw me this pretty pass and we were on the board with a long touchdown catch. Unfortunately, Unitas being Unitas, he answered with a touchdown pass to Lenny Moore and by halftime, we were down 24-7.

We got back into it with a trick play. John David Crow rolled out on the option and threw another bomb to me. We traded field goals and then Brodie and I teamed up on my third touchdown. I think all of my touchdown catches were over 40 yards.

There were still more than four minutes left and we were only down by three points.

I've always believed we had them that day. John kept picking at them and they hadn't really stopped us all day. We were moving the ball and we were making big plays.

Jimmy Johnson intercepted Unitas to give us the ball at midfield in the late going.

We had a great a chance, too, to score. I was wide open downfield and Brodie spotted me and let fly a nice pass right for me. But for some reason, Monty Stickles, our tight end, threw that big old hand up there and knocked the ball away. That was tough. I'm behind him, just there, by myself, waiting in the end zone for the ball, and that happens. That would have been the ballgame right there. It would have been another touchdown.

I can't tell you the precise distance of my touchdown receptions and I can't tell you the patterns I ran to get open. I just remember the one that got away. Because we had a chance to beat Baltimore, and oh, what a win that would have been, because they were an excellent, excellent team.

Dave Parks went to the Pro Bowl in each of his first three seasons with the 49ers, but his career with the team was cut short by a long, bitter contract dispute that proved costly to both sides.

Parks' contract expired after the 1967 season. The 49ers dallied for months before making a move to offer a new one.

"They wouldn't talk to me during the summer and put things off to the last minute and that didn't go well," Parks said. "By then, I had some hard feelings. The wait, the delay, the way they handled the whole thing, just rubbed me the wrong way."

Parks decided to play out his option, accepting a 10 percent pay cut over the previous season's salary for the chance to play elsewhere the next year. He thought he would be free to sign with the team of his choice; R.C. Owens had left the 49ers for the Baltimore Colts in 1961 by pursuing a similar path. But the NFL wanted to clamp down on player movement, and commissioner Pete Rozelle decided the Saints would have to pay the 49ers compensation to the tune of two first-round draft picks for signing Parks.

"I had done everything I was supposed to do to be a free agent," Parks said. "My attorney wanted to sue the NFL and I think we would have won, but that could have gone on for a long time and I just wanted to play ball."

The Rozelle Rule grew, in part, out of the commissioner's decision in the Parks case. The Saints retained Parks, but satisfying the compensation requirements cost them top draft pick Kevin Hardy, who had already spent some time in the Saints camp, and another first-round pick. The 49ers later used it to draft tight end Ted Kwalick.

"That whole thing just put a ton of pressure on me," Parks said. "There were all kinds of expectations because I cost them two first-round picks."

Parks spent five years in New Orleans trying fruitlessly to duplicate the success he had experienced with the 49ers. He failed to develop a solid rapport with Saints quarterback Billy Kilmer—better known as a runner than a passer—and often endured games without a catch.

"John Brodie told me, 'Don't go where you don't have a thrower because you'll be wasted,'" Parks said. "I didn't really understand the throwing end of it, but I learned what it meant the hard way.

"There's nothing worse than people looking at you, like they did in New Orleans, and saying, 'Why did we get this guy?' I was playing just as hard as I was in San Francisco, but I didn't have the same people around me and football is a team sport, not an individual sport."

Going to New Orleans "was something I felt I had to do at the time, but it was a horrible career decision," Parks added. "I was useless there. We had a running back there that caught more balls than me. Billy Kilmer had no time to throw to me. He was running for his life."

From New Orleans, Parks moved on to Houston and ended his career with the Southern California Sun of the World Football League. In 10 years as a professional, Parks played on one winning team—the 1965 49ers, who finished 7-6-1.

But Parks' timing was unfortunate in leaving the 49ers, who had brought in Dick Nolan in 1968 to take over as a coach. A defensive specialist, Nolan basically left one of the league's most productive offenses alone and concentrated on strengthening the defense. By 1970, the 49ers won the first of three consecutive division titles under Nolan. They twice reached the NFC championship game, where the Dallas Cowboys beat them on both occasions, leaving the 49ers one win shy of the Super Bowl.

Parks said he often wondered whether the 49ers would have won their first championship sooner if he had stayed and continued developing his working relationship with Brodie. Brodie, it turned out, felt Parks could have made a difference. Years later, when they were both out of football, Brodie and Parks met up at a celebrity golf tournament at the Prestonwood Country Club in Dallas.

"John, he finally told me I kept him out of the Super Bowl," Parks said. "I've always thought he kind of blamed me, my leaving, for maybe ruining his chance for a championship game—and really, who knows what would have happened?"

Brodie, Parks said, was never angry with him and the two remained close over the years. Parks visited him often when Brodie spent weeks at a time at a Texas rehabilitation center recovering from a near-fatal stroke.

Now and then, though, Parks second-guesses himself.

"John never told me not to leave. He just told me, 'You've got to do what you've got to do,'" Parks said. "I'm the guy who chose to leave John Brodie and a great offensive line. How stupid was that? I was a fool to leave, and I was the one who paid the price."

Chapter 6

LEN ROHDE

Born and raised on a dairy farm outside of Palatine, Illinois, Len Rohde didn't have time for sports at first. Before and after school—Rohde attended a one-room country school—there were chores to be done.

"We had one teacher, eight grades, and 24 kids all in the same place," Rohde says. It wasn't until Rohde began attending Palatine Township High School that he was steered toward football, and the impetus came from an unlikely source: his freshman English teacher, Charles Feutz, who doubled as a coach.

"I come in and I'm bigger than most of the kids and Mr. Feutz says, 'Have you ever thought about going out for football?'" Rohde says. "I told him, 'No, not really. We've got work on the farm. I've got work after school.'"

Turned down initially by Rohde, Feutz decided a more subtle approach was needed to get him to come out for football.

"He was pretty creative," Rohde recalls, laughing. "He told the other guys on the team, 'Listen, if you ever see that the big hayseed guy around school, you ought to befriend him, see if he'd be interested in trying out for football.' By the end of the year, a lot of the guys I hung around with were guys on the football team. So the next year I joined them."

Lanky and tall but strengthened by his labors on the family farm, Rohde spent most of his sophomore season learning to play offensive and defensive line. He hurt his knee as a junior and missed most of the season.

But he came back to have a strong senior campaign that he punctuated by winning the Illinois state heavyweight championship as a wrestler.

"Actually, most of my offers from colleges were to wrestle," Rohde said. "Yet I really wanted to play football. I really didn't care that much about wrestling. Utah State gave me a shot as a football player and that's where I went."

Rohde was a three-year starter for Utah State, spending time playing both offense and defense. He was named captain as a senior, won team MVP honors, and was an all-conference selection. He was selected in the fifth round of the 1960 NFL draft by the 49ers.

As a rookie, Rohde saw action as an offensive tackle, holding his own as a backup to right tackle Bob St. Clair. But he also continued practicing on defense. After an especially strong preseason at right defensive end in 1962, Rohde believed he may have found his playing niche.

"A few weeks before the season started, we'd played the New York Giants at Kezar in an exhibition game," Rohde said. "Y.A. Tittle was playing against the 49ers for the first time since he'd been traded to the Giants the year before. I was playing against him as a defensive end and got a couple sacks on him. Then Leo Nomellini blocked a punt. I fell on it in the end zone for a touchdown. I thought I was going, man. Things were taking off for me."

Red Hickey, the 49ers coach, wasn't entirely convinced, but he went ahead and installed Rohde as the starting right defensive end going into the 1962 season opener against the Chicago Bears at Kezar Stadium.

It did not go well for Rohde, who managed to exert some pressure on the quarterback but also missed some key tackles.

"In my mind, I was this big pass rusher, but I got trapped a couple times and their fullback, Rick Casares, got by me for some big gains. He got a touchdown, we got beat pretty bad (30-14), and I made a couple of mistakes, costly mistakes."

When Rohde showed up for practice on Monday, Hickey told him that he was taking him off the defensive unit and returning him to the offense, where Rohde felt he had failed to establish himself. Clark Miller took over as defensive end.

"I figured it was all over, my career was over," Rohde said. "I mean, how many opportunities do you get? I knew I had been struggling on

Len Rohde *San Francisco 49ers archives*

offense so I didn't think I had a chance. I was about as low as you could go. . . . At that point, I figured I'd wait out the season and if the 49ers didn't want me, I thought I could go play defense for somebody, somewhere. I knew I could rush the passer. But I was down and out, just waiting for the season to get over."

Only by chance, it never came to that.

Eight weeks later, in the middle of a game against the Rams in Los Angeles, coaches reluctantly summoned Rohde from the sideline to fill in for injured right tackle Bob St. Clair. Playing across the line that day was a young defensive end by the name of Deacon Jones. In the years to come, Jones would become a fixture in the "Fearsome Foursome," one of the greatest defensive lines in NFL history. He would be recognized as one of the best pass rushers ever and gain entry into the pro football Hall of Fame.

But that day against the 49ers, after St. Clair left in the first half with a season-ending Achilles tendon injury, the Rams' rising star found himself dealing with a player who was neither comfortable nor confident in his ability as a tackle. But Rohde was desperate. In a hurry, he became desperately good, good enough to change the course of his career and begin a run that put him in the 49ers' record book.

GAME OF MY LIFE
BY LEN ROHDE
NOVEMBER 18, 1962—LOS ANGELES, CALIFORNIA

We were down in L.A. playing against the Rams and all of a sudden, Bob St. Clair got hurt. Bill Johnson, our offensive line coach, was walking up and down the sideline looking at who the hell he could put in there. He looked at me and I could tell he was thinking, "Oh, shoot." He looked over at Leon Donahue, but he was a guard. But I could tell he was thinking, "Maybe I can put the guard in." So finally he said, "Rohde, get in there!" The truth is what he was really thinking was, "You're the only one I've got left. I really don't have anybody else."

Well, their thinking and mine was one and the same: just get through this game and hope you don't get completely run over. It's called survival—just hanging on. And you hope somewhere along the way, things get better.

Maybe in a way—and I've never really figured it out—I had kind of written off my career with the 49ers when I got moved from defense to offense. You see, I had built up a little confidence as a defensive player and I had kind of felt like maybe I could play for some team as a defensive end, that I'd get a job somewhere. So when I was moved to offense, it was kind of like I was going through the motions, like, "Let's get this damn thing over with and get on to the next year."

But all of a sudden, there I was in L.A. playing against Deacon Jones. He was just a young player then, in his first or second year, but people respected him even then. Still, he didn't have the reputation that he developed later. He wasn't a high draft pick either, and he was from a small school. I guess it was probably good that I didn't know too much about him.

Then I got the opportunity and things went pretty well in L.A. I finished the game and I played respectably and we won the game 24-17. I was one of those smaller, faster guys that, as a defensive lineman, you generally prefer not to go against. And I thought, "Wow!" I think I surprised my coaches and I surprised myself.

After that game, nobody was going to come up and say, "Hey, you're our guy." I hadn't really deserved it. I hadn't really earned that. What happened was there were four or five games left, and evidently after playing consistently for those last four or five games, they said, "Well, maybe it's a maturity thing or something." I ended up getting that opportunity, and it somehow worked from there. The rest of the season, I got a little better and a little better and a little better.

It wasn't like this big conscious revelation. That may have been part of it. It may also have been a factor that maybe I matured. Maybe physically I matured and became a better player. It's not like one day you wake up and can jump 10 feet and the day before you could only jump two feet. It doesn't happen like that. It just kind of evolved.

The next week against St. Louis, Rohde started at right tackle in place of the injured Bob St. Clair. He remained in the lineup for the next 13 years, extending his streak of consecutive games played to 208. It's a team record that that still stands three decades later, and in the era of the salary cap and free agency, it's a record that may never be broken.

Rohde started the final four games of the 1962 season at right tackle and played well enough that the 49ers decided to keep him in the lineup when St. Clair came back healthy the following season. St. Clair returned to right tackle and Rohde moved to left tackle, where he remained until retiring in 1975.

"I had reached the point where they felt comfortable enough to say, 'Well, hey, we're going to move this guy to left tackle,'" Rohde said. "I was in their plans, so to speak, to be a starter. Up until that season, it was a case of, 'We've got to wait and see.'"

During the course of his 15-year career, Rohde made the Pro Bowl (1970) and anchored a line that powered one of the NFL's most prolific offenses during a run of three straight division titles under Coach Dick Nolan from 1970-72.

Rohde recalled the 49ers' return to the postseason after a 13-year absence as one of the best moments in his career.

The 49ers clinched their first playoff appearance since 1957 by beating the Oakland Raiders 38-7 in the 1970 regular-season finale. On the floor of the Oakland Coliseum after the game, the offensive line, composed of Rohde at left tackle, left guard Randy Beisler, center Forrest Blue, right guard Woody Peoples, and right tackle Cas Banaszek, took a celebratory photo. It commemorated the win in the 49ers' first regular- season meeting with the Raiders and the group's unofficial record of allowing only eight sacks during the 14-game season. A mural-sized copy of that picture hangs today on a wall in Rohde's Burger King restaurant in Mountain View.

"One of the things I remember most is right after the game, John Brodie just kind of spontaneously said, 'Hey, we're going to have a party,'" Rohde said.

"Call up the Fairmont Hotel," Brodie said before turning toward members of the Morabito family, who owned the team. "If they don't pay for it, I'm paying for it," Brodie said to hoots and hollers from teammates.

Rohde still isn't sure who footed the bill, but it was a heck of a party.

"We had a beautiful room there at the Fairmont, and I mean they had put this thing together in two or three hours," Rohde said. "We were flying high that day."

The feeling carried over to the next week, when the 49ers overcame bone-chilling weather to beat the Minnesota Vikings 17-14 in an NFC playoff game at Metropolitan Stadium in Bloomington, Minnesota. It was the 49ers' first victory in an NFL playoff game.

They returned to Kezar Stadium to host the Dallas Cowboys in the NFC title game but lost 17-10. It was the first of three successive season-ending losses to the Cowboys in the postseason.

Rohde played until 1975, playing through excruciating back pain during his final two seasons. It got so bad, he said, that he bought a hospital-style traction bed.

"[My back] was just sore and stiff as hell," said Rohde, who also overcame a knee injury midway through the 1971 season to keep his consecutive-game streak alive. "It was giving me a lot of trouble. There were all sorts of pulleys and weights on the traction bed that helped support my back and let me get some sleep."

Rohde said his back was killing him during the 1973 and 1974 seasons, but he still managed to play pretty well and kept his consecutive- game streak going, too. He went to training camp in 1975, still unsure whether he would continue his NFL career or start a new one.

"Almost every practice had become a struggle, but I hadn't definitely said, 'Hey, this is it,'" said Rohde. "I had my streak going and I thought I was still playing pretty well."

It was coach Dick Nolan who approached Rohde during the team's 1975 training camp and bluntly urged him to retire.

"He told me, 'You're a hell of a team guy. Why don't you really help the team and retire,'" Rohde said with a laugh. "He didn't quite say it like that, but it was kind of like that. But really, it wasn't like a big revelation," said Rohde, who accepted Nolan's advice. "I knew that retirement was creeping up on me and I already had been looking at other things, so the transition wasn't dramatic."

Rohde had completed work on a master's degree at San Jose State University and had begun looking into different business opportunities even before his football career ended. In 1974, he had interviewed with Burger King and had already been approved for a franchise. Over the years, he became a successful restaurateur, owning as many as 15 different restaurants individually or in partnership.

Rohde continued to remain close with the 49ers, taking part in alumni events and reunions. He was reminded of his best years with the team when the 49ers hired Mike Nolan in 2005 to coach the team that his father, Dick Nolan, had coached for eight years from 1968-75.

"I still enjoy my association with the 49ers," Rohde said. "It's great to see Mike Nolan, Dick's son, coaching the team now. I still remember him as a 10-year-old troublemaker at training camp."

Rohde said the camaraderie with his teammates and competing day in and day out at football's highest level are what he cherishes most from his playing days.

"I had a long career," he said. "The first two, three years, it was survival: get me to the end of the day. Get me to the end of the week, and there were quite a few years like that, though I got in the Pro Bowl one year.

"Maybe I wasn't where I ultimately would like to be—one of the top players and in the Hall of Fame and all that. I wasn't quite at that level, but I was at a level where they weren't looking to replace me all the time. I was there and I was doing my job."

Chapter 7

STEVE SPURRIER

The Science Hill High School football team in Johnson City, Tennessee, was getting ready for the season in 1961 when Chicago Bears quarterback Bill Wade stopped by for a visit. Wade, a native of nearby Nashville, talked to the players about what it took to play the game. He visited with the coaching staff and even drew up a series of pass plays for them after being told that all Science Hill did was run the ball.

Wade urged the coaches to give the forward pass a try, and before leaving, he glanced at the group of players on the practice field and pointed one out, telling the coaches, "That tall kid over there can throw."

Steve Spurrier remembers that moment as the true beginning of his career as a quarterback. Years later, after a Heisman Trophy-winning career at the University of Florida, after playing in the NFL for the San Francisco 49ers and the Tampa Bay Buccaneers, Spurrier wrote a letter to Wade to thank him for helping him get his start. Wade responded with an appreciative note of his own that Spurrier has kept as a reminder of the life-changing impact made by a chance encounter long ago.

Spurrier was a 16-year-old junior at Science Hill and had never thrown a pass in a game before Wade's fateful visit. That all changed over the next two years. By the time he was a senior, Spurrier was throwing the ball regularly. A passing quarterback at the high school level was a sight so rare in those times that he gained notoriety as a sort of football marvel.

He reached a pinnacle in his final high school game, a postseason contest against Church Hill High School. Science Hill found itself trailing 21-0 at one point.

"We started throwing on every down," Spurrier recalls. "We got a bunch of yards and I threw for four touchdowns, which was kind of unheard of for a high school quarterback back then, and we beat them 28-21."

Spurrier had several college scholarships to choose from and eventually selected the University of Florida, where he played for Coach Ray Graves from 1963-66.

"Somebody said to go to a school where you'd like to live and everybody wanted to retire and live in Florida," Spurrier said years later about his decision to play for the Gators. "Mainly, I went there because I thought it was a very good school with a wonderful coach in a super state and I had the opportunity to play quarterback."

Spurrier became a two-time All-American at Florida, piling up 4,848 yards passing. He threw for 37 touchdowns in 31 career games. In 1966, he won college football's top individual prize, the Heisman Trophy, finishing ahead of Purdue quarterback Bob Griese in the Heisman balloting.

"I was lucky," said Spurrier. "We started off 7-0 and just had it going."

The Gators finished that season 9-2 behind Spurrier and beat Georgia Tech in the January 2, 1967, Orange Bowl.

The San Francisco 49ers made him their No. 1 pick in the 1967 NFL draft. The problem for Spurrier was the 49ers had one of the NFL's best—and most durable—quarterbacks in John Brodie.

"When I got there, they told me, 'John will probably be here another four or five years. We'll get you ready to go after that,'" Spurrier says. "And that's just about what happened."

Unable to unseat Brodie, whose 17 seasons made him the longest-serving 49er in team history, Spurrier played quarterback only here and there during the first five years of his nine-year stay in San Francisco. In 1968, he didn't throw a pass. He only had four pass attempts in 1970 and again in 1971, when Brodie led the 49ers to two of three consecutive division titles.

Steve Spurrier *San Francisco 49ers archives*

"I can tell you this about Steve: he was someone who needed to play," said former 49ers receiver Dave Parks. "He looked terrible in practice. You'd never know where the ball was going with him. But you put him in a game, and he'd get things done. He was just a gamer."

The 49ers finally found that out in 1972, Spurrier's sixth year in the league. Brodie suffered an ankle sprain while trying to lead a last-minute comeback in a 23-17 loss to the New York Giants. The October 15 defeat dropped the 49ers to 2-3.

Spurrier started the next eight games, at one point even leading the league in passing, while helping the 49ers go 5-2-1 in that span to get back into playoff contention. He had one of the greatest days by a 49ers quarterback in a 34-21 win at Chicago, throwing five touchdown passes to tie a team record. The victory was part of a season-long three-game winning streak.

But in a chance to clinch the division title in a Monday night game against the Los Angeles Rams, Spurrier struggled, completing 11 of 26 passes for 175 yards in a 26-16 loss. That left the 49ers needing to win their last two games and at least one loss by the Rams to clinch a third consecutive NFC Western title.

Spurrier got the 49ers back on track by leading them to a win against the Atlanta Falcons, but he played so poorly in the finale against the Vikings that he was yanked in favor of Brodie, who led a stirring comeback that clinched the division in what was his first appearance in two months.

Coach Dick Nolan stuck with Brodie for the 49ers playoff game against Dallas, but the 49ers fell victim to the heroics of Roger Staubach, who rallied the Cowboys past the 49ers 30-28.

Brodie returned for one more season then retired, and Spurrier at last went into the 1974 season as the 49ers starting quarterback. But in his final preseason game, he suffered a shoulder separation that sidelined him for all but a handful of plays toward the end of the season. With four different quarterbacks starting games for them, the 49ers went 6-8 for the second consecutive losing season.

Spurrier regained his health for the 1975 season but not the starting quarterback job. Instead, Coach Dick Nolan installed veteran Norm Snead as the starter. Once again, Spurrier found himself watching from the sideline.

Then, midway through another lost season for the 49ers, Spurrier talked Nolan into giving him one more shot, and he made a memorable, if fleeting, return to the lineup.

GAME OF MY LIFE
BY STEVE SPURRIER
NOVEMBER 9, 1975—LOS ANGELES, CALIFORNIA

For having been with the 49ers nine years, I didn't play much. But in 1972, after I'd been there six years, I played quite a bit. Somehow, I threw five touchdown passes against the Chicago Bears that season. That tied the team record by John Brodie and Y.A. Tittle. Joe Montana has broken it since then. He threw six touchdown passes in a game at Atlanta on October 14, 1990. But the game of my career came in my final season with the 49ers in 1975.

We started the season badly, losing five of our first seven games. We were going to L.A. to play the Rams, who were the hottest team in the league. They had won six straight since their only loss of the season in their opener. In my time with the 49ers, we had played the Rams 18 times and we had only beaten them twice.

John Brodie had retired a couple years earlier and Norm Snead was starting at quarterback. We were losing. So at the beginning of the week before we were going to play the Rams, I asked Coach Dick Nolan to let me play.

I remember I said, "How 'bout letting me go play against the Rams down there?"

And he said, "Aww, you never know."

I said, "Come on, I'm serious. I've never had a chance. I've been here nine years and I've never had a chance to play them down in L.A. Just for the heck of it, why don't you let me have a go at it?"

He came back to me on the Wednesday before the game and he said, "O.K., you got it." I got with Gene Washington and they let me put in a few plays and it was a fun week.

The Rams were taking it to us at first. They got up on us 14-0 in the first half. But we got it going in the second half. We went deep on a first-down play during our first series of the third quarter, and Gene Washington caught it for something like a 40-yard touchdown.

Then the Rams fumbled, and just like that, I hooked up with Delvin Williams for another touchdown and we tied it up.

It was in that game that Tom Dempsey, who was known for kicking a record 63-yard field goal while he was with the New Orleans Saints, kicked a field goal and hit our safety, Ralph McGill, on the head. It about killed him because Dempsey hit him right in the temple with that big club on his foot. Ralph was out cold and they carted him off the field and we didn't know if he was going to live or what. They made the field goal and took the lead but all of us were kind of shaken up, including Dempsey.

So, we got the ball back, and on a third-and-1, I hit Gene on about a 70-yard touchdown pass. It was a pretty play, and we were back in front.

With about 90 seconds left, the Rams scored another touchdown on a short run, but Dempsey missed the extra point. Maybe he thought he was going to hit somebody and maybe kill him. He was so shaky, maybe that was why his extra point try went wide.

We were down 23-21, and we got a little ol' drive together and we got to the Rams' 37-yard line. It was about fourth-and-2 and there were less than 40 seconds left. It was a 54-yard field goal try and I was the holder, and I'll be danged, Steve Mike-Mayer made it. And we beat them 24-23 and we were a happy bunch. We were going nowhere, but we beat the damn Rams. We only beat them two times when I was there. Brodie beat 'em the first time in 1970. Then we beat them with that one in 1975. Check the record book. We were 2-15-1 against those guys in the nine years I was there. They owned us. We won the division three years in a row, and our record against the Rams in that span was 1-5. But that day, we beat them. That day was our day.

Safety Ralph McGill didn't see the fantastic finish against the Rams. He was taken off the field and driven by ambulance to a Los Angeles-area hospital, where he spent the next four days being treated for a severe concussion. He rejoined the team after being discharged but missed five of the last six games. He played three weeks later at Philadelphia but fainted on the return trip home, and the team plane made an emergency stop in Chicago, where McGill again was treated for his concussion. He was held out for the rest of the year, though he returned to play two more seasons with the 49ers.

Spurrier remained the starter for the last seven games of the 1975 season. Before the next season, the 49ers acquired Jim Plunkett from the New England Patriots in exchange for three first-round picks, a second-round pick, and quarterback Tom Owen.

The 49ers sent Spurrier to the Tampa Bay Buccaneers in exchange for wide receiver Willie McGee and linebacker Bruce Elia.

Spurrier's only full season as an NFL starter was also his last. He started 12 games for the Buccaneers and appeared in the other two during the Bucs' 0-14 season. They remain the last NFL team to endure a winless season.

"We almost won two or three of those games. It just didn't work out," Spurrier said. "I was released the next summer."

Spurrier hasn't been one to shy away from his part in the NFL's losingest season, though. Indeed, his official biography includes a timeline of his career that reads in part: "1976—Starting quarterback for Tampa Bay, which earns a spot in history by going 0-14."

"It's given me a lot of joke material," Spurrier said. "It gives people a little laugh and gives you a chance to be a regular person. You know, the Tampa Bay Buccaneers booster club named me the team MVP for that season and I did play in every one of those games. But I'd venture that I'm the only quarterback in history to be an MVP who also lost every game of the season."

The Bucs released Spurrier before the start of the 1977 season and he headed into life after football unsure of what he wanted to do. The new direction he would take came to him while he was sitting in the stands at Ben Hill Griffin Stadium watching a football game at his alma mater, the University of Florida.

"I knew I had to do something," Spurrier said. "While I was sitting there, I thought maybe this coaching thing could be fun. That didn't seem like work, and all these other job offers I'd been getting seemed like work."

Spurrier said a mutual friend mentioned his interest in getting into coaching to Florida coach Doug Dickey, and Spurrier was hired as Florida's quarterbacks coach in 1978. Charley Pell took over as Florida's coach in 1979 and Spurrier moved on to become an assistant at Georgia Tech and Duke over the next two years before getting his first head coaching job with the Tampa Bay Bandits of the United States Football League. He began laying the groundwork for his wide-open offense that became known as the "Fun 'N' Gun," going 35-19 over three seasons before the league went belly up.

He took over as the head coach at Duke in 1987 and returned in 1990 to Florida, where he coached the Gators to two national championship appearances, winning one following the 1996 season.

The only person to win the Heisman Trophy and coach a Heisman Trophy winner (Danny Wuerffel in 1996), Spurrier guided Florida to six SEC championships and compiled a record of 122-27-1 in 12 years before leaving. He resigned January 4, 2002, saying simply he had coached at Florida long enough.

Ten days later, Spurrier was hired to coach the Washington Redskins, signing a five-year, $25 million deal that was the richest deal for a coach in NFL history. But his return to the NFL did not go well. His "Fun 'N' Gun" offense didn't get off the ground against more physical NFL defenses, and his laid-back approach to the job was a poor fit in the intensely competitive, driven NFL environment.

Spurrier lasted just two seasons with the Redskins, going 12-20. He resigned within days of a 5-11 finish in 2003 that included losses in 10 of the last 12 games.

"I'm not the right person for this job," Spurrier said at the time. "It's a long grind and I feel that after 20 years as a head coach, there are other things that I need to do."

He took a year off before returning to the college coaching ranks. On November 23, 2005, Spurrier was introduced as the University of South Carolina's head coach. The "ol' ball coach" was back in his element.

"It's good to be in charge of a team again and try to put together a football program," Spurrier said. "We've got nowhere to go but up."

Chapter 8

JOHN BRODIE

No one played longer for the 49ers than John Brodie, but his team-record 17-season stay had a whirlwind start.

Drafted in the first round and third overall by the 49ers, the All-America quarterback from Stanford officially became a member of the team in June 1957 when he signed his first pro contract at the end of a 10-minute meeting in owner Anthony Morabito's San Francisco office.

"We pulled in front. I stayed in the car—John had double-parked on Market Street—and he ran in, signed the contract, and left," Brodie's wife, Sue, says. "He didn't have a representative and Tony was fair. That's the way they did things then."

Just engaged, the couple drove straight from Morabito's office to a jewelry store, where Brodie cashed his $3,000 signing bonus check and bought a ring for his soon-to-be-wife.

A native of San Francisco who was raised across the Bay in Oakland, Brodie came close to delivering a ring of a different sort to the 49ers. Behind one of the most productive NFL offenses of its day, Brodie led the 49ers to three consecutive division titles under Coach Dick Nolan from 1970-72. But Dallas beat the 49ers each time in the playoffs to deny them a championship season. Through it all, through the winning and losing and a roller-coaster relationship with 49ers fans, Brodie left an indelible mark on the franchise, with his forceful personality and with his play.

"He carried the team through some of the roughest times and some of the best of times," said Bill Walsh, who as 49ers coach led the team to its first three championships in the 1980s. "What he could do that you don't see much now in football is he had a touch on his passes. He could throw the soft screen pass or he could throw the ball over someone's head. He could drill the ball if he needed to. He was an absolute technician and an artist. He had the instincts of a great football player and he was one of the great performers at the quarterback position in history."

But Brodie had to wait his turn with the 49ers, whose lofty lineage at quarterback includes three Hall of Famers in Joe Montana, Steve Young, and Y.A. Tittle. When Brodie was a rookie, the 49ers had both Tittle and Earl Morrall already on the roster. Morrall was traded before the start of the 1957 season and Brodie began his career as the backup to Tittle, one of the game's most accomplished passers.

Brodie didn't see the field until the second to the last game of the season against the Baltimore Colts. Needing a win to tie for first place in the division, the 49ers trailed 13-10 with a minute and a half left when Tittle, playing with a groin injury, was taken down hard in a gang tackle by Baltimore's defensive front. He had to be helped off the field, and the call went out for Brodie.

The 49ers were on the Colts' 14-yard-line facing a third down. Brodie ducked his head in the huddle, surrounded by Hugh McElhenny, Billy Wilson, Joe Perry, and Bob St. Clair, among others. At least the rookie quarterback had the presence of mind to ask for their advice.

Wilson told him he'd run an out pattern and to throw the ball to him low and hard. But Brodie's first pass didn't go as low as it should have, and it fell incomplete when a defender hit Wilson just as the ball arrived.

"What the hell do we do now?" Brodie asked after the team huddled for its final play.

McElhenny spoke up and said he would run a quick out and up. Brodie got the pass away just as Colts defensive tackle Art Donovan smashed into him. He was flat on his back when McElhenny turned Brodie's first NFL completion into a game-winning touchdown catch.

Brodie started the finale against Green Bay but was ineffective and Tittle, despite still being bothered by the groin injury, led a second-half

John Brodie *San Francisco 49ers archives*

comeback that pulled the 49ers into a first-place tie in the division with Detroit.

The next week, the Lions rallied past the 49ers in a playoff game bringing an abrupt end to the 49ers' first NFL postseason appearance. But Tittle didn't play well in the second half in the playoff loss and by the next year, Tittle and Brodie would be sharing time. They were part of a long-running quarterback controversy that played out over a couple seasons, before then-coach Red Hickey resolved it in 1961 by trading Tittle to the New York Giants.

Brodie had always chafed for playing time behind Tittle, but he said later that he also learned by watching from the sideline as Tittle ran the 49ers offense. And while Tittle's departure gave Brodie his first fulltime opportunity, it wasn't until Tittle rejoined the 49ers in 1965 as an offensive backfield coach that Brodie's career really took flight.

Brodie said in *Open Field*, a 1974 biography he wrote with James D. Houston, that Tittle revamped the system for calling audibles, giving him greater options in trying to take advantage of any defensive weaknesses. Tittle's instruction and insights, Brodie said, helped him become a more complete quarterback, complementing his passing and competitive instincts with a growing understanding of how to read defenses and what it took to break them down.

Brodie finished the season as the league's most prolific passer, and Dave Parks led the league in receptions, and the 49ers led the NFL in points scored and total offense. He was among six 49ers from the offense making the Pro Bowl.

Despite the sometimes prickly relationship between the one-time rivals, Tittle described Brodie's 1965 season as one of the best years any NFL quarterback could have. But it wasn't enough to break a playoff drought stretching back to 1957, when the 49ers blew a big lead and lost a playoff game to Detroit.

Despite sweeping their season series with the division-rival Rams, the 49ers finished only a half-game above .500 (7-6-1) in 1965. Their defense struggled to limit the damage in many of their losses. The 49ers dropped games by such scores as 42-41 to Minnesota, 39-31 to Dallas, and 61-20 to Chicago. The Chicago blowout remains the most points given up in a game by the 49ers in team history.

Brodie's big year did help him land the richest contract in the league at the time. With the AFL and NFL in the midst of a bidding war for players, the Houston Oilers offered Brodie a record three-year, $910,000 contract. Brodie didn't sign the deal to give the 49ers a chance to match it.

In the meantime, merger negotiations between the AFL and NFL intensified. Many believe the Oilers' play for Brodie hastened the merger, which was worked out in part to avoid the escalating risk of financial ruin to both leagues if the bidding war for players continued unabated. Brodie wound up staying with the 49ers; the Oilers' contract offer, which had been written down on a cocktail napkin, was honored by the 49ers.

There were new pressures and scrutiny that came along with being football's highest paid player, and Brodie's play suffered amidst all the attention and criticism. His erratic play over the next couple seasons opened the door to challenges from George Mira and Steve Spurrier for his job.

In 1968, Dick Nolan, a former NFL defensive back and longtime defensive assistant under Dallas coach Tom Landry, became head coach of the 49ers. He set about fixing the 49ers' persistent defensive shortcomings and after a training camp competition, chose Brodie to continue running the 49ers offense over Spurrier and Mira.

Though Brodie was about to embark on the greatest run of his career, his alliance with Nolan was an uneasy one. Brodie viewed football from the prism of an offensive leader whose gunslinger mentality reflected his willingness to let fly with the ball, and to let that dictate the pace of the game and exert pressure on defenses. Nolan's rugged but close-to-the-vest approach reflected his defensive roots and factored into his more conservative approach on offense.

Despite the philosophical dichotomy, the two co-existed fairly well during a run that saw the 49ers win three division titles from 1970-72. Brodie won the league's MVP award in 1970, leading the 49ers back to the playoffs for the first time since 1957. They twice made it to the NFC championship game, but lost both times to fall one win shy of their first trip to the Super Bowl.

The 49ers headed toward a third consecutive division title in 1972 but an injury would test the resolve of the team and Brodie, who had turned 37. He suffered an ankle sprain Week 5 when he was dragged down awkwardly by New York Giants defensive lineman Jack Gregory. Brodie was hurting so badly that for the first time in his career, at any level, he was carried off the field on a stretcher.

Spurrier started the next eight games, leading the 49ers to a 5-2-1 record and putting them on a brink of a playoff spot if they could beat Minnesota in the finale.

Brodie suited up for the two previous games, against the Los Angeles Rams and Atlanta Falcons, and he seethed privately when Nolan didn't call on him in either instance. Brodie felt he had regained his health and was more than ready to return. He thought he deserved to get his job back because he didn't feel like he had done anything to lose it. But again, Nolan decided to start Spurrier in the finale against Minnesota, a game the 49ers had to win to clinch the division title. Brodie, who felt like he was ready to go some three or four weeks earlier, again watched from the sideline, stewing over Nolan's decision. By then, the relationship between Brodie and Nolan had become so strained that the two barely spoke to one another. When they had something to say to each other, they generally communicated through Jim Shofner, the 49ers quarterbacks and receivers coach.

It was late in the third quarter, after Minnesota capitalized on Spurrier's third interception by scoring a touchdown to take a 17-6 lead, that Shofner let Brodie know that Nolan wanted him to go in the game.

GAME OF MY LIFE
BY JOHN BRODIE
DECEMBER 16, 1972—SAN FRANCISCO, CALIFORNIA

I was still pretty upset over being kept on the bench when I felt like I was ready to play, so when Shofner told me Dick wanted me to go in, the first thing that came into my head was to tell him to take a hike.

But all I did was think it to myself. I never said anything like that. Instead, after a pause, I got up from the bench, ripped off my warm-up jacket, and began throwing some passes on the sideline to get ready to go into the game. And I remember a roar coming from the crowd when they saw me start to warm up.

Our team was in a tough spot, I'll say that. You could see that some people had already given up on us and were heading for the exits. We were down 17-6 to a great Minnesota defense, the "Purple People Eaters," with little more than a quarter to play. Our only chance was to let the ball fly. We knew that, but so did the Vikings.

It didn't start out too well for us either. Every chance I had, I was putting the ball up—something like 15 times within 10 minutes. Two of my first three passes were intercepted. But it wasn't anything I could worry about at that moment. I just had to keep throwing.

Our defense bailed us out by stopping the Vikings after each of my interceptions and forcing them to punt. But on their second punt, they pinned us on our own 1-yard line, where Terry Brown had pushed Mike Eischeid's 51-yard punt out of bounds.

John Isenbarger gave us a little breathing room with a 12-yard catch and then Gene Washington blew past Minnesota defenders for a 53-yard catch to get us within striking distance. A couple plays later, Gene and I hooked up again for the touchdown. There's nothing like a 99-yard drive to restore your confidence.

We got the ball back with about a minute and a half, down 17-13, and the Vikings made some critical mistakes. The biggest was a 26-yard pass interference penalty that gave us a first down at the Vikings' 26. We got down to the 2-yard line on a run and a pass, and from there, I rolled out and found Dick Witcher in the end zone for the touchdown. There were 25 seconds left and we were in front for the first time.

The Vikings had a chance to tie it at the gun, but Fred Cox was wide left with a 43-yard field goal attempt as time expired, and we were division champions for a third consecutive season.

I was pretty giddy considering where I had been at the start of the game, but I was taken by surprise by what happened next. Fans were spilling over the railings and swarming onto the field celebrating our comeback. The next thing I knew I was being grabbed and lifted off the ground by a group of fans. They put me on their shoulders and gave me a dizzying, crazy, jubilant ride. Nothing like that had ever happened to me, before or since. It was wild. I was in the middle of an unruly circle that was jostling me and moving me slowly across the field to the locker room entrance. For a moment, I wondered whether some of the people around me were some of the same ones who had so often booed me over the years and given me grief. But that thought just faded away, overpowered by the joy and grit and emotion from the game of a lifetime, one that had put us back into the playoffs once more.

Looking back, and I've said and written this before, riding off the field triumphantly on the shoulders of fans would have been a nice way to finish my career. I feel that way because everything after the Minnesota game was kind of anti-climactic. But nothing is perfect, and I guess I wouldn't have it any other way. It was, after all, a tremendous ride.

◆　　◆　　◆

The next week in a playoff game against Dallas, the 49ers fell victim to the same kind of comeback they had pulled off against Minnesota.

Roger Staubach replaced an ineffective Craig Morton and rallied the Cowboys, who had trailed 28-10 going into the fourth quarter, to a 30-28 victory. Staubach led the Cowboys to two touchdowns in the last two minutes, with the game-winner coming after Dallas recovered an onside kick.

"That last one was basically just one of those crushing defeats," said Jim Shofner, the quarterbacks and receivers coach.

The defeat was crushing to Brodie as well. He wrote in *Open Field* that he sensed his enthusiasm for the game waning in the aftermath of the 49ers' third consecutive playoff loss to the Cowboys.

"It wasn't that I loved the game any less," Brodie wrote. "It was just that I could no longer bring to it the total energy and effort it would take to overcome what I felt had allowed this defeat to happen."

A month into the 1973 campaign, flying home from a 13-9 win at Atlanta, Brodie told Shofner of his intentions to retire at the end of the season.

"John, you can't do that,'" Shofner told him.

"Nope," Brodie replied. "Enough is enough."

Within a couple weeks, the 49ers were preparing for life after Brodie. Coach Dick Nolan announced that Spurrier would start ahead of Brodie, though in his initial start against New Orleans, Spurrier struggled early and was pulled for Brodie, who led a 40-0 win over the Saints.

But even a big win against the Saints wasn't going to change Brodie's course toward retirement. Before his final game on December 15, 1973, against Pittsburgh, the 49ers saluted him with "John Brodie Day" and his No. 12 jersey was retired. As Brodie walked off the field after the game to meet his family, he noticed a message on Candlestick Park's electronic scoreboard reading "End of an era."

But it was also the beginning of a new one for Brodie. He plunged into a new career as a broadcaster and eventually he embarked on a second professional sports career as a golfer on the Seniors PGA Tour. He beat Chi Chi Rodriguez and George Archer in a playoff in the 1991

Security Pacific Senior Classic in Los Angeles to win his first PGA title. He finished in the Top 10 in more than 10 other tournaments and also became a regular in celebrity tour events across the country.

Football nevertheless remained very much a part of his life, whether as a broadcast analyst or a mentor for family and friends. His family connection centered around his daughter, Diane, who married former NFL quarterback Chris Chandler. Like his father-in-law, Chandler played 17 NFL seasons, though he played for eight teams to Brodie's one.

Brodie's continuing passion for football also came through in his impromptu instructional sessions for friends and acquaintances. Trent Dilfer, a Super Bowl-winning quarterback with Baltimore who struggled earlier in his career while with Tampa Bay, remembers being on the receiving end of one of Brodie's informal training sessions. The two had been golfing at a celebrity tournament in Ocala, Florida, in 1996 and Brodie began ripping into Dilfer, telling him he was a better player than he had shown.

"He was so hard on me, but in a good way, kind of like you want your dad to be," Dilfer recalls. "He would just tear you apart and then build you up.

"We were on the putting green with our golf shoes and he told me to start doing pass drops. I thought it was just going to be a few and we were out there for quite a while … Chris Chandler actually walked down from the dinner and watched us from the balcony and said, 'What the hell you doing, J.B?'" says Dilfer. "I'm sweating. My golf shirt is soaking wet, and the golf green is all torn up. 'Lower! Lower! Lower!' He'd yell at me, 'Get lower! Explode off this leg!' Then he would get the ball—he's 60 years old—and let it rip. He still had it. He really helped me."

That's the way life was for Brodie—family, football, and golf—until it took a devastating turn in 2000. While watching *Monday Night Football* at home in La Quinta, California, he suffered a major stroke that left him with severe speech problems and impaired arm and leg movement on his right side.

"We're not even sure how he survived because it was a massive, massive stroke," says his wife, Sue. "I just think maybe there's a reason he made it. I know that he's influenced a lot of people who have had strokes. We've gotten a lot of people to have checkups who wouldn't have otherwise gotten checkups."

Doctors later determined a blocked carotid artery caused the stroke. Before they could surgically insert a stent to help restore blood flow, Brodie suffered brain damage that basically wiped out his speech. Initially, he couldn't swallow, and doctors implanted a feeding tube in his stomach to help him survive. His right hand was balled up in a crooked fist and he could barely lift his right leg to walk.

Brodie remains in the midst of a long, difficult recovery, but he has also made substantial, and some would say, even miraculous progress. He has worked strenuously in rehabilitation to try to recover as much of his speech and his physical movements as he possibly can.

"He's not willing to give up on anything, and he's still got a good sense of humor," says Sue. "He's really quite amazing."

Years of intense physical therapy and speech therapy have allowed him to regain some movement in his right arm, and his right leg has also gotten more limber. Additionally, Brodie has painstakingly expanded his vocabulary, replacing gruff, one-word remarks with two- or three-word sentences.

In late 2006 and early 2007, Brodie took another step forward in his rehabilitation; he underwent two stem cell treatments in Russia. He further expanded his vocabulary and markedly improved his strength, balance, and flexibility. Brodie and his family remain hopeful that his improvement will continue.

"Considering at one point it was touch and go whether he lived or not, he's doing really well," Chandler said. "No one knows but him how hard it's been. He was a guy who held court. He'd sit around and talk. Everybody observed and listened. Obviously, it's been extremely difficult. But it's a unique challenge for him, because he could have thrown in the towel years ago if he really wanted to. He's just kept battling, and all in all, he's doing extremely well. The laugh is still there. The laugh has never changed."

Chapter 9

RAY WERSCHING

From the sideline, 49ers kicker Ray Wersching watched the drive unfold, almost forgetting it would be up to him to supply the ending. From their own 11-yard line, the 49ers had moved to the Dallas Cowboys' 6, largely on the running of Lenvil Elliott and the passing of Joe Montana.

Now, it was third down with less than a minute to go, and the 49ers were trailing 27-21 in the NFC Championship at San Francisco's Candlestick Park. Three Dallas defenders were furiously chasing a backpedaling Montana. He managed to throw an arcing pass into the end zone, where Dwight Clark made a leaping, fingertip catch to tie it at 27-all.

"After 'The Catch,' I was going nuts along with everybody else on the sideline," Wersching says. "All of a sudden, I'm going, 'Oh, I've got to kick the extra point and I'd better make it.'"

Wersching jogged onto the field, feeling the pressure that went with transforming himself, in an instant, from spectator to competitor.

"In your mind, you're going through your normal ritual of what you do before a kick," Wersching says. "I had to relax. I had to concentrate and focus, take a deep breath. I reminded myself to keep my head down, follow through."

With Randy Cross snapping and Montana holding, everything went just like it was supposed to, and Wersching delivered the decisive point in the 49ers' first conference championship, helping to put to rest the ghosts from three successive playoff losses to the Cowboys during the early '70s.

"As soon as I hit it I knew it was good," Wersching says. "It felt great and it was a relief at the same time. But that was the hardest extra point I've ever kicked.

"When it dawned on us we were going to the Super Bowl, it was jubilation," says Wersching. "You finally realize, 'Hey, we've done it. We've taken the next step, a big step, and we have only one more game to play.'"

That Super Bowl would indeed become a seminal game for Wersching, whose unlikely path toward a career in football arose from an immigrant family's desire for a better life.

Wersching was born August 21, 1950, in a refugee camp in Mondsee, Austria, just outside Salzburg, in the aftermath of World War II.

His parents, Wendell and Theresa Wersching, lived in Belgrade, Yugoslavia, before the outbreak of war. Wersching's father, who was German, joined the German army. He eventually was captured and spent much of World War II in a POW camp in Great Britain, according to his son.

For several years, his father had no idea where his wife was or even if she was alive, Ray Wersching says. His mother had no idea about her husband's fate. It wasn't until Wendell Wersching's release from prison after the war around 1946 that the couple learned each other's whereabouts and reunited.

The Werschings spent several years in Austria at the refugee camp while Wendell Wersching worked on getting immigration papers for the family to move to the United States.

"He heard so much about the United States from the other POWs while he was in England," Wersching says. "They were always talking about what they were going to do after the war. He wanted a better life for us."

Ray Wersching, the youngest of four siblings, was two years old when his family received clearance to come to the United States. They settled in the Los Angeles area, his father working as a carpenter and his mom cleaning houses. They became American citizens.

Ray Wersching *Photo © Michael Zagaris*

But American football was not the sport of choice for the Werschings, at least not initially. Soccer was the family's passion. That's what Ray played growing up, starting at age five, though it was mostly in informal recreational leagues because few schools had any soccer programs in the late 1960s.

It wasn't until his junior year at Earl Warren High School in Downey, California, in 1966 that Ray Wersching played football, deciding to follow the path of an older brother, Randy. He was playing guard for the junior varsity team when one of the coaches gathered the team up and asked, "Can anyone kick?"

"I just raised my hand and said, 'Yeah, I can,'" Wersching recalls. "I knew I could kick because I had played soccer."

So began Wersching's kicking career. He still remembers vividly one junior varsity game where he was called on to try a 48-yard field goal.

"I remember my coach saying, 'I know you can do it,' and hearing guys on the other team saying, 'Yeah, right,' but it went through," Wersching says.

Graduating from high school in 1968, Wersching went on to play guard and kick for Cerritos Junior College for two years, refining his self-taught kicking style along the way. From there, he went to play for the University of California at Berkeley, where his brother, Randy, had also been a kicker.

Ray Wersching often said his brother was a better kicker than he was. Randy Wersching had tryouts with Atlanta, Denver, and the Los Angeles Rams, but never was signed.

Initially, that's how Ray Wersching's NFL career began. He tried out for the Atlanta Falcons in 1972 but didn't make it. He caught on with the San Diego Chargers in 1973, though his kicking lacked consistency and the Chargers "were always trying to get rid of me," Wersching recalls.

He was released and re-signed several times during four years with the Chargers before being cut again just before the start of the 1977 season. Coach Tommy Prothro let him know the Chargers would not consider bringing him back. "This is it," Wersching was told.

During his time with the Chargers, Wersching had made 32 of his 68 field goal tries—a 47-percent conversion rate. Wersching still hoped to catch on with another team and recruited an auto mechanic friend to hold the ball for his self-run practice sessions three or four times per week at a local school yard. But the weeks went by and no phone call came from a team in search of a kicker.

Thinking his football career could be over, Wersching, who graduated with an accounting degree, got a job. He scaled back his practice sessions to one, perhaps two a week.

That was when he finally got a call from Howard Mudd, a former Chargers assistant who had left to become the 49ers offensive line coach in 1977. Wersching was in the middle of auditing a carrot-processing plant on a broiling day in the desert town of Thermal, California, when he fielded the call from Mudd.

"He said, 'Hey, do you want to try out?' I said, 'When do you want me to come up?'" says Wersching.

His boss tried to talk him out of it but Wersching took a "sick" day and flew up to the 49ers' facility in Redwood City the next day for the tryout in front of coach Ken Meyer.

"Something just happened, something just clicked, and it was like I never kicked better in my life," Wersching says. "Everything went right through the middle of the uprights. They signed me that day, and I stuck around for a while."

Wersching, who replaced Steve Mike-Mayer, called up his supervisor at the San Diego accounting firm and told him he had won the job as the 49ers' place kicker, a position he would hold for the next 11 years.

His first game for the 49ers went like his tryout. On October 16, 1977, Wersching hit a then career-best 50-yard field goal against the New York Giants in his first attempt as a 49er.

A month later, at New Orleans, Wersching drilled a 33-yarder in overtime to beat the Saints. When New Orleans visited the 49ers at Candlestick Park, Wersching did it again, nailing a 42-yarder in the final seconds of regulation.

The two field goals were the first of 11 game-winners during his career with the 49ers.

"I think I always knew I could do it. It just took a while to develop," Wersching says.

Wersching finished his first year with the 49ers converting 10 of 17 field goals, including all five from 30-39 yards, to finish with a .588-percent conversion rate. It was a big improvement over any of his seasons in San Diego and foreshadowed even better things to come with the 49ers.

"Maybe I took it wrong, but with the Chargers I never really felt like I was part of the team," Wersching says. "I'd always be off to the side with the punter. When I came to the 49ers, it was completely the opposite. They treated you like you were part of the team. It changed my attitude and gave me the confidence to perform."

That's not to say Wersching did not endure some tumult. The 49ers were purchased in 1977 by the Edward J. DeBartolo family, and the first couple of seasons under his son, Eddie, and general manager Joe Thomas were chaotic.

Over a two-year period, Monte Clark, Ken Meyer, Pete McCulley, and Fred O'Connor were let go as coaches of the 49ers before Thomas' dismissal and Bill Walsh's hiring as coach and general manager before the 1979 season.

"You just didn't know what was going to happen," Wersching says. "There would be times when you would wonder if you're going to be gone, if you're going to be there, or if you were going to have a new coach. Things were unstable. . . . When Bill came, you just knew he was in control of it. Eddie was the owner and he was above him, but it was Bill's team and everybody knew it. And everyone could see they were trying to find talent, trying to improve themselves. We went 2-14 in Bill's first year, but there was some progress. That was the feeling. We may not be winning games, but we're getting better."

The selection of Joe Montana in Bill Walsh's first draft had a lot to do with the 49ers growing success on the field. Montana's arrival in 1979 also was a boon for Wersching, who inherited the then-backup quarterback as his holder.

Montana's sureness in handling the ball on placements inspired confidence in Wersching. He reached such a comfort zone with him as his holder that he convinced Walsh to allow Montana to continue in the job even after he became the full-time starting quarterback in 1981. Montana remained Wersching's holder for seven years until back problems in 1986 forced him to confine his play to quarterback.

"Besides being a pretty good quarterback, he was one dang good holder," says Wersching, who developed a ritual of patting Montana's shoulder and whispering 'help me,' before every field goal attempt.

"Joe had a knack where it didn't matter where the snap was, I knew he would get it down in the right spot," adds Wersching. "It was always going to be there. It's hard to describe, but knowing that, it relaxed me, and I was able to concentrate more and just drive the ball through."

But driving the ball was something Wersching couldn't even think about doing when the 49ers opened the 1981 season. It simply hurt too much.

During preegame warm-ups at Detroit in the Silverdome, Wersching pulled a hip flexor muscle.

"It really hurt. Just hitting the ball was painful," Wersching says. "I told Bill [Walsh], and he said, 'We don't have anybody else. You've got to go out there. The doctor said you're not going to hurt it any worse than it is now.' So we just went for it."

It would prove to be a fateful decision. Wersching couldn't really drive the kickoffs. His knuckleball kicks bounced crazily all over the Pontiac Silverdome turf and the Lions struggled to handle them, something that Walsh took note of and would apply again when the 49ers returned in January to Pontiac to play in the Super Bowl.

The 49ers brought in Matt Bahr to replace Wersching, who was sidelined for a month. He rejoined the club in time to help them rout Dallas in the first of their two meetings during the '81 season.

"No one knew who we were," Wersching says. "No one knew Joe. No one knew Ronnie [Lott]. I think that helped us win but we were also pretty good."

Their drive toward their first postseason appearance in nine years included a pivotal November matchup with the rival Los Angeles Rams at their place. Rams quarterback Pat Haden led a drive resulting in a short touchdown run by Wendell Tyler that put Los Angeles up 31-30 with 1:54 remaining.

"I was on the sideline thinking, 'They left us too much time on the clock,'" Wersching says.

Indeed, they had. Montana drove the 49ers to within field goal range and then held for Wersching as he kicked a 37-yard field goal as time expired, completing a season-sweep of the Rams that had ended a nine-game losing streak to Los Angeles dating back to 1976.

"That was so meaningful because wins had been hard to come by against the Rams," Wersching says.

The victory was the first of five in a row to close out the season. They went on to beat the New York Giants 38-24 in an NFC playoff and then edged Dallas to advance to the Super Bowl.

GAME OF MY LIFE
BY RAY WERSCHING
JANUARY 24, 1982—PONTIAC, MICHIGAN

It was a first for the 49ers reaching the Super Bowl. People did not expect us to be there, but things just seemed to keep falling our way.

We were playing the Cincinnati Bengals, an upstart team just like us. But we had a lot of confidence, especially after getting past Dallas in the NFC Championship game, and we knew if we played our game, no one could beat us.

When we first got to the team hotel, Bill Walsh was there in this funky-looking hat and bellman's uniform. We didn't know it was him at first. He was trying to grab peoples' bags. We grabbed them away from him. I don't think anybody tipped him. Bill was a comedian and that episode helped ease some of the tension.

The day of the game was really cold, ice and snow all over the place. The vice president, George Bush, was there and they closed off traffic for everybody to the stadium because of his motorcade. So we were stuck in the traffic for about 45 minutes or something like that. We didn't know if we were going to make it to the game on time. I remember some of the guys going, "Well, we can walk." But someone said no to that. We eventually made it OK. I remember Bill saying Lindsy McLean, our trainer, was going to start at quarterback if our bus was any later. Anyway, he was making jokes and we finally made it to the stadium.

During the pregame warm-ups, Bill came up to me and said, "Remember the first game of the year against Detroit, when you put the kickoffs on the ground and they had trouble handling it? We're going to do it again."

I resisted. I told him I wanted to kick it off deep. I wanted to show what I could do. This was the Super Bowl. Bill told me again we were going to put the kickoffs on the ground at some point and I finally said, "OK, you're the boss."

Well, it worked. It worked better than I ever thought it would.

We were leading 14-0 and Joe, who was my holder besides being the starting quarterback, had another drive going late in the second quarter. They got down to the Bengals' 5-yard line, and on fourth down I came on and kicked a field goal, a 22-yarder with 18 seconds left. That was when I did the first squib kick. It bounced every which way. It was unpredictable, just like a knuckleball, and the Bengals' Archie Griffin couldn't handle it. Milt McColl recovered it for us at the 4-yard line.

We kicked a field goal right away and I kicked off again, squibbing the ball downfield. It started taking those irregular hops and the Bengals nearly lost it again before finally falling on the ball as we were closing in. Time ran out and we went into halftime leading 20-0.

When I kicked off to start the second half, I had started a fifth play in a row, two field goals and three kickoffs. I guess that's pretty unusual and for a kicker, really an amazing and fun sequence. What was great about it was you felt like you were contributing. Don't get me wrong; kicking a field goal at the end of a game is great, but I wish every game something like this would happen.

Though we had the biggest halftime lead in Super Bowl history, the Bengals began to rally. They scored a touchdown on their first series of the second half and were getting close to another. That was when our defense came alive.

I remember different players making great plays. Danny Bunz made that great goal-line tackle, and then on fourth down, Jack "Hacksaw" Reynolds and the interior line, they stuffed their last run. That was unbelievable. Everybody was going crazy on the sideline. That was a turning point where we finally stopped their momentum and it shifted back to us.

The Bengals did get another touchdown but we went on a long drive of our own that ended with another field goal. Then Eric Wright's interception of Kenny Anderson led to another field goal and we were leading 26-14 with just a couple minutes left.

Dan Ross caught a short touchdown pass with just a few seconds left, but once Dwight Clark recovered their onside kick, the game was ours.

We finally could call ourselves champions. It was just a thrill to win and it was fun. It was a fun game to play. I just felt great to be able to contribute in the way that I did and being a little lucky with those squib kicks. Everybody was emotional and jubilant. It was a great conclusion to a fantastic year.

And it was capped a couple days later with a parade down Market Street in San Francisco. They put us in these motorized cable cars. I remember Bill wasn't all that thrilled with the idea. He was afraid no one would show up. But the number of people was staggering, tens of thousands lined the street as we went down Market Street. It was amazing how many people were there. And I just remember telling Bill, "A lot of people showed up."

Any kicker, any player, is going to have ups and downs, and Wersching was no exception. In 1984, Wersching led the league in scoring with 131 points, but he was bothered for a long time by his last-second miss of a 37-yard field goal try against Pittsburgh midway through the season.

If he had made it, the score would have been tied at 20-all and the 49ers would have had a chance to win it in overtime. Instead, the Steelers hung on, handing the only loss of the year to a 49ers team that Bill Walsh continues to regard as the greatest in the club's 62-year history. The 49ers finished that season with their second Super Bowl championship, beating the Dan Marino-led Miami Dolphins in the title game for their NFL record 18th win of the season.

But with Wersching, he made so many more than he ever missed. He still has the best field goal percentage in team history among kickers with at least 100 field goals attempts (72.8 percent), and his 979 points (409 PATs, 190 FGs) is second only to Jerry Rice's 1,130.

"He was instrumental in countless triumphs and has made the difference in many of our greatest victories," Walsh said in 1988 on the day the 49ers let Wersching go.

Years later, when asked about Wersching, Walsh replied, "He was the best clutch kicker I've been around. In 1981, he was right at the center of our success and when we played in the Super Bowl, Ray was at his very best and it paid off for us. Put it this way: had we had an average kicker or a good kicker, we might not have won. But we had a great kicker. We had Ray."

Wersching continues to reside in the Bay area, with his wife, Christine, daughter Sydney, 18, and son Ray, 15. He works for a San Francisco accounting firm.

Chapter 10

DWIGHT HICKS

Dwight Hicks got the phone call at the end of the Philadelphia Eagles' training camp, just as they were heading into preparations for their 1979 regular season opener.

"I have bad news for you," Eagles director of player personnel Carl Peterson told Hicks. Summoned to a meeting with the head coach, Hicks listened as Dick Vermeil told him he was being cut. It was the second time in a year that an NFL tryout had ended with Hicks' release.

A four-year letterman at the University of Michigan and a former All-Big Ten selection, Hicks was the Detroit Lions' sixth-round pick the year before but was let go by Monte Clark in the preseason. Hicks left Detroit for Canada to play for the Toronto Argonauts before he took another shot at the NFL. He signed in December 1978 with the Eagles, whose team headquarters was only a short drive from Hicks' hometown of Pennsauken, New Jersey.

"I was thinking, 'Yes, I get to go home and play,'" Hicks says.

He got himself in the best shape of his life and had a strong training camp, better, he thought, than some of the safeties the Eagles had kept over him.

"I knew I could play, and to get cut again, it was like somebody ripped out my heart," Hicks says. "I felt like, 'Hey, wait a minute. I'm better than those guys out there. What's going on?' But what could you do?"

Hicks wondered out loud whether he should just quit. His secondary coach with the Eagles, Fred Bruney, who had advocated keeping Hicks, would hear none of it.

"He just looked me dead in the face: 'If you stop playing football, you'll be making the biggest mistake of your life,'" Hicks says. But for a time, Hicks had no choice in the matter.

He moved to Southfield, Michigan, a suburb of Detroit, and began working at a health food store, doing everything from stocking shelves to working the cash register. Hicks worked out sporadically, trying to stay in some semblance of football shape.

One day, between shifts at the health food store, the 49ers called to invite Hicks to a tryout. He was among a handful of defensive backs, receivers, and quarterbacks the 49ers brought in for an evaluation as the season got under way.

"We were in shorts and cleats," Hicks said. "We had to cover the wide receivers and do some drills. I remember these guys were diving and jumping all over the place, just trying to make an impression. I wasn't diving or jumping. I'd just close in on the wide receivers and I think I showed them I could make a play."

The 49ers still sent Hicks home without offering him a contract. Former wide receiver R.C. Owens, who was working for coach Bill Walsh in the 49ers' front office, gave Hicks a ride back to the airport. As he dropped him off, Owens told Hicks, "I have a feeling you're going to be back here."

Three weeks later, Hicks came home from work to find a message on his telephone answering tape from John McVay, the 49ers director of football operations. "There's a plane ticket for you at Detroit Metro airport," McVay said.

When he worked out previously for the 49ers, they had given Hicks a round-trip airplane ticket. "This time, I found a one-way ticket at the airport. That's when I knew I was going to be there for a while," Hicks says.

Hicks signed with the 49ers in late October, joining the team midway through the season. He appeared primarily on special teams until his fourth game, when he came on to play against Denver in place of injured safety Melvin Morgan.

Dwight Hicks *Photo © Michael Zagaris*

Hicks promptly stopped a Denver drive by swiping a Craig Morton pass in the end zone for his first career interception.

"I had realized one of my goals and I thought I'd be ecstatic," Hicks said in a newspaper interview. "But as I caught the ball and was bringing it down, I said, 'Damn it! This is what I should have been doing the whole time.'"

Coach Bill Walsh saw to it that history didn't repeat itself with Hicks. Morgan's season ended with his placement on injured reserve. Tony Dungy, who had fought through injuries after opening the 1979 season as the 49ers' starting free safety, was available, but Walsh opted to keep Hicks in the lineup.

Starting only the final four games of the season, Hicks finished with a team-high five interceptions. By the next season, Hicks entrenched himself as the 49ers' starting free safety, showcasing his instinctive coverage skills, fierce hitting, and leadership qualities on a weekly basis. He was the lone survivor of a relentless attempt by Walsh to upgrade the secondary over the next two seasons. During that span, the three other positions in the secondary were each manned by at least two players.

The most radical changeover occurred in 1981 when the 49ers drafted defensive backs Ronnie Lott, Eric Wright, Carlton Williamson, and Lynn Thomas. Walsh immediately installed Lott and Wright as the starting cornerbacks, and Williamson joined Hicks as a deep back, playing strong safety. Thomas was designated as the team's nickel back, coming in on passing downs as an extra defensive back.

As the lone veteran in the group and "defensive quarterback," Hicks had the job of helping the 49ers' young secondary make their pre-snap adjustments and getting them on the same page with their respective assignments.

"Basically, he just tried to encourage us," Lott told a newspaper reporter. "He knew we were going to make mistakes. I feel a lot of it was because he was in a similar situation. He had been there before."

The 49ers' reconfigured, painfully young secondary endured some growing pains, particularly early on in their first season. But their athletic ability and hunger to produce accelerated the learning process.

"I'm not much of a rah-rah guy. It was just a matter of keeping their spirits up," Hicks says. "You could sense the ability was there. What I wanted to do was let them know that even though they made mistakes early, they had to keep working hard and asserting themselves. I never had anything handed to me and I could appreciate the need not to give up."

The payoff showed itself on the field. With a little time, experience, and patience, the four newcomers weathered their trial by fire and proved to be as good for Hicks as the lone holdover in the 49ers' secondary was for them. Together, the group blazed the championship trail for the 49ers, and in a breakout game at Washington, "Dwight Hicks and the Hot Licks" helped shape the team's Super Bowl destiny.

GAME OF MY LIFE
BY DWIGHT HICKS
OCTOBER 4, 1981—WASHINGTON, D.C.

The Washington Redskins had always been a formidable opponent. They were a very good, very solid team, even if their record at the time— the Redskins had lost their first four games—didn't show it. In some ways, they were like us. They were starting to improve under the guidance of a good coach in Joe Gibbs, who was in his first season in Washington. We were really starting to make strides as a team under Bill Walsh, who was in his third year as the 49ers coach. But we knew that if we wanted to be a team to be reckoned with, if we wanted to break through to join the NFL elite, the Redskins were the type of team that we had beat.

I wanted to do well, too. My mom, two brothers, and some family friends were driving down from New Jersey to see me play.

Going into the Washington game at RFK Stadium, we were 2-2, but we hadn't won on the road yet. We needed a road win to show we could go into a hostile environment and succeed. Our last game away from home a couple weeks before, at Atlanta, hadn't gone well. We didn't play well as a secondary or a defense. We got together as a secondary after that game and we took it upon ourselves to play better and not to make the same mistakes. We knew we were better than what we had showed. We had to just start trusting ourselves as well as our ability to get the job done.

Now, were we young? Yes. I'm sure a lot of people thought Bill Walsh was off his rocker for starting three rookies in the secondary. Actually, we had four rookies in the secondary a good bit of the time because Lynn Thomas was our nickel back. I was the only veteran and I'd been in the league for only a couple years. Our other starters were Ronnie Lott, Eric

Wright, and Carlton Williamson. Lott and Wright were the cornerbacks and Williamson was the strong safety. I played free safety and was kind of the quarterback of the defense. My responsibility was to make the on-field calls and adjustments to try to make sure we were all on the same page.

The 49ers hadn't played the Redskins all that much, and the few times that they did, they hadn't done very well. We'd gone 0-3 in three regular-season meetings since 1973.

But this time, things began to go our way from the start. We got the ball first and Joe Montana led a long touchdown drive. When the Redskins got the ball for the first time, John Riggins carried four or five times in a row and helped them get to about our 20-yard line.

Terry Metcalf came in and he bounced it outside. He was about to turn it upfield but Ronnie Lott was closing in on him and I was coming in to clean up. Metcalf tried to hurdle Ronnie, but Ronnie launched himself right into his midsection and his helmet knocked the ball from his hands. It popped straight up, and I grabbed it out of the air. I went down the sideline 80 yards for a touchdown.

What I liked about it then and like about it now is it was a collaborative effort from our whole defense and in particular our secondary, because we worked as a unit. The fumble return was the longest in team history at the time and it put us in front 14-0. But we were far from finished.

Before the day was done, Redskins quarterback Joe Theismann had been benched. He had only 10 completions in 24 attempts and threw two interceptions. I picked off both of them, and returned one for a touchdown. Tom Flick came on and didn't do any better. He got picked off twice, too, once by Ronnie and also by Milt McColl, who was one of our linebackers. In all, we forced six turnovers by the Redskins.

The thing is, when you get a turnover and you score off it, it's a big change. Put it this way: football is a game of emotion and momentum and when you take away the ball from your opponent and give it to your offense, that is a big boost. That is a huge momentum swing, and you need to do those things when you're on the road.

When I was running that fumble back, the crowd went quiet. I could hear them go quiet.

By halftime, we were leading 24-3. In the third quarter, the Redskins got a drive going but I picked off a pass and brought it back 72 yards. I got pushed out of bounds at the Washington 22 and went to the sideline. Guys were congratulating me on the bench. But right after that, the Redskins intercepted Montana to get the ball back.

We got back in the game on the sudden change and I was still trying to get my helmet on and buckle my chin strap. Theismann tried to hit a skinny post over the middle. He took like a five-step drop, and it was one of those quick-pass type plays where as a defensive back, you have to make a decision and react to whatever is happening. I dropped back, and you can't just break on anything, because if he pump fakes and you bite, you're dead. I was still winded from the previous play, and boom, Theismann throws the ball. I broke on it, picked it off, and took it back about 30 yards for a touchdown. That put us up 30-3. The Redskins scored a couple of fourth-quarter touchdowns, but it did nothing to change the outcome.

After the game, nobody really said a whole lot, but we'd gone on the road and beaten a good team, and we were empowered by that. There was a feeling that we'd done it once, and we were good enough to do it again and again. Really, it was a great game for all of us and that victory had legs. We took from it the lesson that if we played hard, if we competed, we'd win. It was as simple as that. That's how I felt. That's how we felt as a secondary. That's how we felt as a team.

During a Las Vegas reunion party of the 49ers' five Super Bowl teams in 2006, former team owner Eddie DeBartolo remembered the win at Washington as central to the 49ers' climb to the top.

"I think that's when we realized that we had a really good team with a chance to do something special," DeBartolo said. The dramatic turnaround in the secondary reinforced that notion, and Hicks and the young, aggressive defensive backs playing beside him became a focal point of the 49ers' emergence as an NFL power.

It was after their return from Washington that San Francisco sportscaster Martin Wyatt came up with the group's enduring nickname: "Dwight Hicks and the Hot Licks." It was a takeoff from the name of a popular rock'n'roll group, Dan Hicks and the Hot Licks.

"When he told me the name, I thought, 'Oh, that sounds good,'" Hicks says. "It just kind of stuck."

It stuck for a reason. Dwight Hicks finished third in the NFL with nine interceptions—one shy of the team record—and he returned them an NFL-high and team-record 239 yards. Hicks and Ronnie Lott were among six 49ers who went to the Pro Bowl as they helped end a four-year drought without a representative from San Francisco. The two helped lift the team's defense to a No. 2 overall ranking after the defense had languished at No. 27 the previous year.

Though the Redskins dropped to 0-5 after the loss to the 49ers, they validated the quality of the 49ers' victory by winning eight of their last 11 games. The Redskins went to the Super Bowl the next two years, beating Miami following the strike-shortened 1982 campaign.

Following the 1983 season, the Redskins lost to the Los Angeles Raiders in the Super Bowl after advancing to the championship by defeating the 49ers in an NFC title game that would prove pivotal to San Francisco and to Hicks.

The 49ers followed the Washington victory by routing Dallas 45-14 at Candlestick Park, their first regular-season win over the Cowboys since 1972. They never lost a road game the rest of the year after having gone in to Washington with just two victories in the previous 28 games away from home dating back to 1977.

The 49ers' punctuated their NFL-best 16-3 record with a 26-21 victory over Cincinnati in the Super Bowl in which Hicks thwarted the Bengals' first scoring drive with a goal-line interception. It was only the fourth time in NFL history that a team had won 16 or more games in a season.

Though Hicks had emerged as one of the NFL's top safeties, he didn't feel that his salary reflected his level of play or achievement. On their own volition, the 49ers gave Hicks a raise following his contributions toward the team's first championship. But in the weeks leading up to the start of the 1983 season, Hicks asked the 49ers to renegotiate his contract to bring it in line with the league's top defensive backs. He said that Bill Walsh, who was also the team's general manager, had indicated he would re-do his deal if he made the Pro Bowl again, which he did following the 1982 season.

The 49ers refused to negotiate with Hicks or his agent, and the problem between the sides simmered for more than a month before Hicks walked away from the team, two days before an important divisional game against the Los Angeles Rams.

Hicks said he wouldn't return to the team until management agreed to discuss his contract. The walkout infuriated owner Eddie DeBartolo and Bill Walsh, and Hicks was threatened with suspension unless he immediately rejoined the team. But Hicks stayed away, missing the Rams game, which the 49ers won with Ronnie Lott starting at free safety in place of Hicks.

Both sides eventually gave a little bit, and Hicks rejoined the team in time to start the next game against the New York Jets after DeBartolo pledged to "take care of" the contractual issues.

The 49ers, trying to get back to the Super Bowl after struggling through strike-shortened 1982 with a 3-6 mark, closed the season with three consecutive wins to clinch their second NFC West title in three years. They hung on to beat Detroit in a playoff game when Eddie Murray missed a field goal in the final moments and advanced to play the Redskins in the NFC title game.

Washington jumped in front 21-0, but in the fourth quarter Joe Montana threw two touchdown passes to tie it up. The comeback fell short when Mark Mosely kicked a field goal as time expired. The kick came after a Redskins drive that had been aided by two controversial penalty calls against cornerbacks Eric Wright and Ronnie Lott. The pass interference call on Wright and holding call on Lott still rankles Walsh and many of the players who continue to believe the officials botched the calls and cost them the game.

In the locker room after the 24-21 loss to the Redskins, the anger and despair were palpable in the quiet of the 49ers' locker room. Hicks stood up and broke the silence. He told his teammates to remember well their misery. He urged them to do everything in their power not to let it happen again, and to work to excel and dominate in their craft to give themselves the best chance to win games on their terms and keep the outcome out of officials' hands.

The 49ers seemed to take Hicks' words to heart.

"That Washington game was a springboard, just as that '83 season was a spring board," Walsh says. "When we came back to start again the next year, we had tremendous confidence."

The 49ers stormed through the season, winning all but one game en route to their second championship in four years. They finished the season at 18-1, with the secondary playing a major role in their final victory, a 38-16 triumph in the Super Bowl over Dan Marino and the Miami Dolphins.

As much pride as he took in the 49ers' second championship, Hicks said the chance to line up beside teammates Ronnie Lott, Eric Wright, and Carlton Williamson in the Pro Bowl following the 1984 season stands out as a singular honor.

"Super Bowls are great and that's why we play the game and that's why we compete," Hicks said. "But breaking the huddle in Hawaii and seeing the guys I worked with every day, it just doesn't get any better than that."

Hicks played only one more year for the 49ers, and the 1985 season was a struggle for him after he was switched to cornerback to accommodate Ronnie Lott's move to free safety. Walsh had always envisioned Lott's future at safety, and his ferocious hitting gave the 49ers a fearsome presence in the middle of the field. Hicks had a tougher transition moving from safety to cornerback. He did not have the speed to stay with the NFL's fastest receivers in man coverage. When he tried to compensate by playing off them, the opposition kept completing passes in front of him on hitch patterns.

The 49ers let Hicks go and he signed with Indianapolis, where he played the 1986 season before retiring from football after eight years in the NFL.

His playing days, in a manner of speaking, didn't end when he hung it up. Hicks took up acting. He has played parts in such movies as *The Rock* and *Armageddon*, and television shows such as *X-Files*, *The Practice*, *ER*, and *Passions*, a daytime soap opera.

"I feel very fortunate that I found another passion to pursue in the arts," Hicks says. "It's something I want to do and I've worked hard at."

Hicks says he still stays in touch with former teammates from his playing days but has kept only a handful of mementos from football career.

"I've got a few game balls and my Super Bowl rings," Hicks said. "But I gave a lot of the other stuff away. A lot of people thought I was crazy. Were some of those things a part of who I am? Yes. But for some reason, I'm a giver and I wanted to put a smile on somebody's face.

"I still keep in touch with some of the guys, some of my teammates. That's what makes me feel good. That's what it's about. It's great I played a game and got paid for it. It was great to be part of some the 49ers' great teams. That's history and it's a wonderful history. Those were some great moments in my life. But, you know, I've moved on."

Chapter 11

BILL WALSH

While looking for his first coaching job fifty years ago, Bill Walsh came across an opening at Washington Union High School in Fremont, California.

"It was 1957," Walsh said. "They had lost 27 straight games. I don't think there were others who were interested in the job. I took it for $4,650 a year, including an extra $250 for having a master's degree."

As part of his coaching duties, he drove the team bus as well. "When you went to a game, you or one of the guys you worked with had to drive the players to the game," said Walsh, who graduated from nearby San Jose State with a degree in education. "That was just part of the job, so I learned to drive one of those big school buses."

In time, Walsh got to be a pretty good bus driver. He became an even better coach. Washington High went 9-1 and won its conference championship in the second of Walsh's three years at the school.

The turnaround at Washington High foreshadowed the success that would give rise to Walsh's Hall of Fame coaching career in the NFL and his standing today as one of football's great innovators and strategists. He was an early advocate of African Americans in coaching, and sought to heighten minority job opportunities in the NFL through a pioneering internship program.

"You can go through this league and almost every corner of every team is touched by Bill Walsh," said former 49ers owner Eddie DeBartolo, speaking to the *Los Angeles Times*. "I'm talking head coaches to coordinators to sons to cousins." DeBartolo's 49ers won three of their five Super Bowl titles in the 1980s with Walsh as their coach. "I tried to sit down and do his family tree of football once and I just quit," he said. "No one, and I mean no one, has put a mark and touched pro football in the way that Bill Walsh has."

Mike Holmgren, George Seifert, Brian Billick, Dennis Green, Mike Shanahan, Jon Gruden, Sam Wyche, Ray Rhodes, Pete Carroll, and Tony Dungy were among the coaches directly impacted by Walsh's approach to the game. Walsh's influence was felt in many ways: from the way he organized practices, to evaluating personnel, to putting together a game plan and scripting play calls.

"He was the original architect of the West Coast offense and timed passing," said Terry Donahue, the longtime UCLA coach and former 49ers general manager. "And not to minimize his three world championships as coach of the 49ers, but I think his greatest legacies are the fact that his offensive philosophy and system have continued to flourish and spread all over the United States and that he has so many disciples in coaching and management. I think that is an incredible testament to where Bill was philosophically and technically in relation to everybody else."

Walsh's practices were highly organized and he demanded that his players get it right. Over and over again, players heard a familiar refrain from Walsh: "Line it up. Let's run it one more time."

"Bill wanted perfection," said 49ers running back Bill Ring, who played for Walsh from 1981-86. Walsh also sought to practice every conceivable situation players could face in a game to help them perform when the time came to play in a game under pressure. They worked on the two-minute drill, the four-minute drill to protect a lead, red-zone plays, short-yardage and goal-line plays, when to call timeouts and when to stay in or go out of bounds, and on and on.

"We worked on the most intricate details of the game in every possible aspect," said 49ers tight end Brent Jones, who spent the early part of his 10-year career playing for Walsh.

Yet, Walsh's approach was never so regimented that there wasn't room for gut instinct or a foray into the unconventional. That included acquiring his franchise quarterback, Joe Montana, who hardly fit the NFL prototype, in the third round of the 1979 draft. He found a top

Bill Walsh *Photo © Michael Zagaris*

target for him near the bottom of the draft with 10th-round selection Dwight Clark.

Walsh said he knew weeks before the draft that the lean, spindly legged Montana would be NFL worthy after he and quarterbacks coach Sam Wyche saw the former Notre Dame star go through a 15-minute individual workout in Los Angeles.

"I told Sam, 'This is the guy,'" Walsh said. "Because his feet were so beautiful, his athletic ability was so beautiful. He reminded me of Joe Namath in his prime."

He took the same route in gauging Clark during the Clemson receiver's workout.

"Dwight had caught something like 12 passes his whole senior year, but he was big, he could catch the ball, and he could run," Walsh said.

The 1981 acquisitions of linebacker Jack "Hacksaw" Reynolds and defensive end Fred Dean also illustrated Walsh's willingness to defy convention. Where the Los Angeles Rams saw Reynolds as washed up, Walsh saw him as a centerpiece for the 49ers' defense. Where San Diego Chargers owner Gene Klein saw Dean only as a disgruntled star demanding more money, Walsh saw a player seeking and deserving respect as the best pass rusher in the NFL.

When Walsh needed a tight end in 1982, he coaxed the talented but enigmatic Russ Francis out of retirement. He even recruited hurdling superstar Renaldo Nehemiah to play wide receiver for the 49ers in the early 1980s.

Montana led the 49ers to four Super Bowl titles, three of them while he played for Walsh. Clark, Reynolds, and Dean helped Walsh win his first two Super Bowl titles. Nehemiah and Francis were part of a Super Bowl winning team in 1984.

"Who's to say we weren't lucky as heck," Walsh said. "I don't know. But we did make it happen with people that others sort of dispensed with."

That's not to say Walsh didn't do some dispensing of his own. Hired by DeBartolo to coach the 49ers in 1979, Walsh took over a team that had won only seven of 30 games under three different coaches in the two years since DeBartolo's $17.5 million purchase of the club from the founding owners, the Morabito family.

"Having been in the NFL as an assistant for 10 years, I expected an NFL team, and in reality it had been decimated over about a three- or four-year period," Walsh said. "A few turned out to be key players for us, but a very few. I didn't realize until we started playing people, and then it was very evident that we couldn't come close to winning.

"The job was almost overwhelming. My good fortune in taking the position was I had the authority and responsibility for the entire football operation. So I didn't have to have someone else agree with me. Two people couldn't have done it because they would have disagreed. It was so intense and there were so many problems."

Initially, the 49ers' roster turnover was dramatic. Players routinely were brought in one week and gone the next as Walsh relentlessly sought to upgrade the roster. Through all the upheaval, Walsh laid the foundation for the 49ers' dramatic reversal of fortune, with acquisitions of key veterans and the drafting of young stars, from Montana and Clark in 1979, to linebacker Keena Turner in 1980, to defensive back Ronnie Lott in 1981.

After going 2-14 in Walsh's inaugural season, the 49ers improved to 6-10 in 1980. They fought back from an eight-game losing streak to win three of their last five games, including a 38-35 overtime win against New

Orleans in which the 49ers overcame a 28-point deficit. The Montana-led victory endures as the NFL's greatest regular-season comeback. It was also a milestone in the development of Montana's persona as a cool, unflappable player in the face of long odds and the game's greatest pressures.

Moreover, Montana showed a real flair for running the West Coast offense that Walsh had installed upon his arrival. With Montana becoming the full-time starter in 1981 and the offense coming around, Walsh was determined to stop the two-year revolving door with personnel in the secondary. He turned to the draft to solidify the 49ers defense, selecting defensive backs with four of his first five picks. Lott topped the list, with Eric Wright, Carlton Williamson, and Lynn Thomas following in quick succession. The string of four defensive backs in the draft was interrupted only by the selection of defensive tackle John Harty.

Lott, Wright, and Williamson joined holdover safety Dwight Hicks in the starting lineup and Thomas played a key role as a nickel back. That produced the rare sight of four rookies in the defensive backfield for much of the time during the 1981 season.

"There were people that said, 'They're desperate. They're just flailing away, drafting all those defensive backs,'" said Walsh. "But we considered Ronnie to be the best player available in the draft. And from my standpoint, every one of them had been a big-time player who had played in big-time games at big-time programs.

"The whole idea was, 'Look, let's just go out and play the game.' And we didn't have the problem of some veteran saying, 'Hey, you don't know what you're doing.' Nobody told them that," Walsh said. "They just went out and played."

That proved to be the mantra for the 1981 team as a whole, which won 12 of 13 games after a 1-2 start.

The 49ers served notice they would be a force by beating Dallas 45-14 and four-time Super Bowl champion Pittsburgh 17-14 as part of a seven-game winning streak that was the longest to that point in their 31 NFL seasons.

After losing narrowly in Cleveland, the 49ers closed the regular season with five consecutive wins, completing their first season sweep of the rival Los Angeles Rams since 1965.

They headed into the postseason with the league's 13th-ranked offense and seventh-ranked passing attack. Their defense had climbed from 27th overall in 1980 to No. 2 in the league, with their young, aggressive secondary and veteran acquisitions like Jack "Hacksaw" Reynolds and Fred Dean providing much of the impetus for the turnaround.

"That particular year, all of our moves were good ones," Walsh said. "I can't say that was always the case. Really, all I was thinking of was surviving and competing. I didn't have these high-sounding, bravado goals. I never talked about a Super Bowl. I talked about beating the next opponent."

And one after another, the 49ers had beaten the best teams in the league. They finished 13-3 in 1981 and returned to the postseason for the first time in nine years, when the Cowboys ended playoff runs by Coach Dick Nolan's 49ers in each of three consecutive seasons.

The 49ers beat the New York Giants 38-24 in a divisional playoff to move closer to their first title. But standing between them and their first trip to the Super Bowl was a league powerhouse and a familiar nemesis— the Dallas Cowboys.

The Cowboys, who were a couple years removed from consecutive Super Bowl appearances, were anxious to show they were not the same team that had lost to the 49ers by 31 points earlier in the year.

The 49ers unexpectedly were within sight of their first league championship. Ultimately, the 1981 NFC championship played out as a turning point for both teams, with San Francisco's 28-27 victory marking the 49ers' rise as the "Team of the '80s" and a decade-long downward spiral by the Cowboys.

Joe Montana and Dwight Clark provided the game's defining moment when they teamed up for the winning touchdown on a play now known simply as "The Catch." Walsh made the decisive play call on the sideline in the final minute, and to this day views the game and its outcome as the seminal episode in his long, distinguished career as a coach.

GAME OF MY LIFE
BY BILL WALSH
JANUARY 10, 1982—SAN FRANCISCO, CALIFORNIA

We were certainly a Cinderella team, but we also had a lot of confidence. Of course, we had beaten Dallas, badly, earlier in the year.

But they were still "America's Team" and they played a great ball game. For us, a lot of things went wrong—we had half a dozen turnovers—but we didn't, in a sense, self-destruct. We still moved the ball very well against the "Doomsday Defense," as they called it. What kept us in it was overcoming the things that went wrong.

As it worked out, we found ourselves having to drive the length of the field at the end of the game. In the past against the Cowboys, that would have been a Dallas victory, because the 49ers just couldn't muster anything at the end of games and would lose, but there we were. But we really didn't give thought as to what the odds were against us or what had happened to the 49ers before in similar situations with the Cowboys.

There was still tension, a lot of it, although we did have some time to work with. There were just under five minutes left when we got the ball back on our own 11-yard line. We weren't looking for heroic things to happen. At that point in the game, we were depending on our execution. We could have easily said throw three long passes to Freddie Solomon. But no, we intended to methodically move the ball.

That was one positive thing about me; I could really read and understand defenses and we understood their defense totally. They played a defense that was very well coached but stereotyped. There were some flaws in it. I could personally pretty much dictate what they were doing and what they would do. There were a series of plays we used that weren't necessarily the kind of plays that you would call at that time in the game—sweeps, reverses—against their nickel defense. But that's what they were giving us, and we adjusted our sweeps to the defense that Dallas was playing.

They allowed our tight end, Charle Young, to block down, to have a blocking angle on their defensive end. That meant we could block down and pull our guards, and our fullback could come by and pick off the linebacker.

We had Lenvil Elliott in there running for us. The reason he was in there is I had worked with him when we were both in Cincinnati. I knew he wouldn't fumble and he would read the guards' blocks and he would do everything right. Now, Lenvil was well past his prime, but I personally felt very confident that he would run and use the blocks from our guards, John Ayers and Randy Cross, who were our strength. We executed those plays very, very well for moderate gains, and we kept making first downs.

Then we ran a reverse with Freddie Solomon off that action with the sweeps, and that was successful, getting us to the Cowboys' 35-yard line.

We had completed some passes that we had worked on all year, nothing really unique, other than we knew their pass coverage. I felt, and Joe Montana felt, we could complete passes against that coverage if we didn't get anxious. Dwight Clark and Freddie Solomon caught a couple passes and we had a first down at their 13.

Montana just missed hitting Freddie in the end zone on first down and then Lenvil Elliott ran a sweep around left end, almost breaking through but getting to the 6. Now it was third down and there were 58 seconds left. I called timeout to tell Joe what we were going to do and what to think about and what the play will be.

And I'll tell you, sometimes you call a timeout for your own thought processes. That's what people don't quite understand, that knee-jerk calls by coaches sometimes occur, and the coach needs to call a timeout to get his thoughts together because the pressure is incredible. One bad call, and the game's over. The season's over and you've come all this way, down the field, and you can't make a mistake.

The play call there was a sprint right option. It was a good, solid play that had a very high percentage of completions anywhere from the 10-yard line to the goal line. To this day, it's probably the most used pass play in football. It has been for many years. Virtually everybody in pro or college football uses that play. We had been very successful with it during the year. It was the natural thing to do.

The play was primarily designed to go to Freddie Solomon but we also had the outlet to Dwight Clark at the back of the end zone. I told Joe, "We've got two downs to score. So if it doesn't work, look for Freddie, look for Dwight, and then throw it away."

Now, I thought the play would develop differently because I was stupid enough to think we could block those guys and Joe would have a chance to run or pass. But they had a great front four and came off our blocks so fast that Joe had no chance but to retreat and try to find Dwight.

They covered the play to Freddie without any problem. They knew that formation. We had used it before and they knew it was coming. My mistake was not changing the formation somewhat so they didn't recognize what was about to happen. I probably should have used a man in motion. But I just called the slot formation.

Fortunately for us, the sprint right option was a play we had practiced a contingency on, or alternate receiver. Because they zeroed in on what we would do and the pass blocking broke down, they were all over Joe.

Joe knew Dwight would be there on the end line, but to find him and throw the ball under that pressure, and to throw it where only Dwight could get it, that was probably Joe's greatest play ever. Dwight made a great catch, and he had beaten Everson Walls on that play. But thank God for Joe. He was just the greatest player—period.

It was a tremendous relief to score, and I might have been the only one who wasn't celebrating. My God. You're right on the edge of something great. And yet there's 51 seconds left—just enough time for a team like Dallas to complete three passes and kick a field goal and beat us. So our defense has to be given credit as well. Drew Pearson made that catch but Eric Wright made a touchdown-saving tackle. We got the pass rush on the next down. Boy, the place erupted when they fumbled. Lawrence Pillars hit Danny White, and Jim Stuckey recovered for us and it was over. I'll never forget the noise from the crowd. It was just unbelievable. Really, I've not heard anything like it, before or since.

It was a classic game, I'll say that, and overcoming Dallas that day was huge, huge for our franchise. Joe's throw and Dwight's catch continued our momentum to our first Super Bowl. But it was our coaches, players, and team as a whole coming together in the crucible of a pressure game that was central to the ascendancy of the 49ers. That was the breakthrough for us.

A 26-21 victory over Cincinnati in the Super Bowl was a fitting conclusion to the 49ers' storybook season in 1981. The title was the first in the 49ers' 35-year existence, including their first four seasons in the All-America Conference.

It was also the first time a professional sports team had brought a championship to San Francisco. Years later, recalling the public's burst of pride and joy in their championship team, then-mayor Dianne Feinstein said it felt like San Francisco had been covered by a coat of stardust.

The city honored the 49ers by throwing a parade for the team on Market Street, its primary traffic artery downtown.

"I thought perhaps a few thousand people might show up, and it was more like 200,000," Walsh recalled. "My God, it was incredible. And what I remember is one of our players, Charle Young, standing up before all those people saying, 'WE ARE CHAMPIONS!'"

It was vindication as well for Walsh. His long NFL coaching apprenticeship began in 1966, when owner Al Davis hired him as a backfield coach for the Raiders. It included an eight-year stay as an assistant with Cincinnati, the expansion club whose early weaknesses in many ways inspired the West Coast offense.

"That was probably the worst-stocked franchise in the history of the NFL," Walsh said. "So in putting the team together, I personally was trying to find a way we could compete. The best possible way to compete would be a team that could make as many first downs as possible in a contest and control the football.

"We couldn't control the football with the run; teams were just too strong. So it had to be the forward pass, and obviously it had to be a high-percentage, short, controlled passing game. So through a series of formation changing and timed passes—using all eligible receivers, especially the fullback—we were able to put together an offense and develop it over a period of time. In the process, we managed to win our share. The old-line NFL people called it a nickel-and-dime offense. They, in a sense, had disregard and contempt for it, but whenever they played us, they had to deal with it."

Walsh left Cincinnati in 1976, distraught over retiring Bengals coach Paul Brown's decision to pass him over for the head coaching job in favor of Bill "Tiger" Johnson, a former 49ers center.

Walsh moved to San Diego, where he spent one year as offensive coordinator. He left to become the head coach at Stanford, taking them to a bowl game in each of his two seasons before moving on to the 49ers for his first NFL head coaching job at 47.

Having three different jobs over the four years before landing in San Francisco paid dividends for Walsh, allowing him to refine the implementation of his offense in his relentless attempts to make it better.

"The good fortune for me is I installed it and refitted and remolded it in Cincinnati," Walsh said. "Then I installed it in San Diego. A year later, I'm installing it at Stanford, and a couple of years after that I'm installing it with the 49ers. So each year, I was able to process that new offense and deliver it to the team and develop it. The changes forced me to be that much more organized and more specific as to what we taught."

Wherever he went, his quarterbacks were the key to the effectiveness of the offense. "We had Kenny Anderson, Virgil Carter, and Greg Cook in Cincinnati, Dan Fouts in San Diego. Kenny was an NFL MVP; Dan Fouts is a Hall of Famer," Walsh said. "Then at Stanford we had Guy Benjamin and Steve Dils, who both led the league in passing. Benjamin was a consensus All-American. And you know what happened with the 49ers: Joe Montana, Steve Young, Jeff Garcia. The rest is history.

"It takes a quarterback who has the working aptitude to play the game and play within a system. He doesn't necessarily have to have a great arm, but he has to have an accurate arm and a soft touch so the receivers can make the great catches on the pass. Some guys throw it so hard that you can't catch it. You can see all the men we've had from Dwight Clark on through—they've been able to make great catches because the ball is thrown softly."

The approach worked for two more Super Bowl titles under Walsh, the last coming in his final game as 49ers coach following a tumultuous 1988 season.

On the verge of falling out of contention after consecutive losses to the Phoenix Cardinals and Los Angeles Raiders, the 49ers rescued themselves by winning four of their last five to clinch their sixth NFC West title in 10 years under Walsh. But the demands of the job, the constant pressure to win, and the roller-coaster nature of the game had taken its toll on an overwrought Walsh, who had told owner Eddie DeBartolo late in the year that he planned to resign after the season.

Walsh would go out on top, though it took another magnificent drive near the end of his final game to do it. Unlike the 1981 NFC championship game, when Walsh leaned on the run to push the ball downfield against Dallas' defense, Walsh relied primarily on short, quick passes to move the ball in the decisive drive against the Bengals in Super Bowl XXIII.

Joe Montana started the drive by completing three passes, each to a different receiver and none over 8 yards. Roger Craig followed with consecutive runs that went for a total of five yards. They would be the only runs during the 11-play, 92-yard march ending with Montana's 10-yard go-ahead scoring pass to John Taylor with 34 seconds remaining.

"It was the West Coast offense at its best," said Craig.

Walsh walked away from his job as 49ers coach after the Super Bowl and never coached in the NFL again. Years later, he admitted to some regrets about leaving when he did.

"I left them with the youngest team and the best team in football," Walsh said. "I just walked away from something like that, which wasn't very smart. Gosh, I easily could have been involved in a couple more Super Bowls wins, but that's how it ended."

Walsh remains the longest serving coach in 49ers history, going 102-63-1 in his 10 seasons. He closed his tenure with six consecutive winning seasons, becoming the first 49ers coach to win more than 100 games. His legacy also includes a team-record six division titles, a feat later matched by his successor, George Seifert.

He returned for a second coaching tour at Stanford in the early 1990s, following what he said at the time was his "bliss," and rejoined the 49ers as an offensive consultant in 1996. Three years later, Walsh was hired as the 49ers general manager. He helped the organization get through a tumultuous ownership change, daunting salary cap problems, and a changing of the guard in personnel that witnessed the departure of such stars as Steve Young, Jerry Rice, Tim McDonald, Merton Hanks, and Ken Norton.

Terry Donahue succeeded Walsh as general manager in 2001, though Walsh remained as a consultant for two more years before leaving the 49ers for the final time. He again returned to Stanford, where he has worked as a special assistant to the athletic director.

During a family camping trip in 2004, Walsh was overcome with fatigue and struggled with shortness of breath in the high mountain air. He remembered being too tired to do much golfing or hiking or running around with his grandkids.

"The slightest exertion left me utterly exhausted," Walsh said. "I'd have to sleep. Much of the time I was up there, I was flat on my back."

He went to his doctor for a checkup after returning home. Concerned by his anemic condition, doctors performed a test on his bone marrow that revealed he was suffering from leukemia, a cancer of the blood cells.

Walsh kept the news largely to himself for quite some time, letting only his immediate family and closest friends know that he was in a fight for his life. Eventually, rumors that the Hall of Fame coach was gravely ill began to swirl. Walsh finally confirmed those rumors in November 2006.

He sat down with writers Ira Miller and Lowell Cohn, who had covered him for years, and told them he was battling leukemia. Upon hearing the news, former players, coaches, and colleagues rallied to his support, writing him letters of encouragement or coming to visit him in the Bay area.

Walsh remained as active as possible, continuing to work as a special assistant to Stanford's athletic director even as he underwent a grueling treatment regimen requiring frequent hospital visits and regular blood transfusions.

His gallant three-year struggle against leukemia ended quietly at his home in Woodside. On July 30, 2007, Walsh died surrounded by his family. He was 75.

Former 49ers owner Eddie DeBartolo, Joe Montana, Steve Young, and Ronnie Lott were among those who said their goodbyes personally in visits with Walsh in the final weeks and days of his life.

Two days before Walsh died, his good friends John Madden and Raiders owner Al Davis visited with him. Davis said Walsh knew the end was near and had come to terms with his fate.

"He told us that he'd had enough," Davis said. "He'd had a great life."

Tributes for Walsh poured in from every corner of the football world, reflecting his broad impact as a coach, innovator, motivator, and champion of the game and its players and coaches.

"He was not only a great teacher and a great coach, but a great man," DeBartolo said.

"If you gave him a blackboard and a piece of chalk, he would become a whirlwind of wisdom," NFL Commissioner Roger Goodell said.

Outside of his father, Montana said Walsh was the most influential person in his life, and he still marveled years later that Walsh drafted him in defiance of the conventional view that he lacked the size and arm strength to succeed as an NFL quarterback. "But he had a vision and a foresight that was beyond most people," Montana said.

"He knew me before I even knew myself," Steve Young said. "He had such confidence in what I could become."

"There was greatness in the X's and O's," said former 49ers tight end Charle Young. "But what made Bill unique was his ability to bring together different people and unite them for a common goal."

On the football field, Walsh demanded of himself and his players that they work to master skills and scheme alike in a bid to control their fate, to be masters of their own destiny even in the brutally unpredictable, often chaotic environment of the gridiron. It was an expectation Montana alluded to in his Hall of Fame induction speech in 2000.

"There are a lot of things that I learned from Bill throughout my career," Montana said. "But I think the one thing that I continue throughout my life is that want to be perfect, the need for perfection. He pushed me and pushed us, especially the quarterback position, which he was so proud of, to want to be perfect. And if you missed perfect, you end up with great, and that he could handle, nothing else. He taught me to be the same way."

Walsh said he never set out to build a dynasty. It just happened as he sought to transform the 49ers from an also-ran to a consistent winner.

"When I came here," he once said, "I just wanted to build a team that would win more than it would lose. I never envisioned the 49ers of the past three decades would become one of the great franchises in the history of sports. I'm proud that I played a part in it. I walk away knowing I orchestrated it, but also having a special feeling for everyone who worked or played here. We bonded together. It was like Camelot."

Chapter 12

ROGER CRAIG

Wide-eyed and knees churning, Roger Craig took Joe Montana's handoff and swept around left end. It was his first carry during the 49ers' opening series on a sweltering October day at Anaheim Stadium in 1988. He turned the corner and smashed into Vince Newsome, leaving the Rams' hard-hitting safety dazed, en route to a 15-yard gain.

"I hit him so hard that they had to carry him off the field," Craig says, recalling the effort 18 years later. "I was all knees and forearms coming at him. He got crushed. Trust me. I was a violent runner that day. Violent."

Craig's opening carry foreshadowed his career-high 190-yard, three-touchdown performance, which included the tackle-busting, 46-yard scoring run that has come to epitomize his eight-year career with the 49ers. He burst through the middle, veered left, and cut back to the middle of the field, dodging or running through six defenders before reaching the end zone.

"That's highlight reel material forever!" exclaimed 49ers broadcaster Wayne Walker moments after seeing Craig cross the goal line, the ball held triumphantly in his extended right hand.

Says Craig: "I look at that one run and it displayed what Roger Craig was all about. It was the way and how hard I trained. It showed my character, to run, to play with a never-give-up attitude, and to be doing it for the team. I never wanted to go down easy."

From the beginning, that's the way it was for Craig, who said his unorthodox running style was a residue of his time as a high hurdler in high school and college. But the reason he favored it had nothing to do with his history in track and field and everything to do with football.

"This way," Craig says, "I give more punishment than I receive."

He joined the 49ers in 1983, the team's top draft pick out of Nebraska when he was selected in the second round. The pick was part of coach Bill Walsh's attempt to build the 49ers' running attack and bring some semblance of balance to the offense.

Hampered by a rushing game that made little headway—the 49ers ranked 28th in the league—San Francisco quarterbacks put the ball up nearly 80 percent of the time in the strike-shortened 1982 season. Even the year before, when the 49ers won the first of their Super Bowl titles, their leading rusher, Ricky Patton, finished the regular season with 543 yards. It was the lowest total by the team's rushing leader since 1973, when Vic Washington had 534 yards during a 5-9 season.

A day before the 1983 draft, the 49ers acquired running back Wendell Tyler in a trade with the Los Angeles Rams, who then drafted Eric Dickerson with their top pick. Walsh envisioned Tyler and Craig playing together in the 49ers' backfield, with Tyler at tailback and Craig at fullback.

Craig played fullback and halfback while he was at Nebraska. In 1981, he had his best college game, rushing for 234 yards, including a 94-yard touchdown that led Nebraska past Florida State. But by the time he was a senior, Craig spent much of his time as the lead blocker for Heisman Trophy winner Mike Rozier.

With the 49ers, Craig joined a team with a strong fullback tradition. The 49ers' all-time leading rusher, Joe Perry, was a fullback. Ken Willard and J.D. Smith were classic power runners and blockers who buttressed the 49ers' fullback legacy. In Walsh's West Coast system, there was an added offensive dimension with the fullback, who played a pivotal role as a receiver out of the backfield.

Craig caught only 16 passes for 102 yards during his Nebraska career but realized before he even came to the 49ers that he would need to become more accustomed to receiving as a pro.

"I've always worked on my receiving even though Nebraska didn't throw to the backs," Craig said as a rookie. "In school and during summer, I spent a lot of time on it because I knew you had to be able to catch the ball to succeed as a pro. I could always catch the ball. It's been

Roger Craig *Photo © Michael Zagaris*

natural for me. But it wasn't until my first pro mini-camp that I believe they really knew I could catch."

Walsh wasted no time incorporating Craig into the offense, declaring his skill as a runner, blocker, and receiver was "just what the doctor ordered" for the 49ers' languishing attack.

He set a team rookie record with 12 touchdowns (eight rushing and four receiving).

Craig helped clear the way for Tyler's 856 yards rushing while breaking out his high-knee running style by gaining 725 yards on his own in 1983. It was the third highest total by a rookie, behind Vic Washington's 811 in 1971 and Ken Willard's 778 in 1965. He also had 48 catches, the fourth highest reception total by a rookie in the 49ers' history.

During Craig's second season, Tyler carried the bulk of the rushing load, going for 1,262 yards. Craig ran for fewer yards (649) than he did as a rookie, but his 71 receptions led the team, which went 15-1 en route to its second Super Bowl.

"He may be the most versatile back in football," Walsh said in the midst of the 1984 season in which the 49ers' only loss was a 20-17 setback at Pittsburgh.

Craig's versatility and determination reached a crescendo on the NFL's biggest stage. He accounted for 135 total yards and became the first player to score three touchdowns in the Super Bowl, catching an 8-yard pass from Montana for the go-ahead score against the Dan Marino-led Miami Dolphins. He dove in from 2 yards out before catching another scoring pass to close out the 49ers' 22-point victory.

"He thrives on competition," Walsh said. "During the Super Bowl, he had a smile on his face. He was laughing. I heard later he was disappointed because the season had ended."

But the memories endure for Craig, who considers his initial Super Bowl performance as the game of his life.

GAME OF MY LIFE
BY ROGER CRAIG
JANUARY 20, 1985—STANFORD, CALIFORNIA

To this day, I remember the intensity and impact of the first Super Bowl I was involved in with the 49ers. The Miami Dolphins supposedly had this high-powered offense with Dan Marino coming off a record season for a quarterback. We had a lot to prove in the 49ers' first trip to the Super Bowl since the team won its first one after the 1981 season.

We nearly made it back the year before—my rookie season—but lost to the Washington Redskins 24-21 in the NFC title game. Otherwise, we would have had an Oakland Raiders-49ers Super Bowl. That conference championship loss to Washington really left a nasty taste in our mouths.

We were a focused team going into the Super Bowl. We had only one loss all season—20-17 at Pittsburgh midway through the year. But after that, we took it upon ourselves to win it all by winning the rest of the way. We closed the 16-game regular season with nine straight wins and then beat the New York Giants and the Chicago Bears in the playoffs. A Super Bowl victory would give us our 18th win, one more than the 1972 Dolphins' championship team, which went undefeated through a 14-game schedule and the playoffs.

In the days before the game, we were practicing hard and we had a lot of meetings. We all knew what we had to do. I had played in some big games—a high school state championship, the Orange Bowl while I was at Nebraska—but this was something special. At this level, you had to grow up fast. No one was going to hold your hand. You had to think, play, and act like a veteran, but when they introduced me as the starting fullback, I felt like a kid again. I thought I was going to hyperventilate. Here it was, the Super Bowl. Millions of people are watching and 80,000 people are screaming and they call your name out and you run on the field. I got goose bumps.

But once the game started, my body calmed down and relaxed and let me play the way I had practiced. I was focused. I think that was the most I've ever been focused for a game. I might have been just as focused for a game before or after that, but I wasn't more focused.

Every time I touched the ball, I was running with authority. I was running like it was the last time I would touch the ball. When Joe Montana threw to me, I could see the laces on the ball. That's how focused I was. I had two one-handed catches. I caught two touchdown passes. You just get it done; that's the nature of the game. I can remember diving in for another touchdown. I gave up my body and somersaulted into the end zone. It was that type of game. We knew we had a better offense than Miami and we displayed that. Their linebackers just couldn't cover me.

When we went down and scored the second time, we had the ball on Carl Monroe's touchdown catch and our defense started shutting them down, we knew we were in control. Our defense did some cool things as far as shutting down Mark Duper and Mark Clayton. They gave Dan Marino fits with the pressure they put on him. We just had command of the game. Montana controlled the game. We knew we were going to win, plus we were in our backyard, playing at Stanford, and it was foggy. It was San Francisco fog. It was over when that happened. When the fog rolled in, it was over.

You know, I saw O.J. Simpson before the game. He was doing some commentating and he said even before the game I was going to be the unsung hero. He saw something that I didn't even see. That was my second season in the NFL and to be the first to score three touchdowns in the Super Bowl, that's something you just don't forget. That was the game that kind of put me on the map. I'd had a pretty good rookie season. I'd scored 12 touchdowns, second-most to Eric Dickerson (who had 18). But I knew after the Super Bowl I wasn't going to be able to sneak up on anybody any more. I was going to be a marked guy. And knowing that fact really helped me. The following year and the year after that and the year after that, I worked out like a maniac. I didn't want to come back and not perform well for the team. The standard had been set.

The 49ers celebrated their second Super Bowl championship with a ring presentation ceremony for the players at San Francisco's Palace of Fine Arts before the start of the 1985 season.

During the gala, coach Bill Walsh approached his fullback. "Roger," Walsh said, "I need 1,000 yards from you this year."

"Cool. I'm ready," Craig replied, breaking into a laugh as he recalls the conversation years later. "But the thing was, he didn't tell me whether it was 1,000 yards rushing or receiving. So I covered my ass by doing both."

In a powerful encore to his Super Bowl performance, Craig became the first player in NFL history to surpass the 1,000-yard mark in both rushing and receiving in 1985. Craig's breakthrough season included his first 100-yard rushing game as a pro in a September victory over Atlanta followed by his first 100-yard receiving performance when he matched a team record with 12 catches in the 49ers' second meeting of the season with the Falcons.

With three or four games remaining, former *San Jose Mercury News* reporter Charlie Bricker mentioned to Craig that he was within reach of the unique 1,000-1,000 milestone.

"I really hadn't even thought about it and I remember Charlie came up to me and said, 'Man, you have a chance to create a whole new category,'" Craig said. "I thought, 'Wow, that's kind of cool.'"

Craig had combined rushing-receiving totals exceeding 100 yards 11 times during the season, including the finale against Dallas, when he had 72 yards rushing and 50 yards receiving to go over the 1,000-mark in both categories. His 1,050 yards rushing were the most since Craig gained 1,700 as a senior at Central High School in his native Davenport, Iowa. He finished with a league-high 92 catches for 1,016 yards, setting an NFL record for most receptions in a season by a running back.

Four years into his NFL career, Walsh moved Craig from fullback to tailback, where he had his most productive years as a runner. And he maintained his effectiveness as a receiving threat even as the 49ers diversified their offense. In 1985, they added wide receiver Jerry Rice, with fullback Tom Rathman and wide receiver John Taylor joining the team in 1986, and tight end Brent Jones coming in 1987.

Craig ran for a team-record 1,502 yards in 1988 and led the 49ers with 76 receptions for 534 yards. His 2,036 yards in total offense tied Herschel Walker for the NFL lead. He followed with 1,054 yards rushing in 1989, becoming the first player in 49ers history with three 1,000-yard seasons.

"Roger is a marvel," Joe Montana said in a newspaper interview. "He affects nearly everything we do on offense. He helps develop our offense in every way and we go into a game thinking about getting him the ball in the beginning and in the end."

"I was always Joe's safety valve," Craig says. "Joe would dump me the ball. He knew where I was at all times. I mean, I caught some 500 balls from Joe over the course of my career."

The 49ers ended the '88 and '89 seasons by winning the Super Bowl, and Craig played a pivotal role in the last-ditch drive that beat the Cincinnati Bengals in the January '89 title game. Craig handled the ball five times—running twice and catching three passes—before Montana hit Taylor from 10 yards out in the final seconds for the game winner.

The 49ers registered their biggest Super Bowl triumph, 55-10 over Denver the next season, and an exultant Craig kicked off the 49ers' drive toward another one immediately, chanting "three-peat" while he was still on the sideline of the New Orleans Superdome. And the 49ers nearly pulled it off but for what Craig has referred to as "the sorriest moment" of his career.

The 49ers were clinging to a 13-12 lead against the New York Giants with less than three minutes remaining in the NFC championship game. Montana had been knocked out of the game in the late going, and Steve Young was leading a drive to try to run out the clock. Craig had just converted a first down and the 49ers needed just one more first down to secure the victory and the Super Bowl berth that went with it.

But defensive tackle Erik Howard shot through the line and hit Craig an instant after getting a handoff, forcing a fumble that linebacker Lawrence Taylor recovered at the Giants' 43-yard line with 2:36 left. The Giants drove within field goal range, and Matt Bahr converted a 42-yarder as time expired to deny the 49ers' bid for a third consecutive Super Bowl appearance.

Craig was so upset over his fumble that he broke down and cried in the locker room after the game. Teammate Ronnie Lott tried to console him and told him that he loved him.

"I care about Roger Craig more than I care what goes on on the football field," Lott told a San Francisco reporter afterward.

"Without him, we wouldn't even be here," added fullback Harry Sydney.

A grim Craig told reporters he didn't know how or why it happened but that the fumble was "the lowest point ever" in his career.

"All I know is I hit the hole and the ball went out of my hands," Craig said. "This is tough. This is like a nightmare for a running back. I have no excuses. I just have to live with what I did. It hurts really bad."

The ill-fated carry was Craig's last as a 49er. Craig had struggled through much of the 1990 season with a partially torn posterior cruciate ligament, and his 141 carries and 439 yards rushing were both career lows.

After the season, he wasn't among the players the 49ers protected from Plan B free agency. Craig finished his career by playing one season for the Los Angeles Raiders and two with the Minnesota Vikings. Lott was also let go by the 49ers as a Plan B free agent, and Craig took the organization's actions hard, telling the Associated Press at one point that team management had treated him and Lott like "pieces of trash."

Time eventually soothed the bitter feelings on both sides, and in the summer of 1994, Craig became the first NFL player to symbolically re-sign with his old team so he could formally retire as a member of the 49ers. Craig had just one minor complaint—his ceremonial one-day contract had all zeroes in the space spelling out his pay.

"I was like, 'Man, just put a one by it or something,'" Craig said years later, laughing about his last "contract" as a player. "I didn't save it. I threw it away. I had no use for it. All zeroes? It was a dud. But it was the thought that counted."

The ceremonial re-signing was arranged with the help of team owner Eddie DeBartolo and club president Carmen Policy as well as Craig's agent, Jim Steiner. It has now become an accepted practice in the league for teams and former star players who wish to reunite upon the players' retirement. Raiders great Tim Brown and former Washington Redskins wide receiver Art Monk are among the players who followed Craig's lead and came back to their original team in retirement.

DeBartolo welcomed the chance to bring Craig back into the fold.

"When he played, he was the epitome of the San Francisco 49ers," DeBartolo said during Craig's retirement ceremony at the 49ers' training camp in Rocklin. "He did everything that was asked of him, and he did more than was asked of him."

Craig said the symbolic re-signing and retirement allowed his career to come full circle.

"That's one thing I always wanted to do," he said. "This is where I made my mark. My memories are here."

The eight years he spent with the 49ers, Craig said, were a magical time for him, and for the team, which won three of its five Super Bowls during his tenure.

"It was a special time for us," Craig said. "We were like rock stars almost. We were the winningest team in the '80s and it was fun. Bill Walsh put a team together and we understood what it took to work together. Being able to work through all barriers, religion, race. We didn't see color. On our team, we were all one. That was the beauty about the 49ers organization. Eddie DeBartolo was able to assimilate the best management team in the league, get great players to play for them, and Bill helped everyone get on the same page.

"It was a symphony, really. That's how we played. It was beautiful music. We played beautiful music and understood each other's roles—

from Bill Ring to Milt McColl, from Rick Gervais to Joe Montana and Jerry Rice. Everyone took their responsibilities seriously, star players and role players alike. And they were the kind of players I would go to war with any day."

Chapter 13

TOM RATHMAN

Growing up in Grand Island, Nebraska, Tom Rathman was 13 when he got his first job detasseling corn. In the Midwestern summer heat, Rathman slogged through one row of cornstalks after another, pulling the corn tassels out by hand and dropping them to the ground, muddied by the day's irrigation. Popping the tassels out prevented the corn from self-pollinating or crossbreeding, which could affect everything from the strength of the cornstalks to the sweetness of the corn.

The work in the Nebraska cornfields was tedious and demanding. By the end of a shift, Rathman was covered in sweat and grime and had yanked thousands and thousands of tassels.

Detasseling corn wasn't the only labor-intensive job the enterprising Rathman held as a teenager. When he got a little older, Rathman joined a construction crew run by his father and his uncle, and he spent his summers pouring cement.

"The work was hard, the jobs, tough and dirty, just like playing fullback," Rathman says. "But that's where I got my foundation. That's where I got my style of play."

From Rathman's days as a fullback and linebacker at Grand Island High School to his fullback play with the University of Nebraska and then the San Francisco 49ers, power and toughness backed by a relentless work ethic defined his game. He embraced the raw, physical aspects of the position and often said he'd rather help clear a running lane for a teammate than tote the ball himself.

"My forte was the block, running into that wall. Don't blink. Go as hard as you can and don't pull up, because something is going to give, and it wasn't going to be me," Rathman says.

When Rathman did get the ball, though, he tended to make the most of it. He relished collisions with defenders and, when he broke into the clear, he had enough speed to make it tough for pursuers to catch him.

He rushed for 1,425 yards and averaged 6.5 yards per carry during his four years at Nebraska. And he caught the attention of the 49ers with a standout senior campaign. He had three runs of 50 or more yards, including a career-best 84-yarder for a touchdown, and finished with 881 yards and eight touchdowns.

Rathman, a third-round pick, joined the 49ers in 1986 as part of one of the most bountiful drafts in the team's history. Bill Walsh, the coach and general manager, stockpiled draft picks by repeatedly trading down. Though Walsh traded away the 49ers' first-round pick, he wound up with two second-round picks and six selections in the third and fourth rounds. He used the collection on such players as wide receiver John Taylor, defensive ends Charles Haley and Larry Roberts, cornerback Tim McKyer, and tackle Steve Wallace in addition to Rathman.

Training camp, though, was a struggle at first for Rathman, who was trying so hard to do everything right that he began having problems with fumbles.

"I was fighting for everything I could get when I was carrying the ball, every inch," Rathman says. "A fullback has to be an aggressive football player who is in attack mode, so all these defensive backs, they're all trying to get me. Plus, I was coming in to compete with Billy Ring for a job and he was real tight with all the linebackers. Shoot, they were all after me, too.

"But I was fighting too hard and getting careless with the football. I put it on the ground a few times and I remember Bill Walsh saying to me, 'Hey listen, you're not on scholarship any more. We don't have to keep you.' I got the message. I knew I had a chance if I just hung on to the football. I did, and so I made it."

Initially, Walsh envisioned using Rathman on special teams and in goal-line and short-yardage situations. Rathman also backed up Roger

Tom Rathman *Photo © Michael Zagaris*

Craig, something Rathman had done before for a year when he and Craig both played fullback for Nebraska.

That wasn't all, though. For a fullback to be fully integrated into Walsh's West Coast system, Rathman had to become an accomplished receiver so he could serve as an outlet for a quarterback under duress. Rathman had only three receptions as a senior and five in his career at Nebraska. But over time, he became one of the 49ers' surest-handed receivers.

"That's something I developed by working at it," Rathman said. "I had good enough hand-eye coordination that I was able to be a fairly decent and reliable receiving fullback."

Rathman made his mark on special teams during his rookie season, leading the 49ers with 18 special teams tackles. But he also had his moments at fullback, foreshadowing the breakthrough that would put him in the starting lineup.

With Craig banged up, Rathman made his first NFL start five weeks into the season against Indianapolis. In a December game against the New York Jets, Craig suffered a concussion, and Rathman finished in his place. He had 25 yards receiving and 55 yards rushing, breaking through for his first career touchdown on a 29-yard run that stood out as the longest from scrimmage by a 49er in 1986.

"I wasn't thinking of anything, just how hard I was going to spike the ball," Rathman later told a reporter.

He ended his rookie campaign with a 4.2-yard average per carry that led all 49ers running backs, and his 13 receptions more than doubled the reception total that he had in four years at Nebraska.

Still, Rathman's second season with the 49ers started the same way as his first—playing on special teams and backing up Craig. But changes were coming. Midway through the 1987 season, with age and injuries becoming a pressing concern, Bill Walsh shuffled the entire offensive line as well as the backfield. Jesse Sapolu, rookie Harris Barton, Steve Wallace, and Bruce Collie were inserted into the lineup as part of the 49ers' midseason overhaul of the offensive line. Roger Craig, an all-purpose runner and receiver, moved from fullback to halfback.

Rathman left the bench to fill the void at fullback. He cemented a regular spot in the lineup by fighting through bouts of double vision with a solid performance against the Los Angeles Rams that he remembers as the game of his life.

GAME OF MY LIFE
BY TOM RATHMAN
NOVEMBER 1, 1987—ANAHEIM, CALIFORNIA

The week before we played the Los Angeles Rams, I had probably played one of my best games from a special teams standpoint. I had several "de-cleators" blocking on kickoff returns and punt returns against the New Orleans Saints. I'm talking about hitting a guy and his feet going up above his head. I had a couple of those.

And I can remember after the New Orleans game, one of the assistant coaches, Sherm Lewis, came in that next Wednesday, when we were installing the game plan for the Rams. And he said, "OK, guys, here's what we're going to do. We're going to move Roger to halfback and we're putting Tom at fullback." I'd started once as a rookie the year before as an injury replacement. But this start I really view as my first because it signaled to me, at long last, that I would become a regular in the starting lineup so long as I did my job.

For someone who began their career as a role player, becoming a starter was a real milestone. For the first year and a half in the NFL, I'd play special teams, and sometimes in short-yardage and goal-line situations, I'd go in and back up Roger Craig. A lot of people forget that Roger spent the first four years of his career as a fullback. Joe Cribbs had been starting at halfback.

For me, the Rams game defined where I was headed as an athlete. At the time, the Rams were struggling. But as division rivals, we always had some pretty rough battles. Kevin Greene was a young kid that they had and it was really the beginning stage of something of a personal rivalry. I probably played against Kevin about 15 times over the course of our careers. They also had another linebacker, Mike Wilcher. He was very active and athletic. He was part of an outstanding group of guys as far as players and it was kind of the north part of the state versus the southern part of the state. So there was always that battle of who's better. I think any time we played the Rams it was a special game due to the fact you played them twice a year. They're in your division. And you've got to be able to get up for your divisional opponent.

When you crack the starting lineup, there's a lot of things going through your mind. I mean, game day, you start getting in that zone. You go through pregame warm-ups. You're hot, you're sweating. Hopefully, you can calm down in the 10-15 minutes that you have before going back out. But obviously, I was a little bit excited and I got out there and we hadn't even gotten through the first series and I started hyperventilating and my vision started getting jumpy, double vision so to speak. Everything was moving up and down. I don't know what started it or how I could perform. I really hadn't taken a hit or sustained a blow to the head. Sometimes, I think I just wasn't getting enough oxygen because I just hadn't gotten used to playing all the time.

So there I was, hyperventilating and seeing double on a day when I was trying to establish myself as the 49ers new fullback. One thing was for sure. I wasn't going to take myself out of the game. I just kind of got into this zone where I was able to calm my breathing, focus my vision, and just get on with it. That was something I somehow was able to do, block out distractions and get into that zone. For some people, it's kind of like having an on-off switch. That's the way it was for me. I still try to get into that zone when I work out. I've just always had the ability to do that and I think that's one of the reasons I was able to have some success.

Against the Rams, I scored our first touchdown on a trap play, just lunging the final few yards into the end zone. And I caught every ball that was thrown to me. Your instincts just take over. That's the way you have to play this game. You hate to compare it to anything but, man, it's a brutal game. And it could be life and death. That's almost the approach you have to have, being able to survive when your vision isn't there and when you're in pain and you're hurt. You've got to survive but still attack. As a fullback, you're no good if you don't attack.

I remember catching a flat route, not really seeing the ball all the way to my hands. It's wobbling and it's like two balls. I don't know how, but I caught it. Subconsciously, I must have really focused. Just being able to execute in the state that I was in was something special. I mean, if you were an outsider looking at me, you would have said nothing was wrong. You couldn't recognize anything being wrong. A teammate or even a coach, they would never recognize anything was wrong. And I sure never said anything. I just kept playing, but somehow things worked out for the best and I think if you're tough and you're blue collar, you're going to find a way to survive. Really not just survive but excel, and that's what I strived to do. I wouldn't do it any other way.

◆   ◆   ◆

The 49ers' pairing of Tom Rathman and Roger Craig in the same backfield began with the Rams game, and they continued as a tandem for four years. They were a part of some of the best teams and most productive offenses in 49ers' history, including back-to-back Super Bowl-winning teams following the 1988 and 1989 seasons.

Brought together midway through the 1987 campaign, Rathman and Craig helped the 49ers finish the season with the league's No. 1 offense, ranking first in both rushing and passing yardage. The next year, the 49ers had the league's second-ranked offense, and Rathman was the primary lead blocker for Craig's then-team-record 1,502 yards rushing.

Running behind Rathman, "I just see people disappear," Craig said at the time.

In 1989, Rathman became a focal point of the passing attack as a chief outlet for Joe Montana. Rathman led all 49ers running backs with an NFC-high 73 receptions, always running with attitude after the catch.

"I think I most like to take a pass in the flat and turn up field on a defensive back," Rathman told *The San Francisco Chronicle*. "It's always nice when you find those 190-pound DBs trying to take on a guy who's 235 pounds and in full stride. I don't try to put a move on them. I just try to go right through them."

Rathman spent eight years catching passes, blocking and running through the opposition for the 49ers. In 1994, he became a free agent and wasn't re-signed. He moved to the Raiders, playing one more season before deciding to hang it up, in part because of a nagging neck injury.

The next year, the 49ers, needing help at fullback, tried to convince Rathman to come out of retirement. Midway through the season, the 49ers lost starting fullback William Floyd for the rest of the season when he tore knee ligaments.

"I talked to [coach] George Seifert about it," Rathman says of coming back. "I just felt I wasn't going to be able to play to my standards ,and my body was wearing down. It was a combination of those two things really."

Rathman instead continued coaching running backs at Serra High School in San Mateo.

The 49ers, meanwhile, seemed to be heading for a fourth consecutive meeting with the Dallas Cowboys in the NFC Championship game. But they were upset in the divisional round 27-17 by Green Bay Packers and a pivotal play involved the 49ers' backup fullback.

Adam Walker, who was playing with a cast over his broken hand, caught a swing pass from Steve Young on the first play from scrimmage. But linebacker Wayne Simmons hit him an instant after the ball reached him, jarring the ball loose, and cornerback Craig Newsome returned the fumble 31 yards for a touchdown, and Green Bay never looked back.

Rathman never played again, but he eventually returned to the 49ers as an assistant coach. During the team's training camp in 1996, Rathman served as a coaching intern for the 49ers and spent the rest of the year as Menlo College's offensive coordinator. When Steve Mariucci replaced Seifert as the 49ers' coach before the 1997 season, he hired Rathman to coach running backs.

"He was a coach when he was playing. All he did was graduate to what he really was," quarterback Steve Young said after Rathman's addition to the staff.

Rathman said he always took pride in knowing not just his responsibilities on a play but also the responsibilities of all those around him. He brought to coaching the same intensity, seriousness, and high expectations that characterized his tough-minded approach to the game as a player.

"I would expect the players that I coach to be able to go out and do the same things I did—play hurt and concentrate and attack and get it done," says Rathman, who began coaching running backs for the Raiders in 2007. "Everything I do is related to that. My players, they know where I come from and they know what my experiences and expectations are. The game, I've learned, is more mental than it is physical."

In five of Rathman's six years as 49ers running back coach, the team produced a 1,000-yard rusher, including Garrison Hearst's then-team-record of 1,570 yards in 1998. The team also twice led the NFL in rushing (1998-99).

But Rathman is also remembered for a notable run-in with a player, running back Lawrence Phillips, during his coaching stay with the 49ers. A talented but troubled player, Phillips drew a suspension while playing for the University of Nebraska for dragging an ex-girlfriend down some stairs by her hair. The St. Louis Rams still drafted him in the first round in 1996 only to cut him loose little more than a year later. He also spent time with the Miami Dolphins, who also released him.

Phillips was coming off a stellar showing in NFL Europe when the 49ers signed him in 1999. They had recently learned that running back Garrison Hearst would miss the season with complications from an ankle fracture suffered in a season-ending loss at Atlanta in the divisional playoffs. The 49ers also added running back Charlie Garner in free agency.

Garner eventually beat out Phillips for the starting job, and as Phillips' playing time decreased, he became increasingly troublesome and clashed with coaches and teammates. It all came to a head during a Friday practice heading into the November 14, 1999, game at New Orleans. Phillips, who had missed a crucial block Week 3 at Arizona that led to the hit resulting in Steve Young's career-ending concussion, refused Rathman's request to take reps during team drills.

Phillips' explanation at the time was, "I'm not going to do it in a game. Why should I do it in practice?"

The team responded by suspending Phillips, leaving him behind and heading to New Orleans to play the Saints.

Three days later, coach Steve Mariucci announced that Phillips would never again play for the 49ers, and he was subsequently released. Phillips filed a grievance but nothing came of it, and he never played for an NFL team again.

"He seemed to have everything under control and as the season progressed, he just started to lose focus," Rathman says. "When he was focused, I enjoyed coaching him, but when things went bad, with a player like that, sometimes you've just got to anticipate trouble. I never have spoken to him again."

Rathman left the 49ers after Mariucci was fired following the 2002 season. When Mariucci was hired to coach the Detroit Lions, Rathman joined him as his running backs coach.

Mariucci was let go by the Lions midway through the 2005 season. Rathman left Detroit after that season and took a year off before being hired in 2007 as the running backs coach for the Raiders, the only other team he played for in his nine-year NFL career.

Chapter 14

JERRY RICE

The night before the 49ers played at Houston in 1984, coach Bill Walsh was in his room watching college football highlights on television. Public relations director Jerry Walker dropped by to give him some credentials just about the time a Mississippi Valley State University wide receiver named Jerry Rice flashed across the screen.

"Check this out," Walsh told Walker, and hurriedly returned to his seat by the television set. "Look at this guy, look at the way he runs," Walsh said. "Look at the way he catches the ball. This kid is really playing well. He's just the guy we need."

The team's general manager, John McVay, came by minutes later and Walsh repeated to him his earlier observations of Rice.

"There was absolutely no doubt that Jerry Rice had won his fancy," Walker said.

Just how much became evident six months later in the 1985 NFL draft. Walsh traded No. 1, 2, and 3 draft choices to the New England Patriots in return for their first-round pick, the 16th overall. He used it to draft Rice in what certainly became the most fortuitous pick ever by a team coming off a championship season.

In 16 years with the 49ers, Rice helped them win 10 division titles and three Super Bowls while becoming one of the league's great players and the most prolific wide receiver in NFL history.

He retired in 2005 after making the Pro Bowl 13 times in a 20-year career that also included stops with the Oakland Raiders and Seattle

Seahawks. When Rice left the game, he was the NFL's all-time leader in touchdowns (208), receptions (1,549), and yards receiving (22,895). He holds the NFL's single-season receiving yardage mark, going for 1,848 yards in 1995.

"He did some amazing things," said Mike Holmgren, who coached Rice in San Francisco as an assistant in the late 1980s and early '90s and in Seattle as the Seahawks head coach during the receiver's final season in 2004.

"I think that if you are a football coach, you didn't have to watch him for very long before you get the idea that this guy was special," Holmgren said. "In the day and age when some receivers are getting their notoriety by being controversial, he was just the opposite. He certainly let his play speak for himself, and he was such a hard worker.

"I can remember taking him out of practice a couple of times just because I felt that he might run himself into the ground. But if I didn't do it he would just go and go and go. He and Roger Craig seemed to have this competition of who could work the hardest, which is something very special on any team."

Though it's hard to imagine now, Rice was the third receiver taken in the 1985 draft. The New York Jets drafted Al Toon at No. 10, and the Cincinnati Bengals took Eddie Brown at No. 13, underscoring the divided opinions on Rice's NFL prospects at the time.

He was downgraded by some scouts because they felt his gaudy numbers at Division II Mississippi Valley State—he had 28 touchdowns and 1,845 yards receiving as a senior—reflected the weaker competition. They also felt Rice, who lacked elite speed, wasn't fast enough to be anything more than an average receiver.

None of those concerns were enough to dissuade Walsh or trouble Rice.

"I never gave into that," Rice says. "When they told me I was too slow, that I couldn't play in the NFL—I think I've proven everyone who said that wrong."

But Rice wasn't able to say "I told you so" right away. His rookie season included dealing with some nightmarish problems with drops. Those were among the reasons that Rice said he wrestled with self-doubt early in his career. There were times when he was so down on himself that

Jerry Rice *Photo © Michael Zagaris*

he called back home to Mississippi to his girlfriend, Jackie (whom he later married) practically in tears over his difficulties hanging on to the ball.

"When I came here, I was like a deer in headlights," said Rice, who struggled to adjust to the big city pressures and scrutiny after a lifetime in rural Mississippi. "I came from Crawford, Mississippi, population 74. When I came to the 49ers, I was overwhelmed by so many things. I was terrified. I felt like I had stepped into something that was too big, coming from a small school like Mississippi Valley State University, and all of a sudden coming here.

"But guys like Roger Craig, Guy McIntyre, Joe Montana, Ronnie Lott, Eric Wright, all those guys, they kept pushing me. They kept saying, 'Everything's going to be OK. You're pressing, but you're working hard. Things are going to work out.'"

With Rice at a low point late in the 1985 season, Walsh, too, lent his support. Though Rice was under intense media criticism for continual drops, Walsh declared in late November that he would continue to play extensively and predicted "at some point, the boos will turn to cheers."

Roger Craig agreed with Walsh's long-term outlook on Rice.

"He found a way to fight through those tough times as a rookie," said Craig, a 49ers running back. "He had a lot of pressure stepping into a role that Dwight Clark did a great job in for years. Freddie Solomon was no slouch either.

"When Joe throws him the ball, we're expecting him to catch it, so times when he was struggling, he felt like he was all by himself. But I was always encouraging him, getting in his ear, 'It's going to be OK. Just hang in there,' and he worked that much harder."

And he got that much better, breaking out in the 14th game of the season, a Monday night affair against the Los Angeles Rams. Though the 49ers lost 27-20, Rice signaled his emergence as a go-to receiver for Joe Montana by torching the Rams' secondary for 10 catches and a team-record 241 yards.

"That was like my coming-out game, and after that, it was never enough," says Rice. "We just kept working during the off-season and kept trying to win Super Bowls."

Craig says Rice's performance against the Rams convinced teammates he was a special talent: "That's when we knew he could play this game, when he destroyed the Rams defense like that as a rookie. It was pretty incredible."

Rice finished his rookie season with 49 catches for 927 yards, earning NFC Rookie of the Year honors. The next year, he broke through for 86 catches for 1,570 yards, the first of 11 consecutive 1,000-yard receiving seasons.

In 1987, Rice led the league with a team single-season record of 138 points. He followed that up in 1988 by averaging a career-best 20.4 yards per catch.

Former 49ers tackle Steve Wallace remembers one 1988 touchdown in particular. It was a last-minute strike from Joe Montana to Rice that beat the New York Giants and captured the greatest elements of his game, melding the catch, the run-after-catch, and the score: "We were backed up and Joe just chucked the ball as far as he could. I could see it was well past Jerry. But he outran the ball while it was in the air. He grabs it, the two defenders knock each other down and he takes it to the house. The only other [player] that I saw catch up with the ball like that was Bo Jackson."

Rice wrapped up the 1988 campaign in grand style in the postseason. He tied a playoff record with three receiving touchdowns in a victory over the Vikings and added a pair of scores in the NFC title game victory over Chicago.

But he was at his best in his first Super Bowl appearance, stamping himself as one of football's great clutch performers and the preeminent receiver in the game.

GAME OF MY LIFE
BY JERRY RICE
JANUARY 22, 1989—MIAMI, FLORIDA

You know, on a platform like that, I have always been able to somehow elevate my game, kind of like *Monday Night Football*. I used to love *Monday Night Football*, and the Super Bowl, you visualize situations the night before that you might be in. The repetitions you take during the week, you know you're going to have opportunities in the game, and now you've just got to go out and execute, as a player and as a team.

But what made Super Bowl XXIII so special is what we were able to accomplish with some three minutes left in the game.

John Taylor made the game-winning catch at the end, but in a situation like that, where we had to basically go the length of the field, anything can go wrong. If we make a mistake along the way, the ballgame is over. That's when you really have to focus. Also, you have to depend on your teammates, knowing we have been in situations like that before, and for one and all, to be able to perform at a very crucial time.

We were in the hole, down 16-13, and we were backed up at our 8-yard line after a holding penalty on the kickoff return. We had a long way to go, but Joe Montana and Roger Craig got us started, connecting on a pass to get us some breathing room. Then we hit two passes in quick succession, the first going to John Frank for a first down, and then I caught my first pass of the drive, in the right flat.

There we were at the 30-yard line, getting there all on passes. Just like that, we ran for the first time. Roger got only a yard and that put us at third-and-2. We went back to Roger and he ran for a first down and I remember the clock stopped for the two-minute warning. Roger's second straight carry was the last run Bill Walsh called in the drive.

I got open running down the left sideline and Joe hit me for a 17-yard gain. That was a nice chunk, good enough to get us into Bengals territory at their 48-yard line. We were clicking. Our confidence was building.

Roger caught a pass for another first down, and Joe threw the next pass away, the only time the ball hit the ground in Joe's nine passes during the drive.

We had a little bit of a glitch on the next play when a catch by Roger was negated by an ineligible receiver downfield. But that set up our longest play of the drive. Joe hit me coming across the middle. I made the catch in stride and I took off down the left sideline. I wasn't knocked off my feet until I got to the Bengals' 18-yard line. I thought for a while that I was going to break free and I very nearly did.

Roger caught a pass to get us down to the 10-yard line and we called a timeout on second-and-2 so we could decide what to do.

On that play, I went in motion so I was like a decoy, and I think I helped the play work. I was watching old highlights and the Cincinnati coach, I could hear him saying, "This is going to Rice. I know this is going to Rice." But we threw it to John Taylor on the post and we got the winning touchdown with just seconds to spare.

With that drive, I think we had everybody on the edge of their seats. Look, everything was on the line. And for us, just to be able to function amid all that pressure and scrutiny was an accomplishment and something I remain very proud of. We were able to block everything else out, to really focus on winning the game and perform with distinction on football's grandest stage. That's about as good as it gets for a player and for a team. And whenever I run into a tough spot, whenever I start thinking that something is too hard or maybe even impossible, be it on the golf course or competing on *Dancing With the Stars*, all I have to do is look at our Super Bowl ring from that game. It's a constant reminder that when you pull together as a team, and when you do your job as an individual, so many things are possible, including something as special and as hard as a championship.

Jerry Rice was named Super Bowl MVP after an 11-catch, 215-yard performance that included a tying touchdown receptiom in the 49ers' 20-16 victory over Cincinnati. And though over the years Rice took some criticism at times for seeming selfish, Bill Walsh said there was always a purpose behind his demands for the ball. That included a key moment in the 49ers' 92-yard, go-ahead drive during the waning minutes of Super Bowl XXIII.

Before Rice took the field for the decisive drive, he told Walsh that he could get open on a deep "over" pattern. Walsh called the play and Joe Montana hit Rice, who turned his 11th reception of the game into a 27-yard gain that brought the 49ers to the brink of a score. Rice's catch stood out as the longest advance in the 11-play march, and two plays later from 10 yards out, Montana hit John Taylor for the game-winner with 34 seconds left.

"Jerry is the one who set it up," said Walsh, who coached his final game for the 49ers in the Super Bowl. "He had an incredible game in the Super Bowl but that's the way he was. In the big games, Jerry was at his best. He was truly a great player."

Rice's contributions always went beyond what he did on the field on game day. He raised the level of play of those around him by setting an example with his rigorous off-season workouts, his tireless study of game film, and his own head-turning plays that inspired teammates to reach for the stars in their play as well.

Former 49ers defensive tackle Dana Stubblefield was a rookie in 1993 when he saw Rice leap over two defenders and haul in a pass one-handed in a game against the Los Angeles Rams.

"I was like, 'Wow!'" Stubblefield says. "And our coach, George Seifert, said, 'He's one of your teammates. Now, go out there and make him say the same thing about you.' I just shook my head and I was amazed. Him catching the ball in that game raised my level of expectations for myself."

Hall of Fame quarterback Steve Young, who teamed with Rice 85 times for touchdowns, once an NFL record, credited the receiver's conditioning and game preparation for much of their success and on-field rapport.

"I remember times when we'd be playing in a noisy dome and he couldn't have heard the play," Young said. "But I'd drop back and throw the ball. He'd catch it and we'd move on. It wasn't dumb luck. It happened because of all the right things."

A year later, near the end of a lopsided season-opening win over the Los Angeles Raiders in 1994, Rice broke new ground. He scored his third touchdown of the night, making a leaping grab of a long pass from Young for his record-setting 127th career touchdown. It put him one up on Hall of Famer Jim Brown as the NFL's all-time leader.

"I think that was very special because of the way we did it," Rice said. "George Seifert gave Steve and I one opportunity to do it. I think everybody in the stadium knew it was going to happen. And still the Raiders couldn't stop it.

"Steve threw the ball up, and I was able to go up and attack the football. This is something Bill Walsh taught me when I first came. He said, 'Always go up and attack the football. Never wait on the football.' I went up and I attacked the football, and I was able to come down with it."

Supremely conditioned throughout his career, durability was also a hallmark of Rice. He played 12 years without missing a game due to injury before tearing ligaments and damaging cartilage in his left knee on an end-around in the 49ers' 1997 season opener at Tampa Bay. Rice made an ill-fated attempt to return for a mid-December game against the Denver Broncos that coincided with the retirement of Joe Montana's No. 16 jersey at halftime. But his unlikely comeback was short-lived. He fell on his surgically reconstructed knee after making a touchdown catch against the Broncos and cracked the knee cap, finishing him for the year and setting off a second round of rehabilitation.

Rice came back to play three more seasons for the 49ers but endured a wrenching departure. Bill Walsh, who was general manager at the time, signaled the end was coming in the days leading up to the 2000 home finale against Chicago. He advised 49ers fans to treat the game as "Jerry Rice Day" and to come out and show their support and appreciation for the 49ers great.

Rice made a public farewell after the game from a platform set up on Candlestick Park's field, and he rode into the locker-room on the shoulders of his teammates. But Rice's farewell game is also remembered as a coming out for Terrell Owens, who caught an NFL-record 20 passes in the 49ers' victory over the Bears.

Six months later, in June 2001, after Rice rebuffed a $1 million offer from the team to retire immediately as a 49er, he was cut in a salary-cap move.

Later that same night, Rice drove to the 49ers' Santa Clara headquarters to clean out his locker and gather up all of his football belongings. Dozens of Rice's shoes, game pants, jerseys, gloves, and footballs were piled into a laundry cart. Assistant equipment manager Nick Pettit pushed the cart out to the car, followed by Rice, who was carrying a couple of shoe boxes, and Terrell Owens, who had been in the midst of a solitary workout at the facility when Rice came by for his things.

They packed Rice's car and trunk with the accoutrements from Rice's 16 seasons with the 49ers. Before Rice drove away, he rummaged through the trunk, pulled out a football and handed it to Owens. It was the game ball he had been presented with after he had played in his final home game as a 49er—the same game in which Owens had the record-setting 20-catch performance.

"He deserved it," Rice said years later, when asked why he gave Owens the game ball. "That was an amazing game, so that was out of respect to that."

During his final four years in the league, Rice, at age 40 in 2002, helped the Raiders to a runner-up finish to Tampa Bay in the Super Bowl and became the oldest wide receiver ever to earn a Pro Bowl berth.

But he also saw his NFL record streak with at least one catch snapped at 274 games in September 2004 when he was shut out against Buffalo. A month later, the Raiders traded Rice to Seattle in return for a conditional draft pick. There was a final distinction in what proved to be his final season. Between the Raiders and the Seahawks, Rice became only the fourth player of the modern era to play in 17 games during the regular season.

Rice went to training camp with the Denver Broncos in 2005 but after coach Mike Shanahan, who had previously worked with Rice as the 49ers offensive coordinator in the mid-1990s, told him he was no better than fourth or fifth on the depth chart, Rice decided to call it quits.

"I never thought I would see this day," said Rice, who was closing in on 43 when he announced his retirement at Denver's team headquarters. "But it's here and I feel pretty good about it. The tears you see are because I've really enjoyed this ride. It's been great. It's been fantastic."

Rice played longer than any other wide receiver in NFL history. Plunging into new ventures right after he stepped away from the game helped him adjust rapidly to life without football. He began working as a sports talk show host on satellite radio and renewed his pursuit of golf as an avocation.

He also took the plunge into Hollywood, taking part in television's second season of *Dancing With the Stars*. The show paired novice celebrity dancers, like Rice, with professional partners, and the couples faced off in a nationally televised competition that became a primetime hit.

"After playing the game so long, a lot of guys can't really cross over. They can't make the transition," Rice said. "But I had so many other opportunities on my plate, it got me through it. I never sat around, saying, 'Oh, I can still play.' I've been busy doing other things with my life, with my family."

On the show, Rice struggled in some of his early dance routines with partner Anna Trebunskaya, but he survived the rough spots and some harsh criticism from judges by connecting with the voting public and becoming a more polished dancer over time.

"In football, I always started slow," Rice says. "By midseason, I was getting strong and towards the end I was at my best. It was the same thing with *Dancing With the Stars*."

Rice said one of the things he was proudest of from his *Dancing With the Stars* experience was his willingness to step out of his comfort zone into a new, different but also very public arena. And even though Rice was out of his element, he persevered on the show for a second-place finish.

"I have always been the type of person to take risks," Rice says. "We were all rooting for each other in the ensemble but it was still competition, and I knew that the media and my peers were watching. You're going to have some people for you and you're going to have some people waiting for you to fall on your face. I just put the same work ethic into dancing that I had put into football."

Throughout the competition, dangling from a chain around Rice's neck was a reminder of what he could accomplish when he put his mind—and body—to it: his ring from the 49ers' victory over Cincinnati in Super Bowl XXIII.

"It was like my security blanket when those judges were ripping me apart, trying to mess with my ego," Rice said. "I put it on and I've kept it on ever since."

He was still wearing it when he returned to the 49ers' Santa Clara headquarters in August 2006, and with owner John York looking on, signed a ceremonial one-day contract, allowing him to come full circle and retire as a 49er.

Six years earlier, after his release, Rice had driven away from the team's facility into the night, accompanied only by the football keepsakes he had stuffed into his car. Finally, at least symbolically, he was back where he belonged. And when he said goodbye this time, he was surrounded by hundreds of familiar faces.

"I feel like this is home," Rice said. "This is where my heart started and this is where I'm going to end it."

Rice said he walked away knowing that in his 20-year career, "I never felt like I cheated the fans. When they came to the stadium, I wanted them to leave the stadium feeling like they had witnessed something that was really special."

In that, Rice was a masterful success. His teammate and workout partner, Roger Craig, seconds that notion, saying, "There was no other player on the planet who had the passion that he brought to the field every day."

Chapter 15

JOHN TAYLOR

In his 10 years with the San Francisco 49ers, John Taylor tended to shy away from talking about his play. He preferred to let his actions on the field speak for themselves. From that perspective, Taylor had a wonderful way with words.

Playing opposite the great Jerry Rice, Taylor emerged as a game-breaking receiver and clutch performer in his own right. Yet Taylor's path to NFL stardom did not come easily or quickly. It included some painful detours, plenty of hurdles, and an unconventional proving ground in his youth—the local cemetery in his hometown of Pennsauken, New Jersey.

"That's basically the only place we had to play," says Taylor. "There were a couple of parks, but the majority of them had broken glass laid throughout the field. We knew the only place that wasn't going to have any broken glass would be the graveyard. The only thing we had to worry about when we caught a pass was running into a tombstone. That was our main concern. We really didn't worry about anything else."

Taylor's neighborhood was an incredibly rich source of NFL-caliber talent. Four of his contemporaries, including his younger brother Keith, would go on to play in the league. Another was David Griggs, who as a San Diego Chargers linebacker played against Taylor and the 49ers in the January 1995 Super Bowl. Griggs' brother, Billy Griggs, and Todd McNair, also went on to play in the league. Incredibly, the five lived within a few blocks of each other in the south New Jersey community.

When Taylor got to Pennsauken High School, he played safety on the football team—"I used to light people up," he says—and he displayed his athleticism on the baseball team. Taylor, who admits that baseball was his best sport, used his speed to cover a lot of ground as a second baseman and become an offensive catalyst as one of the region's top base stealers.

But sports were little more than an afterthought when Taylor graduated from high school in 1980. He passed on a college baseball scholarship in favor of continuing to work as a delivery truck driver for a liquor warehouse, dropping off shipments in Atlantic City and other points in South New Jersey.

"I was making $800 a week. I was living at home with my parents, had no kids," Taylor says. "I had no need to go to school, you know?"

That was the approach Taylor took for about a year. Eventually, he took stock of himself and his future, and became determined to change the course of his life after making some "wrong choices," as Taylor puts it.

"I came home one day and I just told my dad, 'I've got to get out of here. I'm going to school,'" Taylor says.

With the financial support of his parents, Alice and John Taylor, John enrolled at Johnson C. Smith University, a predominantly black college in Charlotte, North Carolina. He stayed there a year before transferring to Delaware State, where he decided to walk on to the football team as a wide receiver, though he was a novice at the position.

"I had played baseball a majority of my life, and if you can catch a little ball like that, I thought I should have no problem catching a ball that was about eight times the size," Taylor says.

Taylor had no problem convincing himself he could be a capable receiver, but his coaches at Delaware State initially were unsure what to make of him.

"Of course, they gave me a helmet that was too big and shoulder pads that were too big. Basically, I looked like a clown," Taylor says. "They put me in on the demo squad. My first pass, I beat a couple of their DBs, so they looked at me and said, 'Who is that kid?'

"They actually never knew my real name for quite a while. I'd only told them J.T. and that's all they knew me by. For the longest time, my position coach used to call me Jake. I guarantee you it went on for a year or so. Then one day he was calling me Jake and I just said 'Listen, why

John Taylor *Photo © Michael Zagaris*

are you calling me Jake? My name is John.' So he says, 'Why did you let us call you that for all this time?' I just said, 'I saw no reason to interrupt you until just now,' and let it go like that."

Taylor's decision to play wide receiver was a boon for him as well as for Delaware State. He played in a handful of games in his first year and then started each of his last three seasons. He totaled 2,426 yards receiving on 100 career receptions, 33 of which went for touchdowns. He also returned four of 48 career punt returns for scores.

Intrigued by Taylor's big-play potential, the 49ers made him the last of their three third-round selections and the 76th player selected overall in the 1986 draft, regarded by some as Bill Walsh's greatest draft. As part of eight draft-day moves, Walsh traded away the 49ers' No. 1 pick in order to stockpile selections in lower rounds. The draft-day bounty produced eight future starters: Larry Roberts, Tom Rathman, Tim McKyer, Taylor, Charles Haley, Steve Wallace, Kevin Fagan, and Don Griffin. They were at the core of 49ers teams that went on to win back-to-back Super Bowls in 1988 and 1989.

For his part, Taylor wasn't really expecting to be drafted into the NFL: "I knew during the year there were some pro scouts around," Taylor says. "And I played in the Senior Bowl, the Blue-Gray game, and the East-West Shrine game. Still, I really wasn't thinking about playing professional football.

"The actual day of the draft, I was upstairs asleep. My older brother came running up and said, 'Hey man, you just got drafted by the Niners in the third round.' I said, 'Yeah, OK.' I went back to sleep. Then my dad came in and said, 'Hey, your brother isn't lying. You just got picked.' I said, 'Oh, really.' So that's how I wound up going to San Francisco."

Taylor's rookie season was a wash, however. He suffered a back injury trying to recover a fumble by Tom Rathman in an exhibition game against Denver and spent the rest of the season on injured reserve.

In 1987, he arrived at the 49ers' training camp healthy, but with Jerry Rice, Dwight Clark, and Mike Wilson on the roster, Taylor found himself far down on the team's depth chart. So when the team issued a try-out call for any player interested in punt returning, Taylor answered it. But as Taylor fielded punts at practice, Coach Bill Walsh turned to his special teams coach, Lynn Stiles, and said, "He'll never be a punt returner. He's too much of a long strider."

"Lynn told me what Bill said," Taylor says. "I asked him, 'Can I still try?' He said, 'Sure.' So I just said to myself, 'I'm going to show you what a long strider does.' My first opportunity came when we played in the Hall of Fame exhibition game against Kansas City. I ran a punt back for a touchdown and damn near ran two others back. The next day, when we got back to training camp and looked at the game film, I said to Lynn Stiles, 'Hey, that guy returning those punts really can't return them because he's too much of a long strider.' Lynn just looked at me and started laughing.

"I ate stuff like that up. I used that stuff. You can say what you want to about me. I'm not going to get ticked. I'm not going to run up to you and do a whole bunch of arguing. I just take care of it on the field."

Taylor didn't play much in 1987, but he scored his first career touchdown by advancing Harry Sydney's fumble. He eventually made his first two career starts and played well enough to put himself in position to compete for the opening in the lineup left by the retirement of Dwight Clark.

But Taylor missed the first four games of the 1988 season while serving a suspension for what the NFL said was a violation of its substance abuse policy. Initially, Taylor declined commenting about the incident—and just about everything else—for seven years before finally telling *The New York Times* his side of the story. Taylor admitted to the paper that he'd "made a mistake" and received a warning from the league and the team after a positive drug test.

A subsequent drug test by the team came back negative, but one by the league was positive, leading to the NFL-imposed suspension despite his contention the results were inaccurate. Taylor has said that the league later admitted to him in private that its test results were flawed, though the NFL never has said anything publicly about the matter.

Unhappy with some of the public coverage of his problems, Taylor largely maintained his silence with the media and quietly resolved to try to make the best of a bad situation. "When I was suspended," Taylor said in a newspaper interview, "I knew there were people out there who felt I'd be another black guy who fell by the wayside and came up short. I set out to prove that wasn't true."

When Taylor returned a month into the season, he never looked back. He returned a punt 77 yards for a touchdown in his first game back October 2 against Detroit. Down the stretch, Taylor returned a punt a team-record 95 yards against the Washington Redskins, igniting a victory that started the four-game winning streak that carried the 49ers to the NFC West crown after 6-5 start.

Taylor finished the regular season as the NFL leader with a 12.6-yard punt-return average. He demonstrated his knack for the big play, scoring all four of his touchdowns on plays of 65 or more yards.

He capped his breakthrough year by making one of the most important catches in 49ers history in the last and most important game of the season. With 34 seconds remaining in the Super Bowl, Taylor ran a skinny post and Joe Montana hit him in the end zone for a 10-yard touchdown that lifted the 49ers past the Cincinnati Bengals for their third championship in eight years.

"At some time or another, as a kid, you always say or imagine, 'If I make this catch, we're going to win the Super Bowl.' I can honestly say it actually happened to me. It was a great feeling," says Taylor.

The championship-winning catch came at the end of an 11-play, 92-yard drive, and was Taylor's only reception of the game.

"It was funny, because we went in and there were only a few minutes left, and we were sitting in the huddle, and Joe walked in the huddle and he was laughing and cracking jokes," Taylor says. "I was just listening to what he was saying, and he joked around and said, 'Aww man, listen, let's do what we've got to do and let's go home.' Then he said, 'Yeah, there's John Candy over there in the first row.' We turn around, and sure enough there's John Candy. And time came back in and he marched us right down the field. He basically just picked them apart."

Taylor headed into the 1989 campaign entrenched as the 49ers punt returner and their No. 2 receiver, but all of that became an afterthought after his mother, Alice, died suddenly. She collapsed during a summer outing at a New Jersey amusement park. She died several days later of complications related to a brain aneurysm. She was 47 years old.

The grief-stricken Taylor began his first full year as a starter for the 49ers by dedicating the season to his mother. He went on to earn his first trip to the Pro Bowl, establishing career highs with 1,077 yards receiving and 10 touchdowns while helping the 49ers to an NFL-best 14-2 regular season mark under first-year coach George Seifert.

In an important game against the Los Angeles Rams, Taylor also pulled off something no NFL player has done before or since: turning a pair of short passes from Joe Montana into two touchdown plays, each covering more than 90 yards. Seifert later called Taylor's display the most spectacular individual performance he had seen in some 30 years of coaching.

The coach recalled the feat in 2006 during a lavish Las Vegas reunion of the 49ers' five Super Bowl teams organized by former owner Eddie DeBartolo. "I still remember the Monday night game against the Rams in Los Angeles," Seifert said as he addressed a gala dinner celebration.

"We were behind and Joe threw two short passes to John Taylor and he went 90-odd yards for touchdowns each time to win that ball game. Georgia Frontiere, the owner of the Rams, was walking along the sideline holding her glass of wine up to all the fans, and then she had that taken away from her by the great play of our team in the second half."

What Taylor remembers most is the unspoken communication between him and Montana that led up to the plays and opened the door to transforming a routine and predictable pass route—the slant—into an eloquent mix of timing and surprise, precision and instincts, strength and speed.

GAME OF MY LIFE
BY JOHN TAYLOR
DECEMBER 11, 1989—ANAHEIM, CALIFORNIA

Going into the game, we knew whichever team won would take the division and earn a bye the first week of the playoffs. It was a huge Monday night game and everyone was watching. Our mind-set was all about business. We just wanted to do what we needed to do to get a win and stay on track toward getting back to the Super Bowl for the second straight season.

L.A. beat us in our first meeting at Candlestick Park, and things didn't start too well for us the second time around. We fell behind early, down 17-0 after the first quarter. It seemed like no matter what we did, things came out badly. We finally got it together a bit and had a first-and-goal at the 2-yard line, but we couldn't punch it in. We settled for a field goal for our first score.

The Rams went on the move again and when they got down to our 4-yard line, they went for the jugular to try to put us away right there.

They faked a field goal on fourth down from the 4, but Michael Walter tackled their holder, Pete Holohan, a yard shy of the goal line.

A short pass to Brent Jones gave us a little breathing room, and on third down from the 8, the call from Joe Montana was for me to run a slant pattern. On that particular play, it just so happened that we both noticed the cornerback was kind of cheating, not really playing the pass honestly. Joe and I both said the same thing to each other at just about the same time. The cornerback was looking at me, but not really paying attention to me. I mean, he knew I was out there, but he really wasn't worrying because of the score and because we were backed up close to our own end zone. They weren't looking for a pass per se as much as they were looking for a run because that was the tendency of most NFL teams when they get backed up. The first thing an offensive coordinator wants to do is run and in my opinion, it's, "Hey, that's what they're thinking we're going to do. So let's pass it, you know?" You always try to keep them off guard.

At the snap of the ball, Joe saw that the cornerback wasn't really paying attention to me and he hit me as soon as he got a handle on the ball. I caught it and right away the DB was in a chase mode. But I knew where I was going; he didn't. Once I got up to speed, I just put that one move on, let him slide by me, and cut back inside. It became a foot race to the end zone and I wasn't going to let anyone catch me.

We felt pretty good going into halftime, behind 17-10. But the Rams got it going again, and with a little more than 13 minutes left they were leading 27-10.

That wasn't going to be enough for the Rams, though, because we scored the next three touchdowns in a hurry. Joe connected with Mike Wilson for a touchdown to get us back in the game. The Rams got all the way down to our 4-yard line, but Jim Everett fumbled the snap, and Matt Millen recovered for us at the 5.

Here we were, backed up again close to our own end zone. In the huddle, Joe said, "Let's go with the slant." I looked at Joe and he looked at me, and when I came off the line, the Rams were playing off of me and to the outside. If they were going to take that outside away from me, I was going to keep them outside of me, but I'd come hard across the middle. I was going to get as much separation as possible, and Joe saw that. He saw the coverage and at the snap of the ball, he looked at me and nodded toward me. He hit me in that gap and I caught it in stride.

I just picked up blockers as I was going downfield; Jerry Rice was out in front of me. I made a couple people miss, and then it became another footrace. I wasn't going to lose that one either.

That got us to 27-23 after we missed the extra point, but that didn't matter after the Rams fumbled the kickoff. We got it at their 27, and we mixed running and passing. Roger Craig ran it in from up close to give us the lead late and we had the win, another division title, and the inside track on the road to the Super Bowl.

From a personal standpoint, though, the most satisfying thing out of the deal for me was that the next day, my dad called me. He's retired now, but he was a postal worker in South New Jersey for more than 30 years. He said he had been looking at the game the night before and we were getting blown out so bad that he'd said, "Oh, I just went and cut the television off and went to sleep because I had to get up early and go to work." He got in to work the next day and he said everybody, all his co-workers, were running up to him and congratulating him. He told me, "I had no idea what they were congratulating me about until one of them said, 'Man, how did your son manage to pull off those two 90-yard touchdowns?'" That's when he realized we had come back and won. Prior to that he had no idea what had happened. I still get a kick out of that. And sometimes, when people say the Rams moved from Los Angeles to St. Louis, I just say, "Yeah, I ran them out of L.A."

Taylor finished with 11 catches and 286 yards receiving against the Rams. At the time, it was a team record for yards receiving in a game and the fifth highest total in NFL history.

It was emblematic of a season in which Taylor also had a 70-yard catch-and-run as part of a furious fourth-quarter rally that toppled Philadelphia and averaged a team-record 32.5 yards per catch, helping the 49ers win at Atlanta.

He caught a touchdown pass in each of the 49ers' three postseason victories, including a conquest of the Rams in the NFC championship and the blowout of the Denver Broncos in their second consecutive Super Bowl triumph.

"He was just a tremendous player, an exquisite talent," said Bill Walsh, whose final play call as 49ers coach was the "20 halfback curl X-up" pass that Montana completed to Taylor for the winning touchdown in the previous Super Bowl.

After the 1989 campaign, Taylor spent six more seasons with the 49ers. His 97-yard touchdown catch from Steve Young against Atlanta in 1991 remains the team record, and he helped the 49ers win their fifth Super Bowl title following the 1994 season. He played one more year before calling it a career and starting a new one.

Nowadays, Taylor goes back and forth across the country three or four times a month as an independent long-haul truck driver. In a refrigerated tractor-trailer rig, Taylor typically hauls California produce to the East Coast and returns with a load of chicken.

In many ways, the work is a return to his blue-collar roots. "I grew up around trucks," Taylor says. "I used to ride up and down the freeways all over the place with my grandfather. He used to haul for a farming outfit. I always said that when I got done with football, I'd be driving a truck. It was second nature to me. I just love that stuff. I got my license in 1998, and I've been driving ever since."

Taylor operates a W900L Kenworth that is equipped for the long hauls. In the cab, he has a bed, a small sofa bed, a closet, a dresser, a microwave, a refrigerator, and a television set. "It's the greatest," Taylor says.

Taylor enjoys his trucking career and traveling the open road as much he enjoyed playing football. He's had a chance to meet people and see the country and get paid for it, just like he did playing pro football. And, just as he did with his charitable work as a player, he's had a chance to help people along the way as well. Taylor once bumped into a trucker at a truck stop and the two of them decided to travel part of the country together. While driving in the middle of nowhere, his friend's rig began having transmission problems.

Taylor stuck with the trucker for hours as they coaxed the sputtering rig along until reaching a town where it could be repaired. To show his appreciation, the trucker offered to take Taylor to dinner.

Taylor, needing to make up for lost time, suggested another way to repay him: "I told him if he sees someone in the same predicament tomorrow, or the next week or the next year, just stop and help them."

And with that, Taylor was off, back on the road again.

Chapter 16

JESSE SAPOLU

A couple weeks after another loss for the 49ers in the NFC title game, center Jesse Sapolu found solace in Honolulu; ten years into his NFL career, Sapolu's play in 1993 drew long overdue recognition in the form of his first Pro Bowl berth.

George Seifert and the rest of his 49ers coaching staff were in Hawaii, too. Coaching the NFC's Pro Bowl team was their consolation in losing a second consecutive conference championship to the Dallas Cowboys.

It was while they were in Hawaii that Seifert and offensive line coach Bobb McKittrick set in motion one of the first changes aimed at strengthening the 49ers' chances against the Dallas Cowboys, who were the greatest obstacle to another championship season for the 49ers. They asked Sapolu to return to guard and began recruiting New York Giants center Bart Oates, who was also in Hawaii as a member of the NFC Pro Bowl squad before heading into free agency.

Sapolu's willingness to give up his position and the subsequent signing of Oates allowed the 49ers to solidify their line while filling the hole left by the loss to free agency of Guy McIntyre, a five-time Pro Bowl guard. But it was not an easy move for the prideful Sapolu.

"It's really tough when you're one of the best at a position, and now they're asking you to go back again and virtually start over," Sapolu said in a 1994 newspaper interview. "Your family's asking, 'Why'd you do it?' Your friends are asking, 'Why'd you do it?' They're almost saying you're stupid for making it because you're now in the Pro Bowl. But those people don't have to weigh the importance of the Pro Bowl compared to the Super Bowl.

"If our chances were hurt because I was selfish enough to stay, it would have been something lingering in my heart. It's thinking of that that made me willing to make the sacrifice."

But the change turned out well for Sapolu, and even better for the 49ers. Despite playing guard for the first time in five years in 1994, Sapolu's season ended with a second successive trip to the Pro Bowl.

"He risked his own personal goals for the good of the team," Oates said. Seifert added, "He could have balked at the move but he didn't. The thing that really made me feel good is that he was rewarded by not only playing well at guard, but being voted to the Pro Bowl."

Oates and eight other 49ers joined him, matching a team record for most Pro Bowl players. The 49ers also sent 10 players to the Pro Bowl in 1984 and 1995.

"The reason I made the move," Sapolu said, "was not to go back to the Pro Bowl. It was to go back to the Super Bowl."

That's where the 49ers went, helped by a reconfigured line and the No. 2-ranked offense central to the scoring of 66 touchdowns and 505 points in 1994, both team records. The 49ers beat Dallas for the first time in three consecutive meetings in the NFC title game before winning their fifth Super Bowl in as many trips to the NFL pinnacle, routing the San Diego Chargers 49-26.

The next season, Sapolu remained at left guard and Oates remained at center. Sapolu was the "Iron Man" of the group, standing out as the only member of the offensive line to start every regular-season game and a divisional playoff. Indeed, Sapolu wound up logging the most playing time of any 49ers in 1995, taking part in 1,077 snaps, or 99 percent of the plays.

It was in the middle of that season that Sapolu displayed the gumption and leadership that made him one of the most respected figures in the 49ers' locker room. After a 5-2 start by the 49ers, back-to-back losses at home to lowly New Orleans and expansion Carolina left the defending Super Bowl champions reeling. Steve Young remained sidelined by a shoulder injury and charismatic fullback William Floyd was lost to a season-ending knee dislocation in the loss to the Saints.

Jesse Sapolu *Photo © Michael Zagaris*

Next up, with their season hanging by a thread, was a game at Dallas, the 49ers' longtime nemesis. And no one was really giving the 49ers a chance to win against a surging Cowboys squad out to reclaim its moniker as "America's Team."

GAME OF MY LIFE
BY JESSE SAPOLU
NOVEMBER 12, 1995—IRVING, TEXAS

This is a game that I remember vividly because of the situation we were in at the time. We were the defending champions, nine months removed from our fifth Super Bowl title. But we had lost two in a row at home. New Orleans came in with the worst record in the league at the time and beat us and then we lost to expansion Carolina. I remember it was the first time that an expansion team playing its inaugural season had defeated a reigning Super Bowl champion. We dropped to 5-4 and we had to go to Dallas to play a Cowboys team that, at 8-1, had the best record in the league to that point. We had to go against "Primetime," cornerback Deion Sanders, who was in Dallas after winning the championship with us the year before. They had Troy Aikman, Emmitt Smith, and Michael Irvin, "The Triplets," who had given us so many problems throughout the '90s.

On top of that, we were without Steve Young. He had a shoulder injury, so Elvis Grbac was starting in his place. And we had lost William Floyd, our fullback and our emotional leader, to a season-ending knee injury in the New Orleans game. It was almost like the demise of the 49ers was taking place before our very eyes. Nobody was giving us a chance against Dallas. We were 13 1-2 point underdogs against the Cowboys. But inside, I felt enough was enough. After we lost the Carolina game, I told a reporter, "I promise you, we're going to win this next game in Dallas." He just looked at me.

I remember calling in the guys that week for a team meeting. I said, "We're up against the wall, but all we need is 11 people who believe. If you don't believe, you can still get your check next Monday, but we don't need you on that plane to Dallas." We got together again in the locker room before the game. We felt as if it was us against the world. Nobody believed we could go in there and beat the Cowboys—nobody but us.

When we got out there on the field, it was so loud we couldn't even hear the snap count. The call on the second play was a quick slant to Jerry Rice. I had Leon Lett on my outside shoulder, and Charles Haley was on the outside shoulder of Kirk Scrafford, who was next to me at left tackle. Lett and Haley did a looping stunt to try to create a split between Kirk and me, and if Kirk had set up to the outside, that's what would have happened. But Kirk stayed home and stopped Lett. Haley came charging and I got just enough of him for Elvis to get the ball off to Jerry. I looked up and all I could see was Jerry's heels. He was already 30 or 40 yards downfield. He ended up going 81 yards for a touchdown. It was the second play of the game. We had the lead and the crowd went silent. Our defense scored on the next series. Merton Hanks returned a fumble by Michael Irvin 38 yards for a touchdown. Their next series ended in an interception by Rickey Jackson and that set up a field goal. We didn't stop. We just kept scoring. We had a 24-nothing lead before the Cowboys finally scored. We ended up winning by 18 points.

After the game, Carmen Policy, the team president, gave me a hug and told me it was one of the most satisfying wins in his involvement with the 49ers because we had shown the heart of a champion. It was one of the most satisfying games for me as well. We didn't win a championship that year. In fact, we lost the first playoff game we played in the divisional round against the Green Bay Packers. Winning a championship indeed is the ultimate for an NFL team, but there are certain things that satisfy you as a competitor, and one of those things is earning the respect of your peers. We went into Dallas undermanned, but we kept the team together. For me personally, as a senior member of the team, I felt like I'd arrived as a leader. I had matured not only as a player but as someone who could help hold that team together and win a huge game that the whole world thought we were going lose.

You know, the 49ers were always sort of known as pretty boys who play finesse offense. But we pushed people around that game. The feeling was, "Hey, finesse this." That's the kind of feeling we took from that game, and it stayed with us for a long time.

Sapolu played 15 years with the 49ers and was part of 14 playoff teams during an especially dominating stretch by San Francisco. He remains one of only six 49ers players to win four Super Bowl rings. That he played so well for so long didn't seem at all likely early in his career, when a succession of foot and leg fractures cost him virtually all of three seasons.

Sapolu played both guard and center during his four-year career at the University of Hawaii, breaking into the NFL in 1983 as the 49ers' 11th-round pick. He was the 286th overall selection and the last player drafted by the 49ers. But he impressed coach Bill Walsh and offensive line coach Bobb McKittrick with his versatility and athleticism, beating long odds to make the team as a backup at both positions.

As a rookie, he played in every regular-season game as well as two postseason games. The last was a 24-21 loss to the Washington Redskins in the NFC championship game marked by a memorable 21-point rally in the fourth quarter by Joe Montana that fell just short.

Sapolu's initial season included his first career start. He was thrust into the lineup in place of right guard Randy Cross, who missed a November 13, 1983, game at New Orleans with a toe injury.

"We don't believe we're taking that big of a step backwards when he is in the lineup," coach Bill Walsh said at the time. "He doesn't have the ballast that Randy has in pass protection and he doesn't carry quite the body girth. But he's quick and active and very aggressive."

The promise Sapolu showed as a rookie helped to tide him over during the grim three-year period that followed. Sapolu fractured his right foot during a workout in Hawaii shortly before the start of the team's training camp in Rocklin. He spent the first 10 games of the 1984 season on the "physically unable to perform" list. He was activated for a November 11 game at Cleveland but rebroke the foot the next week during practice. He spent the rest of that year on injured reserve.

After a grueling rehab, Sapolu went into the training camp in 1985 vying for a starting job only to break the same foot for a third time while pass blocking during an intra-squad scrimmage. Sapolu left the field with the help of team trainer Lindsy McLean. He was so discouraged and upset that at one point he told McLean, "Linz, this is it for me."

Neither Walsh nor McKittrick was ready to give up on their star-crossed lineman. They convinced Sapolu to give football another go. He grudgingly agreed, unaware that even bigger trials lay ahead.

He reported to the 49ers' Rocklin training camp in 1986 in the best shape of his career, but during a July 29 scrimmage, disaster struck Sapolu once more. His left leg became tangled in a pileup and he suffered a left tibia fracture when a teammate fell on the back of the leg. "It felt like I was hit by a two-by-four," Sapolu said at the time.

Sapolu was taken to a hospital in nearby Davis, where doctors inserted a metal rod into the leg to stabilize the fracture and promote healing. Once more, Sapolu was consumed by thoughts of retiring.

McKittrick went to visit him in the hospital and told the shell-shocked Sapolu that he still thought he could have a stellar career. McKittrick assured Sapolu that he still believed in him and would do everything he could to help him get back on the field: "I told him a lot of guys could throw it in and I'd understand … but I encouraged him to give it one more try," McKittrick said, recalling his hospital visit several years later.

Sapolu said McKittrick talked him out of quitting. "Bobb said, 'If you have it in your heart to come back from another injury, I'll be there to develop you into the player that I know you can become,'" says Sapolu.

Sapolu, who was born in Apia, Western Samoa, and at age eight came to the United States, unfamiliar with the English language or football, spent three months with his parents in the Los Angeles area rehabilitating the leg fracture.

When Sapolu looks back on the injury and the rehabilitation that followed, he considers it a blessing because it allowed him to spend additional time with his father, the Rev. Pa'apa'a Sapolu, who passed away later in 1986.

"We had a really enjoyable time," Sapolu says. "That was the outcome I was searching for and the Lord showed it to me."

Sapolu reported to training camp in 1987 fit and strong and had his first injury-free season since 1983, playing in all 12 non-strike games. He took over as left guard on November 1 against the Los Angles Rams and remained in the starting lineup at either guard or center for the next 10 years. It was an extraordinary demonstration of durability following his string of injuries earlier in his career.

Before he retired following the 1997 season, Sapolu made one more comeback, and it was even more remarkable than the fortitude he displayed through three foot fractures and a leg fracture in the mid-1980s. Following the 1996 campaign, Sapolu decided the time had come to repair a leaky heart valve, a problem that arose from a bout of rheumatic fever during his childhood in Western Samoa. The condition had prevented him from participating in sports and physical education activities throughout much of his elementary and middle school years.

"When you play sports, when you start running and sprinting, your heart has to work a lot harder to pump the blood because of the leakage in the aortic valve," Sapolu said. "Your heart gets bigger and swells and that was the danger the doctors were concerned about. They didn't let me play at all. I'd sit under a tree at recess and take roll call when we'd go back to class. That was so hard. That was the most excruciating thing I ever went through."

When Sapolu reached the eighth grade, the condition had eased to the point where doctors finally cleared him medically to take part in physical activities. However, doctors continued to monitor his damaged aortic valve throughout high school, college, and his time with the 49ers.

In 1996, doctors noticed that the leakage worsened and open-heart surgery became necessary. Dr. Bruce Reitz performed the surgery in January 1997 at Stanford Hospital.

"One of the most encouraging things was the day after the operation, I was still in ICU, and they came in to listen to my heart and for the first time since we discovered it, the doctors said, 'Oh, no more murmur,'" Sapolu says. "That was refreshing to hear."

The medical reports were so encouraging and he felt so good that Sapolu sought one more shot at football. However, 49ers officials were wary of bringing him back after the operation. They released him in February and made fifth-year pro Chris Dalman the starting center.

But Sapolu still had his backers, including one Bobb McKittrick, the team's offensive line coach who had persuaded Sapolu to stick with football as a troubled young player beset by injury.

"Jesse got married [in March 1997] and when I was at the wedding, one of his agents came up and asked me if I thought Jesse would get a chance to play," McKittrick said. "I told him my guess is his best chance of playing is if somebody's center somewhere in the league gets hurt and they need a veteran and Jesse's ready to go. Well, that's what happened, and the somebody was us."

Dalman suffered torn ligaments in his left knee during an August 9 exhibition, an injury that sidelined him for the first three games of the regular season. The 49ers lacked an experienced backup at center—the position responsible for calling out the pass protection schemes—and

McKittrick urged general manager Dwight Clark and coach Steve Mariucci to bring back Sapolu.

Just before the last exhibition, the 49ers re-signed Sapolu, who showed up for work with a stark reminder of his January open-heart surgery: a foot-long scar running from his lower neck to the tip his rib cage. But there he was on opening day, starting at center for the 49ers in a game at Tampa Bay.

Sapolu started two more games before Dalman regained his health and reclaimed his job as the starting center. Sapolu nevertheless remained grateful for the opportunity to add one more chapter to his career.

"I look at things differently," he says. "I'm just appreciative of the moment. When you're younger and you win all those Super Bowls, you always think, 'Well, I've got this many years to go.' You know, I've played a long time and with a heart like new, I feel great.

"But there's a time when you have to move on with your life. . . . As far as I'm concerned, this is it."

That sentiment was driven home in the hours before the 49ers played Denver in a late December Monday night game in 1997. Tight end Brent Jones spotted Sapolu in the training room at Candlestick Park. Sapolu was already decked out in his full uniform and seemingly lost in thought as he approached what would be his last regular-season home game.

"You look like you're thinking about all the memories you've had here," Jones told Sapolu.

"That was exactly right," Sapolu says. "He hit it right on the spot. There are so many."

Chapter 17

DERRICK DEESE

Derrick Deese's senior season at Culver City High School didn't go very well. The team lost 10 straight games at one point and then had to forfeit its only three wins after it was learned that an ineligible player had taken part in those games. Their coach was fired.

Deese would only become even more discouraged about football in the days and weeks that followed. While cleaning out the desk of the school's fired coach, officials found recruiting letters from dozens of colleges that were intended for Deese and one of his teammates. Neither Deese nor his teammate had been made aware of them.

"At that point, I didn't care about playing football. I was upset about the things that went on at my high school," Deese said.

Gene Engle, the offensive line coach at El Camino Junior College in Torrance, California, had seen Deese play offensive and defensive line for Culver City High and believed Deese had a promising football future. But Engle first had to convince Deese, who was considering a career as a police office, to get back in the game.

Engle spent time talking with Deese, telling him he believed he could become a top-flight lineman and continue his education to boot. He also sought out Deese's mother and his high school counselor, enlisting their support in getting Deese to keep playing.

"I had to encourage him," Engle said. "I told Derrick, 'You'd really regret it if you didn't give it a shot.'" Engle finally persuaded Deese to enroll at El Camino JC. Both strong-willed individuals, the two butted heads at times over Engle's insistence on a disciplined approach to the game, but they got through it.

"If I made a bad play, if someone made a sack or something, he would yank me right out of the game," says Deese. "I'd be mad. Everyone made mistakes. Then I realized I didn't run anything. He said I was there to play, not coach."

Under the tutelage of Engle, who was a former tackle at Stanford University, Deese blossomed into one of the finest offensive linemen ever to play for El Camino JC. He became one of the most sought-after offensive linemen in the country in the process, fulfilling Engle's promise to Deese that he would have his choice of colleges if he played for him for two years.

"Out of 111 Division I-A programs, I'd received letters or offers from all but two of them," Deese says. "I chose USC because I thought they could help me become an even better lineman. USC was known as 'Running back U,' but they also had an appreciation for linemen."

Deese played tackle at El Camino JC but moved to guard when he joined the Trojans. It was soon after he arrived at the school that he first began to think seriously about a future in the NFL.

"I was at practice and one of my coaches, John Matsko, told me, 'If you'll just let me coach you, you could make some money at this,'" Deese said. "It was like a light went off in my head: 'I could play in the NFL.' That was something that I had never, never even thought about."

Deese's junior year was solid, and he earned honorable mention All-Pac-10 honors. But he dislocated his elbow as a senior and rarely played. He was passed over in the NFL draft, but Engle contacted 49ers offensive line coach Bobb McKittrick. Engle knew McKittrick from having had a brief tryout with the 49ers after graduating from Stanford in 1979. He told McKittrick that Deese had the athleticism, smarts, and strength that he favored in his offensive linemen.

Acting on Engle's recommendation, McKittrick urged the 49ers to sign Deese and he was brought in to training camp in 1992 as an undrafted free agent.

"If it wasn't for Gene Engle, I would have never gotten to the NFL," Deese says. "If it wasn't for Bobb McKittrick, I would never have played in the NFL."

Deese was gaining the 49ers' attention with his strength and quickness as well as with his effectiveness as a blocker, but he dislocated his elbow

Derrick Deese *Photo by Terrell Lloyd*

again while blocking defensive end Dennis Brown in a team drill. By then, Deese had shown McKittrick enough potential that the offensive line coach fought to keep him around over the objections of coach George Seifert, who wanted to give him an injury settlement and release him.

The 49ers wound up retaining Deese—but not playing him—for the first two years of his career. He spent 1992 on injured reserve because of his elbow problems and returned to injured reserve the next year after breaking his wrist in practice midway through the season. He had been inactive for the first six games of the 1993 season.

But there were injuries and changes in the offensive line that left an opening for Deese heading into the 1994 campaign. Starting left guard Guy McIntyre was allowed to leave as a free agent, and starting right guard Ralph Tamm had suffered a torn plantar fascia in his foot, leaving him unable to take part in training camp.

The 49ers, meanwhile, were gearing up for a major Super Bowl push. They had fallen one step short of the Super Bowl in each of the past two seasons, losing to Dallas in consecutive NFC championship game meetings with the Cowboys.

They brought in a dozen free agents, largely to bolster a defense that had let them down against the Cowboys. But the 49ers also signed center Bart Oates in free agency and had incumbent center Jesse Sapolu slide over to left guard to replace McIntyre.

Deese was having his strongest camp yet, and with Tamm nursing a bad foot, Deese had climbed to the top of the depth chart at right guard. Even Seifert had begun singling Deese out for his solid play in the line during the team's exhibition games.

Nonetheless, when the season opened, Tamm got his job back and Deese found himself back on the bench. Little did Deese know that he was about to get the chance he had been waiting for, and it would become the starting point for a long and distinguished NFL career.

GAME OF MY LIFE
BY DERRICK DEESE
SEPTEMBER 5, 1994—SAN FRANCISCO, CALIFORNIA

Going into our regular-season opener against the Raiders, I was a little mad. I'd started at right guard all through the preseason. Ralph Tamm was the starter there the year before, but he had missed training camp after tearing the plantar fascia in his foot. You just get to the point where you're thinking you're going to start, but a few days before we played, my line coach, Bobb McKittrick, told me Ralph felt OK and that he was going to start.

You have to understand, I was itching for my chance. I hadn't played for the 49ers at all during my first two years in the NFL because I was either inactive or on injured reserve. My first year, I dislocated by elbow in training camp, and in 1993, I was inactive for the first six weeks before I broke my wrist in practice.

Still, the last thing I expected was to get thrown into the game, but that's what happened when Ralph re-aggravated his foot injury on the third play against the Raiders. I remember Bobb coming up to me on the sideline to tell me to go in, and he said, "This is your time to shine. Show them what you can do."

Now, our offensive line was a tight group. I got to the huddle and Jesse Sapolu and Harris Barton and the rest of the guys encouraged me. Harris said, "Hey, just do what we did all through camp," and Jesse told me, "Remember, all your friends are watching, so go to work."

Basically, though, I was thrown into the fire without any practice. Once you start practicing for regular-season games, the starters get all the reps. I never really doubted myself, whether I could play in the league. I just wanted a chance. I just wanted to get my shot. But once I got my shot, I knew wanting it wasn't enough. You had to do your job and you had to do it well. That was the 49ers way, and when I look back, that's what I take pride in, because I think that's what I was able to do.

We were playing against a good defensive line and I was matched up against the Raiders' Scott Davis, who was a big, tough interior defender. But I held up well enough from the moment I went in. I mean, it doesn't get much better than blocking for a 69-yard touchdown pass from Steve Young to Jerry Rice on the first NFL play of your career. That was the start of a big night for Jerry and for me and for us as an offense and as a team. Jerry was going for the all-time touchdown record and his first touchdown was the 125th of his career, one fewer than Jim Brown's NFL record, with more than three quarters left to play.

At halftime, we were only leading 23-14. But we were about to break out for a 21-point fourth quarter, and Jerry scored the last two touchdowns, to tie and then overtake Brown with his 126th and 127th career touchdowns.

Jerry scored for the second time on an end around early in the fourth quarter. After the Raiders were stopped short on a fourth-and-3 play, we took over at the Raiders' 38-yard line. Coach George Seifert wanted to get the hype surrounding Jerry's chase of the touchdown record out of the way. So even though we were leading by 23 points with just over four minutes left, George sent Steve and Jerry back on the field specifically to try to get the record.

For all the records we set, the focus of our season was never about records. The season was always about winning the Super Bowl. We'd gotten to the NFC Championship the previous two years but those seasons were considered failures because we didn't make it to the Super Bowl. That was the 49ers way, too. Getting Jerry the record was part of it in the sense that George wanted us to refocus on the big picture.

The Raiders had Jerry double covered, and Steve just had to put the ball up. Jerry outjumped cornerback Albert Lewis and safety Eddie Anderson at about the 5-yard line. The Raiders defenders came down awkwardly, and Jerry just kind of walked into the end zone for the record breaker.

It was an amazing feeling to be on the field for that slice of football history. Ricky Watters and I ran for the end zone—we were the first ones down there—and we gave Jerry a bear hug and I lifted him up to celebrate the moment.

I think it happened initially because, for me, anyway, you're just so ecstatic about playing the game after waiting your turn over the previous two years. And just the way he scored—in the last few minutes of a big win when everybody in the stadium had to know it was going to him, most especially the Raiders. It was a defining moment, not just in his NFL career but in 49ers history and in the history of the NFL, and I was happy to be part of that.

It was wild and it also started a tradition for Jerry and me. From then on, whenever he scored a touchdown, I'd run down there and give him a bear hug and lift him up in the end zone to celebrate. It didn't matter whether it was a 10-yard pass or a 50-yard pass or an 80-yard pass. I was always there to congratulate him and he was always there to share it.

We were together for a lot of end-zone celebrations and it became a special bond between us. But it started on that September night against the Raiders when he made history and I got my chance and made the most of it. Because that was the game that allowed me to really establish myself as a player.

◆   ◆   ◆

Deese started the 49ers' next 18 games at guard, including their final victory 49-26 against the San Diego Chargers in the Super Bowl at Miami. In the process, he went from an untested, inexperienced reserve to one of the anchors holding together a 49ers offensive line battered by injuries during the 1994 season.

Three starters in the offensive line went down at one time or another, resulting in 26 regular-season starts by replacements, including 15 by Deese. Still, the 49ers scored a team-record 505 points en route to their fifth championship, and their offense finished as the second most productive in total yards.

Deese's ability to step in and fill the void was a key element in the continued productivity of the 49ers offense. "I can't say that he's surpassed Bobb McKittrick's expectations, but I have to admit that he has surpassed mine," 49ers Coach George Seifert said. Said McKittrick: "He's got unique balance, quickness, speed, and smarts. He's big enough to do everything we want him do."

That would come to include every position on the line over the course of his 12-year stay with the 49ers. There were even times when Deese played two or three positions in a single game.

His versatility and willingness to take on the challenge of playing difference positions first came into play in 1996, when he was the swing guard backing up starters Ray Brown and Chris Dalman. During the team's training camp in 1997, Deese practiced extensively at center and started an exhibition at the position after Dalman injured his knee. When the 49ers decided to re-sign center Jesse Sapolu to fill in for Dalman, Deese resumed substituting at both guard positions.

He saw duty at both positions before being moved to left tackle a month into the season to relieve an ineffective Tim Hanshaw. For Deese, it was the first time he had played tackle since his days at El Camino Junior College. At 289 pounds, Deese was the lightest tackle in the league, but again he had a stabilizing impact for a 49ers team that reached the NFC championship game before being eliminated by Green Bay.

The 49ers allowed an average of 2.3 sacks in the 13 games Deese started at left tackle after allowing an average of 4.7 before he moved into the lineup.

"He's so athletic. He can do almost anything with his feet," McKittrick said. "He never takes a wrong step. He's a better athlete than probably any other tackle in the league."

The 49ers moved Deese again at the start of the 1998 season, switching him to right tackle to accommodate the acquisition of left tackle Jamie Brown in a trade with Denver. But Brown's struggles led to his benching five weeks into the season, triggering a three-way rotation among Deese, Dave Fiore, and Kirk Scrafford at the two tackle spots. Deese was the only one in the rotation who saw time at both tackle positions, finishing with eight starts on each side.

"People ask me to state my position," Deese once said. "I just say, 'Derrick Deese, offensive lineman.' Year in, year out, I don't know where I'm going to be playing."

Deese's ability to adapt to position changes was valued and appreciated by his team and his teammates but it probably cost him in terms of recognition. He never gained Pro Bowl recognition, even after he finally settled in at left tackle during his final four seasons in San Francisco. He closed out his 49ers career by not allowing a sack in 35 consecutive games, protecting the quarterback's blindside while facing some of the toughest pass rushers in the league.

Deese was released by the 49ers after the 2003 season, part of a salary-cap-driven purge that also saw the departure of such players as running back Garrison Hearst, quarterback Jeff Garcia, and wide receiver Terrell Owens. Deese went on to sign with the Tampa Bay Buccaneers. He played one more season in the NFL before starting a new career as a football analyst.

"I look back on my career with the 49ers and I think it was a great career," Deese says. "Whenever the team had a fire on the offensive line, I tried to put it out. That was what being a team player required. You get known by playing one position in your career, and maybe moving around like I did cost me some individual accolades. But I don't think there are a lot of guys in the league who could have done what I did as well as I did. My approach was, 'Wherever they need me to play, whatever they need me to do to help the team win.' That's what I was going to do. Those are things that I'm very proud of."

Chapter 18

ERIC DAVIS

Eric Davis jumped, twisted in the air, and blindly tussled for the ball with Alvin Harper. The 49ers cornerback and the Cowboys wide receiver fell to the Candlestick Park turf together. Harper clutched Troy Aikman's pass to his chest. Davis was left to wonder how he came up empty.

"I can still see it like it's in slow motion," Davis says, recalling a pivotal play in the Cowboys' NFC championship victory over the 49ers following the 1992 season. "I knew it was coming but I couldn't tell when it was coming because the last few feet, it was directly in the sun. It went through my hands and bounced off my helmet. I turned and I saw Alvin grab it and I tried to knock it out as we went down, but he made a great, great catch."

Davis still recalls the advice he later received from Hall of Fame wide receiver Lynn Swann: "He told me, 'If the sun's in your eyes, you know what you do? You've got to catch the sun. You've got to catch the sun, man.'"

In time, Davis would indeed catch the sun for the 49ers. But he first endured the scrutiny, questions, and criticism that came with being at the center of a series of pivotal plays in the drawn-out struggle for NFL supremacy between the 49ers and Cowboys.

"We knew those guys so well. They were the only ones we thought would even give us any type of competition," Davis said. "I still remember sitting in training camp in Rocklin at a restaurant where the DBs would go eat lunch. They had a schedule up and we would sit there, year after year, look at the schedule and say, 'OK, we play Atlanta, we have the Saints, the Rams, Buffalo, blah, blah, blah. We should be 11-0 and oh, here's Dallas in Week 12. We've got to get that so we can have home-field advantage against them in the playoffs.' That was our mind-set."

From 1992-94, the teams met in three consecutive NFC championship games. The Cowboys won two of them; the 49ers took the other. In each instance, the victor went on to win the Super Bowl.

The games featured many of football's brightest stars, from Steve Young, Jerry Rice, John Taylor, and Brent Jones for the 49ers, to Troy Aikman, Emmitt Smith, Michael Irvin, and Daryl Johnston for the Cowboys. Some of the teams' best players went at it from both sides. Linebacker Ken Norton, defensive end Charles Haley, and cornerback Deion Sanders won Super Bowl rings for both the Cowboys and the 49ers.

"These were great players in their prime," Davis says. "We were all in the prime of our careers, and we were better than most at what we did. And sometimes, someone was just better than you on a play."

Davis speaks from personal experience, taking his lumps early in the 49ers-Cowboys rivalry. Harper's leaping 38-yard reception over Davis led to a short scoring run by Johnston in the third quarter that snapped a 10-10 tie. Though the 49ers pulled to 24-20 on Young's 5-yard touchdown pass to Rice with 4:22 left, Aikman's precision passing and a quick, crisply run post pattern by Harper cut off the 49ers' rally. He ran about 10 yards downfield straight at Davis before veering inside, where Aikman hit him in stride. With a wide-open alley in front of him, Harper cut away from Davis and headed downfield ahead of safety Dana Hall for a 70-yard catch and run that set up Dallas' clinching score in its 30-20 victory over the 49ers.

"When I saw the man coverage, I thought we were going to get a completion, but there's no way I thought we were going to get a 70-yard gain out of it," said Norv Turner, who, as the Cowboys offensive coordinator, made the play call. He recalled the moment in 2006 when he presented Aikman for induction into the Pro Football Hall of Fame, calling the supremely accurate throw that beat Davis and Hall one of the defining passes of Aikman's career.

Eric Davis *Photo © Michael Zagaris*

Davis says Aikman's passing always presented a challenge to defenders: "In the NFL, no one should ever be wide open. Open in the NFL is a matter of inches. There were times I could see my hands inside of the receiver's hands." But even that kind of proximity didn't always mean an interception.

"Troy was the most accurate quarterback I'd ever played against, and I played against Warren Moon and John Elway and Steve Young and Joe Montana," he says. "As far as time after time after time, when it came to putting the ball in a spot, he was the most accurate guy I ever played against." Aikman's pinpoint passing cost Davis and the 49ers in the first of their three-successive conference championship meetings with the Cowboys.

A year later at Texas Stadium, they were done in by the unexpected. Down 28-7 at halftime, the 49ers knocked Aikman out of the game with a concussion before driving to a touchdown midway through the third quarter. Bernie Kosar was in for the injured Aikman, and the 49ers needed only a third-down stop to get the ball back.

"We had fought back and got it to within 14," Davis says. "We make that play and we could get it to a 7-point game."

Davis and safety Merton Hanks both read Harper's slant route and broke toward the inside, anticipating a tough-to-defend low, inside throw.

"Bernie always threw his slants low and inside, so the worst case was they catch the ball, take the hit and get maybe 7 to 9 yards," Davis says. "Then I see the ball going over my head. I remember thinking, 'Who is he throwing to?' It was so high that I thought he was throwing it away, that it was going out of bounds. But all of a sudden, I hear everybody screaming."

Up in the press box, Turner was among those who were screaming.

"When Bernie turned to throw, I started yelling, 'No!'" Turner said. "I knew where the corner was and I thought Eric was going to intercept it. But Bernie, being a veteran guy, put it where only Alvin would be able to get it. It was a maximum blitz and Bernie knew what to do. He just threw a perfect ball."

Davis says, "I still don't know if it was luck or a great play. Bottom line, they made the play and that was it. After that, it was up to 21 again. We were still fighting. We were still trying, but they were the better team that year."

It was the third time in four seasons the 49ers were tripped up a step short of the Super Bowl, dating back to their NFC title game loss to the New York Giants 15-13 following the 1990 campaign.

As the clock ticked down on the 49ers' second successive NFC championship loss to the Cowboys, 49ers owner Eddie DeBartolo and club president Carmen Policy boarded the press box elevator and headed down to the team's locker room. A disconsolate DeBartolo told Policy he never wanted to see the Cowboys embarrass the 49ers again and further told him to do whatever it took to overtake the Cowboys as the league's preeminent team.

In the months leading up to the 1994 campaign, the 49ers took the free agency plunge at the dawn of the salary-cap era. They splurged to acquire cornerback Deion Sanders, linebackers Ken Norton and Gary Plummer, and defensive ends Richard Dent and Rickey Jackson, among others.

Davis, however, was among the holdovers. By the end of the season, Davis had earned the admiration of teammates and the respect of opponents. With teams trying to avoid throwing toward Sanders, Davis led the 49ers with a career-high 22 passes defensed and ranked fourth with 73 tackles.

"A lesser man would've folded" under the pressure of being a constant target, Davis once said. "But Deion's coming here has given me the opportunity to really do some things."

Davis expected to be targeted again going into the 49ers' third consecutive NFC championship match up with Dallas. He didn't talk about it with reporters in the days leading up to the game, though. He saw no point in rehashing the failures of the past.

"I didn't feel like going into that stuff," Davis says. "I didn't want to have to hear about anyone saying, 'What about this?' and trying to bring up all the ghosts of NFC championships past. Really, it wasn't that big a deal to me. I always knew getting beat was an occupational hazard for a DB. I could live with that, if you beat me. But I was going to make you earn it and my thinking always was, 'I'll get you next time.'"

That was very much Davis' mind-set as the 49ers approached their third NFC championship meeting in as many seasons with the Cowboys, even if he did avoid the subject in the days before the matchup.

"Eric was a hell of a player," Turner said. "You play as long as he played and you're going to have the good and the bad. Unfortunately for him, a couple of those bad things came at the wrong time. But he redeemed himself."

Even more fitting for Davis, his redemption came against the team that had tormented him and the 49ers for so long.

GAME OF MY LIFE
BY ERIC DAVIS
JANUARY 15, 1995—SAN FRANCISCO, CALIFORNIA

Everyone was harping on what had happened to me before, but it didn't weigh on me as much as it weighed on everyone else. I didn't put that much into it because I knew I was ready to play. I knew I was in position to make those plays, and it was just a question of making them. It was never a question that they were so much better than us, that we were not even in the picture, that we were not even there. I was right there, but we had to finish it. And I knew that. I wasn't going to be one to make excuses. I was never one to place blame.

I will say we had had so many intense battles with the Cowboys, and of course I felt like I was right in the middle of them. Those guys had ended our season by beating us in the conference championship the previous two years. Here we were meeting them in the conference championship for the third straight time.

I studied film of them so hard. I knew their routes. I knew what side of the field Troy Aikman liked to throw to, and where he was likely to go with his first read, his second, his third. It had become a rivalry and reflected the competitive nature that was in all of us.

The competition extended into our practices and probably into their practices as well. We had colossal battles in practice, both throughout the season and also in the days leading up to the game. It was about competing. It was about proving we were the best, no matter who we happened to line up against. So what if it was in practice, against your own guy? The Cowboys might have been the only other team that understood that.

At the same time, our fans were spoiled, and rightfully so. They expected us to win and we expected to win and we fed off that. They can say all they want about how 49ers fans were more into their wine and cheese. But for that game, on that day, that place was alive. You could just feel it.

Early in the game, things just started to come together. The first third down in the first series, there was a play that Troy would throw to Kevin Williams. Williams would get in the slot and basically get down to the first-down marker and break out. Tyronne Drakeford was playing him in the slot. I was outside lined up on Michael Irvin.

But this is the thing: we were in an underneath zone and I didn't have deep responsibility. It was a great call by Ray Rhodes, our defensive coordinator. So I was there, fighting with Mike off the line and then I turned my back to him like I was running down the sideline with him. But I ran with Mike just long enough for Troy to look over at me and get his first read. As far as he was concerned, I was playing man coverage. Which meant Tyronne was inside playing man coverage on Kevin Williams, so Troy must have thought, "OK, I've got him."

I just flipped around and here came the ball. Well, I've got *him*. All I had to do was catch it. I ran into Kevin but I was ready for it. He wasn't expecting anyone to be there because Troy never made those kinds of mistakes; you had to bait him into one.

But honestly, that 44-yard interception return for a touchdown was my play to make. I wanted him to throw that ball. I didn't want to just make the tackle. I thought I had the chance to make a big play. But did I think the game was over? No.

We came out the next series and what did they do? They threw at me again. Troy threw one of those balls that was right on Mike's hands. I was breaking and I saw the ball in the air and I realized I was not going to be able to get there to get my hands on the ball while it was in the air. But I got there right when the ball hit Mike's hands and I came down hard on his arm and knocked the ball out. Tim McDonald was there to recover the fumble.

If there was any more reassurance we needed that it was going to be our day, that fumble was it. We set the offense up. They went down and scored again on Steve Young's touchdown pass to Ricky Watters.

We kicked off for the third time in the first five minutes, and Adam Walker slammed into Kevin Williams and forced a fumble that our kicker, Doug Brien, recovered. I was standing on the sideline next to Tim McDonald. Sometimes, when things would get intense, Tim would bite his lip so bad, I had to tell him to stop because it would start bleeding. He turned around after the fumble and said, "Here we go again. We've got them." He was pumping his fist, yelling, "Yes! Yes!"

We took over at the Cowboys' 35, and a few plays later, William Floyd went in for a short touchdown run. That made it 21-0 and we were barely halfway through the first quarter. Don't misunderstand me: no one relaxed and no one thought it was over. We knew Dallas understood what was at stake. They were the world champs, and their 1993 Cowboys team was the best team I had ever played against in my life. We basically had to put together an all-star team to beat them. It was phenomenal how well they played, and this basically was the same team that we were playing. They weren't going to quit fighting or give up, just like we hadn't the year before.

The Cowboys kept trying. Before we knew it, we had a defensive breakdown, and Mike caught a long touchdown pass from Troy. Emmitt Smith added a touchdown run, and suddenly we were only up 10 points midway through the second quarter.

Jerry Rice gave us some breathing room when he caught Young's 28-yard touchdown pass over Larry Brown just before halftime. But the Cowboys outscored us two touchdowns to one in the second half, getting within 10 points again midway through the fourth quarter.

They were driving on us with five minutes left in the game. If they scored a touchdown, they'd try an onside kick, and if they recovered, all they needed to do was get a field goal to force overtime. But with a couple minutes left, they had a fourth-down play from our 46-yard line.

Tim McDonald and I came out of the huddle. He looked over at me and he was like, "We have to get off the field. NOW! NOW!"

Aikman completed a pass on the right side to tight end Jay Novacek. They needed 18 yards. He got 16. He came across the middle and tried to turn it up on me. And I was like, "No, I was not missing that tackle." I came in and took him down.

Bill McPherson always used to say tackling is "want to." And really that's it. A 180-pound man like me is either going to run full speed and stick his nose into this 6-4, 6-5, 260-pound tight end or he's not. They can't make you do that. But there was no way I was not going to do it. I knew we were going to get that game and guess what? I had a chance to put the nail in the coffin.

More so than the interceptions, more so than that conversations I had with guys or coaches, that tackle—stopping Jay Novacek two yards shy of a first down in January at Candlestick—that's the play I'll remember more than any other. It gave us a chance to be the best. That's the tackle that made us champs. I knew that when I got up off the ground.

After we beat the Chargers in the Super Bowl, a reporter asked me when did you guys feel like you had the game? If you look back, I said right after we beat Dallas. Nothing against San Diego: that's just the way we felt, and that's what made that game and that tackle so special.

Someone once said that until you do something special, you're just a guy. That tackle of Novacek, its time and place and situation, was something special. I knew that the guys would always respect me for that. I was no longer just a guy. I knew that I had earned my spot, and our team had earned its place among the best.

Eric Davis' solo stop of Jay Novacek was his seventh tackle of the game, matching linebacker Ken Norton and safety Tim McDonald for most on the team. He also had two passes defensed and two of the 49ers' three interceptions of Troy Aikman.

Deion Sanders had the other interception and five passes defensed, limiting Alvin Harper—who had averaged nearly 100 yards receiving in the Cowboys two previous conference title wins—to one catch for 14 yards.

Michael Irvin was matched up for part of the game against Davis. He tied an NFC championship record when he caught 12 passes, including two that went for scores. But Davis saw to it that it didn't matter, offsetting the Cowboys play-maker with plays of his own. Davis picked off his second pass just before halftime. Aikman's deep throw was intended for Irvin and followed his interception return and forced fumble that keyed the 49ers' 21-point first quarter.

Davis wound up as the 49ers' postseason leader with four interceptions. He had at least one interception in each of the team's three postseason games, the last coming in the 49-26 victory over the San Diego Chargers in the Super Bowl.

"He's the best corner I've ever played with in the NFL, and I've played with a lot of people," Sanders told reporters after the 49ers beat Dallas to advance to their fifth Super Bowl.

After the 49ers' final victory of the season, Davis' secondary teammates, cornerback Deion Sanders and safeties Tim McDonald and

Merton Hanks, told Davis to pack his bags and join them in Hawaii, where the three of them were playing in the Pro Bowl.

The three felt Davis, the only member of the 49ers starting secondary left off the NFC's Pro Bowl roster, had been slighted in the vote by his peers. So they each chipped in and flew Davis to Hawaii for an all-expenses-paid vacation as their guest.

"They were like, 'Just make your arrangements. No matter what anyone says, no matter what the voting says, you belong and you're coming. You're supposed to be here and there's no way we're going without you,'" Davis says. "I just hung out with them for the week. It was something."

But the talent-laden secondary that had played so well together during the 49ers' championship season didn't stay together for long. Sanders left as a free agent before the next season, joining the Cowboys in 1995, when Dallas became the only team to win three Super Bowls in a four-year span.

The 49ers seemed headed for a fourth consecutive matchup with the Cowboys in the NFC championship only to be stopped short by the Green Bay Packers, who upset them in a divisional playoff. Davis had another strong campaign in 1995, earning his first trip to the Pro Bowl in what proved to be his final season as a 49er.

The highest pick out of Division II Jacksonville State when he was drafted in the second round by the 49ers in 1990, Davis became an unrestricted free agent before the 1996 season. Confined by salary cap problems, the 49ers failed to field a competitive offer for Davis, who signed a four-year, $11.4 million deal to join the Carolina Panthers.

Davis went on to play for seven more years and remains Carolina's all-time leader in interceptions, with 25 in his five seasons with the Panthers. He played one season each in Denver and Detroit before retiring in 2002.

Davis returned with his family to the Santa Cruz area, south of San Francisco, and runs a variety of businesses, including a jewelry store. During a March 2006 reunion in Las Vegas of the 49ers' five Super Bowl winning teams, Davis had a chance to reconnect with Sanders and other members of the 1994 championship team.

"He and I just talked about how it used to be and the bond that developed during that one season," Davis said. "And we both wondered how much more we could have done if the 49ers had kept us together longer. Neither of us wanted to leave, but neither of us was given the choice to stay."

The 49ers haven't been back to the Super Bowl since the '94 team added a fifth Lombardi Trophy to the shimmering glass case in the lobby of the 49ers' Santa Clara headquarters. And Davis savors the thought he helped put the championship trophy there.

"I always felt like we were supposed to do it and I was supposed to be a part of it," he says. "I wanted to be there to earn it and feel it, and I validated all those feelings."

Chapter 19

STEVE YOUNG

When Steve Young showed up for his first practice as a 49er, he was outfitted with a helmet, shorts, a jersey, and cleats. Then he went outside and was introduced to Joe Montana.

"Joe says to me, 'Nice shoes,'" Young says. "I didn't think much about it. They looked a little ratty and worn to me."

It was only later that the reasons for Montana's keen interest in the shoes became apparent. Young was taking off the cleats after practice when he noticed the No. 16 embossed on the heel of the shoes that were given to him by equipment manager Bronco Hinek.

"They were Joe's shoes," Young says. "I wasn't there 15 minutes and they're playing practical jokes on me. I about shot Bronco."

By the next practice, Young had his own cleats. But filling Montana's shoes, into which he'd slipped so easily the day before, would become a long trial punctuated by success and failure, frustration and fulfillment, and ultimately a Super Bowl triumph.

The protagonists in one of the most riveting quarterback controversies that the NFL has ever seen, Young and Montana had an uneasy co-existence in their six years together on the 49ers roster.

"As competitive as possible without letting it come between us," Montana once said in describing the rivalry between the two.

"Everybody wants to play. I want to play desperately and I'm going to drive everyone nuts until I get a shot," Young once said of his relentless push to play.

Yet it's worth noting that some of Montana's greatest work coincided with Young competing with him for his job. And Young's most productive seasons followed four years largely spent watching and learning from the sideline while Montana played, adding two more championships to his Hall of Fame résumé.

"Joe arguably had the greatest career in history and wanted to continue it, and I was trying to start what I hoped would be a very good one," Young says. "You had two hyper-competitive guys trying to figure out how we were all going to do it.

"We had to practice every day. Yet we golfed and laughed. We were talking every day. I was the backup and acted that way and tried do that role as best I could, and we got through it. We never argued or had a cross word, but it was hard. It was difficult, probably for both of us."

That Young tolerated such a long apprenticeship in the prime of his career had a lot to do with his topsy-turvy football past. He began his career at Brigham Young University as the eighth—and last—quarterback on the depth chart. One coach told Young he'd probably never play quarterback at BYU and suggested he switch to defensive back. Young shrugged off the coach's advice and instead took the advice of his father, Grit Young, who counseled patience even as he urged his son not to give up on his dream of playing quarterback.

Within a year, Young had ascended to the No. 2 job at BYU behind Jim McMahon. As a senior, he threw for at least 300 yards in all but two games and completed 71.3 percent of his passes, a single-season NCAA record at the time. He was a consensus All-American and finished second to Nebraska running back Mike Rozier in the balloting for the 1983 Heisman Trophy.

But he took a detour on his way to the National Football League, signing a $42 million contract to play for the Los Angeles Express of the United States Football League.

There were some benefits to that decision, besides the big contract. Young had the chance to learn from Express coach John Hadl, a former San Diego Chargers quarterback, and his offensive coordinator, Sid Gillman, a former head coach of the Los Angeles Rams and the Chargers and a highly regarded innovator in the passing game.

It was while Young was with the Express that he showcased his dual skills as a runner and passer. He became the first player in the history of

Steve Young *Photo © Michael Zagaris*

pro football to rush for 100 yards and throw for 300 yards in the same game in 1984 against Chicago.

But the USFL struggled to compete against the established NFL and eventually went belly up. Young recalls times when there were not even enough towels to go around for the players to take their postgame showers. On one occasion, Young said, the team bus driver for the Express refused to move until he got paid. Young dug some cash out of his pocket and collected some more dough from his teammates on the bus. He turned over about $500 to the driver, and only then did the team bus pull away.

According to agent Leigh Steinberg, Young decided to exercise a buy-out clause in his contract with the Express, freeing him to sign in September 1985 with the Tampa Bay Buccaneers. A year earlier, the Bucs had made Young the first selection in the NFL Supplemental Draft.

The move brought freedom, then misery to Young. The Bucs won only four of 32 games in Young's two seasons in Tampa Bay; Young went 3-16 in his 19 starts. A 1986 game played in whiteout conditions in Green Bay was the low point.

"He was running for his life but really couldn't even see his receivers to throw them the ball in the snow because the Bucs' uniforms were all white," Steinberg says. "I can still see him getting knocked down and getting his face shoved into the turf. When he got up, his helmet was filled with snow and ice and he couldn't see a thing."

Giving up on Young after a second disastrous season, Tampa Bay selected quarterback Vinny Testaverde with the No. 1 overall pick in the NFL draft, setting the stage for Young's trade to the 49ers.

"Steve had a choice to let his Express contract run out or exercise a buyout and he bought it out under Hugh Culverhouse's promise that he would be the quarterback in Tampa Bay for the rest of his career," Steinberg says, referring to the Buccaneers' former owner. "The rest of his career turned out to be two years after they drafted Testaverde.

"I told Culverhouse that we wanted to decide where he goes in a trade. St. Louis and San Diego were two of the teams that wanted him and they had offered first-round picks. But Bill Walsh did a secret tryout of Steve back in Utah, and then the 49ers made their pitch."

Tampa Bay took the 49ers' offer of second- and fourth-round picks and about $1 million in cash for Young. Steinberg says that price would have never been accepted over the superior offers by other teams "were we [Steinberg and Young] not heavily dictating the trade."

The prospect of becoming the quarterback for a successful team that was two years removed from a championship was a powerful lure for Young, whose career was in tatters after two years of struggle in Tampa. Moreover, Steinberg said Walsh told Young that it appeared likely Montana would have to retire because of a bad back, leaving the way clear for Young to take over as the 49ers starter.

"No way on the face of the earth would I have allowed Steve Young to walk into that situation otherwise," Steinberg says. "I understood the love affair between the Bay Area and Joe Montana. He was already iconic, legendary, and even coming in to replace him because of injury or retirement wasn't exactly a desirable situation. Controversy was inevitable for anyone following Joe Montana, and there would be constant comparisons.

"Then we get there, and my goodness, guess what? Joe Montana is healthy and Steve Young was stuck in a nightmare. His only desire was to be in the middle of the fray and he watched as Montana went on to have some of his most stellar years."

Young said he knew on the same day he unwittingly donned Montana's shoes that the scenario laid out to him by Walsh before the trade wasn't quite accurate.

"That first practice, I realized Bill kind of led me astray when he told me Joe's back was not going to get better," Young says. "Bill made it feel like this transition was definitely going to happen. But that first day, I saw Joe jog off to practice, and I thought, 'He really doesn't even look hurt.' By the end of practice, my thought was, 'He's not hurt at all.'"

Still, Young says, he only had to think of his awful experience in Tampa Bay to know he was in a much better place with the 49ers, his standing on the depth chart notwithstanding. He resolved to make the best of it.

"The Tampa Bay experiences were profound, because I had never realized how bad football could be, how tough and disorganized it was, and how difficult it could be in every way possible," Young said. "The elements of teamwork were just not there. Once I got to San Francisco, I knew if I complained too much, I could go back to a place like that. So, despite my disappointment at not really playing for those four years, I knew I had just come from the worst to the best.

"I don't look at the tutoring for those four years as being all good for me. I'd say a little of it was good and a lot of it was unfortunate. It was hard because I knew those were some of the prime years of my career, but that's the way it was.

"Despite my frustration, it was an experience that taught me a great deal. And what I hung on to was the thought that if I could get going by the time I was 27 or 28, I could have 10-12 good years, which was just the case."

Walsh said Young's initial standing with the 49ers reflected where he had been as a quarterback more so than where he could be once he became familiar with the West Coast system.

"When he came here, Steve was pretty shaken related to his self-confidence and shaken up as to what he might accomplish on a football field," Walsh said. "Really, Steve had spent a number of seasons just being totally frustrated and maligned. By the time we got him, he was extremely anxious to be part of this organization because this was really his last chance to become a viable NFL player. Down the road, there was greatness, but at the time, he really didn't have a grasp of the offense."

That would come gradually, as Young learned to shed his over-reliance on his running, which characterized his play with the Express and Buccaneers, and embraced the central premise of the West Coast offense to spread the ball around to his playmakers.

"Those were my roots [at BYU]," Young says. "I scrambled a little bit, but we threw the ball. I mean, we'd drop back 30 or 40 times. We'd pick, pick, pick at a defense and then make a big play. Or, we'd pick, pick, pick, run. I'd had that kind of beaten out of me because I had to make plays.

"I was the $40 million man with the Express. I was the savior of the Tampa Bay franchise. It was like, 'OK, I'll take that on and move the ball any way I can.'"

Young had his moments as Montana's understudy as well. He was thrust to the forefront of the mushrooming quarterback controversy when Walsh benched a struggling Montana in the third quarter of the 49ers' shocking loss to Minnesota in a divisional playoff following the 1987 season.

Midway through the 1988 season, Young started against the Vikings in place of an injured Montana. He connected on a 73-yard touchdown pass to John Taylor and won the game with a twisting, tackle-breaking 49-yard touchdown run, staggering into the end zone to complete one of the most memorable plays in 49ers' history.

Young started ahead of Montana the next week at Phoenix but the 49ers blew a big fourth-quarter lead. Walsh went back to Montana the next week, and Montana reasserted his grip on the job by leading the 49ers to back-to-back Super Bowl titles.

With Montana once again in command, Young had to wait for his chance to become the complete quarterback. But even as he bided his time, Young was learning and getting a better grasp of the offense.

"There was still a sense of, 'You'd better make this ball go,' because Joe was so productive," Young says. "Bill, he would always harp on me, 'Let your teammates know what you're doing. If you're playing crazy, they don't know what to expect. They need to know what to expect from you.' So it was a process. I had to get back what I had lost."

Young got his chance to apply those lessons in 1991, when elbow problems forced Montana to miss the season. Montana missed most of the next season with a recurrence of the elbow injury.

"When you're playing 16 games in this offense, you don't want linemen saying, 'Where is he going?' Or Jerry [Rice] saying, 'What is going on?' It's totally discombobulating," Young says. "My saying during that entire time was, 'Don't end up with the ball. Get it into somebody's else's hands.' It was psychological and stylistic. It's kind of like, 'I know I can get those four yards with my feet, but don't do it. Drop it off.' And obviously I learned watching Joe. I mean, Joe was a major part of that."

Once he became the starter, Young put up phenomenal numbers. He won four consecutive passing titles from 1991-94, all with a passer rating above 100, which was an NFL first. He threw for 4,023 yards in 1993, becoming the first 49ers quarterback to reach that benchmark. The quarterbacks he surpassed included John Brodie, Y.A. Tittle, and Montana, who had been traded to Kansas City prior to the 1993 season.

"In retrospect, it was the right thing for everybody," former team president Carmen Policy said of trading away Montana. "It would have been very difficult, almost impossible, with both of them here."

Even though Montana was gone, he cast a huge shadow on his successor and a daunting legacy as a four-time Super Bowl winner.

In two of his first three years as the starter, Young led the 49ers to the NFC championship game but they lost to the Dallas Cowboys both times. Young came under withering criticism, from both fans and the media, questioning whether or not he could ever win the big one.

Though stung by the ferocity of the criticism, Young said he understood it as a product of the great expectations that came with following a four-time Super Bowl champion like Montana.

"It was the standard," he said. "You play great in '92, but get beat at home by the Cowboys" in the NFC title game. "Because of where we'd been as a team, that runner-up trophy was not worth that much. It was like kissing your sister. It's not going to get it done.

"I realized if I wanted to take my individual awards and kind of make out my statement, that wasn't going to work. You need to put this team into a championship. But no quarterback ever does that by himself."

In 1994, Young did his part, and the 49ers helped out by broadening his supporting cast on both sides of the ball, with the acquisition of a dozen free agents. He went on to win his second NFL MVP award and fourth straight league-passing title, setting a single-season league record with a passer rating of 112.8. His 35 touchdown passes were a club record at the time.

Young went beyond the numbers to help quash the 49ers' greatest nemesis, leading the 49ers past Dallas 38-28 in the NFC championship. In the process, he became the only other 49ers quarterback besides Montana to lead the team to the Super Bowl. It was an emotional victory for Young, who celebrated with a manic postgame circling of Candlestick Park, thrusting his arms up in exultation and high-fiving fans along the way.

"It was an amazing feeling running around Candlestick Park," says Young. "I think I did it because of the pain and anguish of losing to the Cowboys over the previous couple of years. It doesn't go away and you can't begin to fix it for another year.

"When we beat Dallas, we felt like we had just beaten the best team in football besides us," Young adds. "We found out we were going to play the Chargers in the Super Bowl. For us, it was, 'Now, let's go finish this.' And I don't remember when we were ever more sure we were going to get this done."

GAME OF MY LIFE
BY STEVE YOUNG
JANUARY 29, 1995—MIAMI, FLORIDA

Mike Shanahan, our offensive coordinator, had this crazy, kind of evil smile on his face in the days leading up to the Super Bowl. Mike was smiling because, as he made clear to us, he felt like he had the San Diego Chargers' number.

In drawing up his game plan, Mike believed he had unlocked the secret to their defense. His plan was very bold, maybe more so than I'd ever seen in the three seasons we were together. He kept telling us through the week, "You have to execute it. I'm going to be very aggressive. Don't think for one second we're going to let up. We're going to attack from the first second to the last."

That attitude was underscored during the ritual we used to go through about an hour and a half before every game. Mike would quiz us on the game plan, and the Super Bowl was no different. We went over formations, personnel groupings, and hundreds of plays for every conceivable situation: short-yardage, red zone, goal-line, plays for down and distance. I would always try to be perfect and for once I got everything right. I remember Mike telling me right before we took the field, "Steve, don't worry. We're going to crush these guys."

Going out to play in the Super Bowl itself was a great feeling. It was fun. There's so much extra glitz. There's all kinds of things going on around the stadium. It's special. There's this buzz. But we were so locked in. We just felt we had too much to lose. You couldn't be a 49er and lose this game. I think our team knew that even our victory over the Dallas Cowboys in the NFC championship would be empty if we didn't beat the Chargers in the Super Bowl. We were like, "Let's just win this. Then we can celebrate."

It was pretty warm and humid in Miami, but that didn't bother me. It actually helped me get a better grip on the football. I felt like I could never get a better grip on the ball, and I was just really going to let it fly and let it fly with confidence.

Our first 20 plays were scripted, but Mike was true to his word. His play-calling was aggressive from the start. We were about a minute and a half into the game when he called a play-action pass with Jerry Rice as the primary receiver. The Chargers were playing two-deep coverage, and Jerry cut between the safeties going right down the middle. We had a good formation to get Jerry open downfield, which we really hadn't done before. He just went by them and that was it.

I remember thinking it was so early in the game. There was still smoke and fog from all the pregame hoopla. It was almost ethereal. It was like Jerry went running off into the fog. I turned to Harris Barton and asked if he could tell what happened. We both went running down there to see, and sure enough there was Jerry in the end zone. Touchdown!

For us, a 44-yard touchdown pass was a great way to start, but I also think our first score was very debilitating for the Chargers.

We really were at our peak as an offense, as a team. I think it would have been tough to beat us had you put us up against anybody that day. Mike's thinking was driving us. He didn't want to give the Chargers a chance to breathe. He wanted to be attacking on every play. We scored on the third play of our first drive and the fourth play of our second, another big play that went to Ricky Watters for a 51-yard touchdown. We were leading 14-0 before I threw my first incomplete pass. We had just one third down on the first two drives and I was able to convert with a scramble.

San Diego managed to score but we just kept about our business. Our third drive was more methodical, and still Mike remained aggressive with his play calls. We'd gotten a first down at the Chargers' 5-yard line but rather than pound it, Mike had me put the ball up again. I dropped it to our fullback, William Floyd, and he was in the end zone. We were barely into the second quarter and we were leading 21-7. We got another touchdown on a short pass to Watters and we went into halftime leading 28-10.

I remember it being pretty matter of fact, pretty business-like during halftime. We felt like everything was moving in the right direction. We were kind of like a train rolling down the track, and we knew it was going to be tough to stop this train. Really, a lot of our work was done, and the worries were kind of over. It was more about finishing it up and just playing well in the second half. But don't forget who was calling the plays. Mike Shanahan wanted more, and it was our job to get more.

I'd thrown for four touchdowns in the first half, but I remember Mike asking me, "You got four more?" I said, "Of course I do, if you keep calling them."

The first time we got the ball in the third quarter, we drove to a touchdown with Ricky Watters running it in for the score. Later in the third, I threw another touchdown pass to Jerry, and we were up 42-10. The Chargers scored on a kickoff return only to see Jerry get open for his third touchdown catch and the sixth overall scoring pass. We even had the luxury of using Deion Sanders on offense. He came in as a wide receiver during my last fourth-quarter drive. I passed incomplete to him for my final Super Bowl throw before being relieved by Elvis Grbac.

The celebration began in the final few minutes on the sideline, but there's one part I regret. I kind of turned around and said within earshot of teammates and television cameras something like, "Please, somebody, take this monkey off my back." Now, there was a lot of pressure, a lot of scrutiny, that came with following Joe Montana. Still, all through the years I had never talked about having a monkey on my back. I always had tried to turn it into a positive by embracing it as an opportunity and refusing to look at it as a burden. I guess it was a moment of insanity that made me say that on the sideline.

Really, I had lived with it for so long, it wasn't like I needed it to survive. I mean, I was relieved, no question about it. But I viewed it then as I view it now: it was a challenge that I accepted. It was a challenge that I met, but I had so much help from all the people around me. Whatever I did, whatever we did, we did it together.

One of the perks Steve Young enjoyed after the Super Bowl win was a celebratory parade at Disney World in Orlando. But he learned that while he could go toe-to-toe with Joe Montana's legacy, neither he nor Jerry Rice was bigger than Mickey Mouse. As he rode in a car with Rice and Mickey Mouse, he heard a youngster watching the parade complain that he wished the two big guys would get out of the way so he could see Mickey Mouse.

The venture to Disney World brought Young back to earth after a post-Super Bowl exultation that his agent, Leigh Steinberg, described as "a moment of pure joy and liberation" for Young from the expectations and the long shadow of Montana. Young was named Super Bowl MVP after passing for 325 yards and a record six touchdowns, including three to Rice, who played much of the game with a separated shoulder.

Montana threw for five scores in the 49ers' 55-10 Super Bowl win over Denver following the 1989 season. The 49ers didn't quite match their previous Super Bowl outburst, but they came close and Steinberg said Young told him later that then-offensive coordinator Mike Shanahan deserved credit.

"Steve told me Mike Shanahan called the perfect game," Steinberg says. "What he did was he changed all their normal plays and made them look a little bit different. Every single play that the Chargers would have been looking at on film were all changed enough that the linebackers were running into each other. Shanahan had cleverly disguised every aspect of what they were going to do and took them completely by surprise."

The game represented the culmination of Young's relationship with Shanahan, who left after the Super Bowl to become head coach of the Denver Broncos, later winning a pair of Super Bowls in his own right.

"He needed to be a head coach again, but you take those three years of our offense when he was there and it would be a challenge to find three years like that by any offense ever," Young said. "His last game coaching the 49ers, in many ways, was a reflection of him and his approach."

Young played five more years for the 49ers, but the team didn't return to the Super Bowl in that span. In retrospect, Young said the failure to keep the 1994 team intact for at least couple more years was costly, damaging the team's chances to put together another title run.

"We made some personnel decisions that hurt us, especially losing Ricky Watters," Young said of the 49ers' decision to let the running back go in free agency. "In hindsight, that was a tough one to overcome."

The 49ers reached the playoffs in four of the next five seasons but suffered three postseason losses to Green Bay and another to Atlanta before Young suffered a career-ending concussion at Arizona in September 1999. He announced his retirement before the start of the 2000 season.

In 2005, Young became a first-ballot inductee to the pro Football Hall of Fame in Canton, Ohio, joining his one-time rival, Joe Montana, in the pantheon of football greats. His father, Grit Young, presented him at the August 2005 induction. In his induction speech, Young returned to what he regarded as the seminal moment of his career: the team huddle in the locker room in the minutes after the 49ers' Super Bowl triumph in January 1995.

"My favorite moment was still the five minutes after the Super Bowl when we were alone in the locker room," Young said. "Just the 50 players and coaches kneeling in the Lord's Prayer, then looking up at each other and realizing that, yes, we were world champions. No media, no one, just us. That feeling when you do something great together is like no other. No MVP or passing title can compare to that feeling."

Recalling years later the last time the Super Bowl-winning team was together, Young adds, "All the challenges that we had faced as a team that season came to my mind. We had overcome them. And the people that tried to knock us down, which is just human nature to me, came to mind. But we persevered. It was just a special moment there in that locker room."

Chapter 20

GARY PLUMMER

As a teenager growing up in the San Francisco Bay area city of Fremont, Gary Plummer became a devotee of Sylvester Stallone's *Rocky* movies. Whenever he and his younger brother went to the theater in the late 1970s to see the tale of the underdog boxer and the sequels that followed, they each would find an aisle seat. Being near the aisle was a must for the brothers; they needed the extra room to jump, yell, and cheer in support of Rocky Balboa's improbable championship quest. Invariably, by movie's end, the Plummer brothers had plenty of company.

"The entire audience was jumping with us," Gary Plummer says.

There was, of course, a reason why Plummer identified so strongly with Stallone's blue-collar "Rocky" character and the fighter's long shot climb to the top. He applied Rocky-like fervor, determination, and perseverance to keep his pursuit of football alive.

A highly decorated player on a highly successful team at Fremont's Mission San Jose High School, the undersized Plummer nevertheless went virtually unrecruited by major colleges. Plummer still hoped to get a scholarship to play at nearby Stanford, but George Seifert, then a Stanford assistant coach, took one look at the rail-thin 6-foot, 200-pound linebacker and laughed.

"You can't play in the Pac-10," Seifert told Plummer.

Plummer never forgot what Seifert said to him that day in 1978. And he used Seifert's harsh assessment of his football potential as motivation during a long career that brought the two together again 16 years later: Plummer as a 49ers linebacker and Seifert as his head coach.

The path Plummer blazed toward that unlikely reunion was filled with twists and turns. Determined to gain strength and size, the high school senior worked out furiously, a practice he would continue throughout his football career.

Plummer walked on at Ohlone, a local junior college in Fremont in the shadow of the old Mission San Jose. He played two years there, finishing as the school's career leader in tackles. But again, no college offered him a football scholarship. So again Plummer walked on, this time at the University of California, Berkeley, where he developed into a fierce defender as the team's starting nose guard.

Passed over by NFL teams in the 1983 draft, Plummer "walked on" with the Oakland Invaders of the rival United States Football League. His original signing bonus with the Invaders was a bench press, another reflection of Plummer's relentless commitment to conditioning.

He made the team as a linebacker and was reunited with Invaders defensive coach Ron Lynn, who had been Cal's defensive coordinator when Plummer played for the Golden Bears. Playing in a league that included such players as Steve Young, Herschel Walker, and Reggie White, Plummer became the Invaders' career leader in tackles, including 162 stops during his rookie season.

When the USFL folded three years later, Lynn went to the San Diego Chargers as a defensive coach and brought Plummer in for a tryout. Plummer finally broke through to reach the NFL pinnacle, laying claim to the middle linebacker job and developing into one of the league's premier run stoppers.

"First and foremost, I'm a guy who likes to play smash-mouth football," Plummer said.

His numbers in eight years in San Diego showed it. He averaged 100 tackles per season and led the Chargers in tackles three seasons in a row.

In a display of toughness and durability, Plummer didn't miss a game due to injury during his final seven seasons in San Diego, including 1991, when he played most of the year with steel pins in his hand after fracturing his thumb in a September game against Kansas City.

A free agent in the spring of 1994, both the Chargers and the 49ers sought out Plummer. The 49ers were intent on bolstering a run defense

Gary Plummer *Photo © Michael Zagaris*

that had given up a league-worst 4.5 yards per rush the previous season, which had ended in San Francisco's second consecutive loss to Dallas in the NFC title game.

Plummer saw firsthand how serious the 49ers were about overtaking rival Dallas when team brass turned out in force to watch him work out. The audience for what Plummer had been told would be "a little workout" included team president Carmen Policy, general manager John McVay, assistant head coach Bill McPherson, linebackers coach John Marshall, and one George Seifert, the 49ers head coach who as a Stanford assistant had told Plummer he was too small to play major college football.

A couple years earlier, during a training camp scrimmage between the 49ers and the Chargers, Plummer had re-introduced himself to Seifert. He reminded Seifert he had once told him he wasn't good enough to play football for a major college. But Plummer also thanked him, telling Seifert his words fueled his pursuit of football for many years.

At the end of an impressive workout by Plummer, Seifert hearkened back to their first meeting.

"You might not be able to play in the Pac-10," Seifert told him, "But you certainly can play for the 49ers."

Within days, Plummer rejected San Diego's counteroffer and signed a two-year, $1.8 million deal with the 49ers. He proved to be the first in a parade of free agents signed in 1994 by the 49ers, who were driven by a "Super Bowl or Bust" mantra going into that season.

Other free agents added to the roster included linebacker Ken Norton, defensive ends Richard Dent and Rickey Jackson, and cornerbacks Deion Sanders and Toi Cook. The collection of talent gave the defense the same kind of star quality that the 49ers' offense possessed with the likes of Steve Young, Jerry Rice, Brent Jones, John Taylor, and Ricky Watters.

Playing behind the standout tackle tandem of Bryant Young and Dana Stubblefield, Plummer and Norton helped to shut down the running lanes. They contributed to a turnaround that saw the 49ers rush defense improve to No. 2 in 1994, up from 16th the previous season.

The 49ers went on to beat Dallas for the first time in three successive tries in the NFC title game, and advanced to the Super Bowl, where they defeated Plummer's old team, the San Diego Chargers, 49-26, for their fifth championship.

In 1995, the 49ers were even better against the run, allowing a team-record low of 3.0 yards per rush to finish at the top of the league rankings for the only time since 1970. In the four seasons Plummer and Norton teamed up as 49ers inside linebackers, San Francisco never ranked lower than fifth against the run and was either ranked No. 1 or No. 2 in the three other seasons. Twice, in 1995 and 1997, the 49ers finished No. 1 in total defense.

No play epitomized the stopping power and fierce physical play of the 49ers defense in that span more than a hit Plummer delivered during the final month of the 1995 campaign in a nationally televised Sunday night game against Buffalo.

Plummer forced a goal-line fumble by Darick Holmes by literally launching himself over the line and smacking head-on into the running back's chest, dislodging the ball. Fellow linebacker Lee Woodall picked it up on the fly and ran 96 yards for a touchdown, providing a 14-point swing in a key game with the second longest fumble return in team history. Only Don Griffin's NFL-record 99-yard return against Chicago in 1991 was longer.

Holmes said afterward the hit was one of the hardest he had ever experienced. "I never saw him," Holmes said at the time. "I just felt it and the ball came out."

Woodall had a fellow linebacker's appreciation for the force of the blow. "Those are the kinds of hits you dream of," Woodall said. "If you look at the film, it was a real nasty hit." That's the way Plummer remembers it, too.

GAME OF MY LIFE
BY GARY PLUMMER
DECEMBER 3, 1995—SAN FRANCISCO, CALIFORNIA

At the time, the Buffalo Bills were an offensive juggernaut. They had a Hall of Fame quarterback in Jim Kelly. They had a Hall of Fame running back in Thurman Thomas. They were a team that had reached the Super Bowl four consecutive times.

I remember the preparation that week for what they called the K-Gun. Essentially, they didn't huddle. Jim Kelly would just gather them around in what they refer to as a "sugar" huddle; the offensive linemen are already up to the line of scrimmage, and the wide receivers just come in toward the ball, close enough to be able to hear what Kelly is calling. It's a loose huddle that is probably about 15-20 yards wide. That way, the wide receivers can split out as quickly as possible and get back in and run another play. They averaged running a play every 22 seconds, the fastest in the league. So it was a huge deal during the week in terms of the preparation. Pete Carroll was the defensive coordinator and he told us that was essentially what was going to happen. They loved to do the K-Gun, sugar huddle, and often you couldn't change the defensive personnel groups.

So they got the ball. It was a tie game, 10-10. It was a critical situation midway through the third quarter: they'd driven the length of the field using the K-Gun, one play after another, every 22 seconds. I was just exhausted. I was used to playing maybe three or four plays in a row, coming out for a third-down pass situation, getting a drink of water, and then being able to go back in a bit rested. They reached our 16-yard line and they gave the ball to running back Darick Holmes. Their All-Pro guard, Rueben Brown, came out and just engulfed me. That's not anything unusual. Offensive linemen are going to hold you. When Holmes ran by me, I couldn't get off the block. Normally, you can continue to fight, to try to run down the ball carrier. But Holmes got down to the 1-yard line, and I didn't run to the ball. I literally could not run to the ball between Brown's block and my physical exhaustion.

As a player, you get graded on every single play: a zero, a plus, or a minus. You get a minus for what they call loafing, which is not running to the ball or having a missed assignment. At that point in my career, it was my 13th year, and I'd never had a "loaf," not in college, not in the pros—not anywhere, ever. It was one of those pride things. I used to grade myself as the plays happened, literally during a game, and I could not stop cussing myself out. Thirteen years of professional football and four years of college football and I'd never had a loaf. Well, I had just gotten my first "loaf" and I knew it.

At that point, the Bills had a first and goal from the one. Again, it was a critical situation in a game late in the season with playoff implications for both teams. For us, we were fighting for home-field advantage in the NFC. They were fighting for home-field advantage in the AFC. We were supposedly going to be the teams that met in a Super Bowl. But I was still angry with myself from the previous play. I decided to line up seven yards deep in the end zone so I could really size up the situation.

And I recognized the formation, recognized what they liked to do in that situation. And I just said, "You know what? I'm going to make up for not running to the football the play before."

One of the things you can do is launch yourself, just like a missile, at a lead blocker in a goal-line situation. Sometimes, if you launch yourself high enough, you can go right over the top of the lead blocker and hit the running back.

I knew with 90-percent certainty that they were going to run what's called a lead draw, or a New York draw. So at that point, it's like the hair on the back of my neck was standing up and I was excited because I knew what was coming at me. The other thing in the back of my mind was, I'm going to make up for letting my teammates down.

I saw the lead back and I saw the running back take a jab step and I knew it was exactly what I thought it was going to be: the lead draw. I noticed the fullback coming in low. One of the things that Kenny Norton and I always tried to do was to make a fullback quit. And the way to make him quit is to put your helmet under his chin; you only have to do that a couple times before a fullback starts to cut you—and this fullback was not going to let that happen again. He was going to come in low and try to cut me. By my first step, I'd recognized the draw. By the second step, I'd recognized that the fullback was going to try to cut block me. By the third step, I knew I was going to be able to launch myself over the top of the lead blocker.

Darick Holmes took the handoff and I don't think he even took a step with the ball, and I had completely launched myself over the top of the lead blocker. He never touched me, and it was just the full force of 255 pounds in the air on the helmet right on the guy's chest and it knocked the ball out. I saw the ball come out. I just didn't know where it ended up because he landed on his back and I landed on top of him.

As soon as I jumped up, I saw Lee Woodall about five yards off to my left. We always did a drill called "Scoop and Score," and he literally scooped the ball up on the run. I started to run for him to have a blocker but he was already so far ahead of me and there was nobody else from Buffalo that was even close. I just stopped, probably, after five yards and I just put my hands up in the air because I knew it was going to be a touchdown. It was just cool. Everything we'd learned and practiced came together; there was the ability to recognize formations, the ability to recognize tendencies. It was just neat to prove our skills in a situation like that, on national television, when it meant the world to 49ers fans and to us as a team.

Probably 50 people a year, easily, will just remind me of that one moment. Obviously, it was a great game. It was a 14-point swing for us at a crucial time. And we went on to win the game. It was huge.

Plummer played professional football for 15 years, spending the last four years of his career with the 49ers. Though he won a Super Bowl ring and continues to view his time with the team as the most rewarding of his career, his final two years in the game were not easy.

Heading into the 1996 season, Plummer fractured his left wrist in the exhibition opener when he wound up at the bottom of a pile-up. He was sidelined for six weeks after surgery to repair a series of cracks in the wrist. Plummer's consecutive-game streak, dating back eight years, was snapped at 139 when he missed the opener.

A month into the season, Plummer was back in action, using a special leather brace to protect his still-healing wrist fracture. Following the '96 campaign, Plummer turned 37 and was caught up in the changes that swept through the organization after the 49ers ousted George Seifert as coach and hired Steve Mariucci to replace him. Team officials informed Plummer they were giving his starting job to a younger player, fourth-year veteran Kevin Mitchell. Plummer wasn't happy with the decision but swallowed his pride and accepted a 50-percent pay cut, throwing himself into the special teams role that the team envisioned for him.

However, Mitchell's play in the exhibition season was erratic, and a week before the opener at Tampa Bay, Mariucci returned Plummer to the starting lineup.

"I've always had to prove myself. It seems I've never been big enough or fast enough or strong enough. This year, I wasn't young enough," Plummer said. It didn't take Plummer long to show that he was still good enough, though.

The 49ers lost Steve Young and Jerry Rice to injuries in a season-opening setback at Tampa Bay. Rice missed all but one game the rest of the year after tearing knee ligaments when Tampa Bay defensive tackle Warren Sapp tackled him by the facemask. Young suffered a concussion and backup Jeff Brohm a hand injury, leaving rookie quarterback Jim Druckenmiller to start the next game against the St. Louis Rams.

With Druckenmiller struggling in what would be his only career start, Plummer and the 49ers defense put the game on their shoulders. They kept the Rams out of the end zone and forced four fumbles, offsetting the four giveaways by the 49ers, including three interceptions by Druckenmiller.

Still, the Rams needed only a couple inches to keep driving toward the go-ahead score in the game's waning moments. But Plummer dove over the pile to stuff Tony Banks' fourth-down quarterback sneak for no gain. He ran off the field screaming, "They can't block me! They can't block me!"

The stop preserved the 49ers' 15-12 victory over the Rams and started an 11-game winning streak that remains the longest in team history in a single season.

For Plummer, though, the Rams game marked the beginning of the end of his career.

After the team returned from St. Louis, Plummer visited team doctors because of nagging soreness in his hip. The doctors discovered Plummer was suffering from osteoarthritis in his left hip and told him he would eventually need hip replacement surgery because of the degenerative condition.

Anti-inflammatory medication and pain-killing injections helped Plummer make it through the rest of the 1997 season. The 49ers' season ended with their third consecutive loss in the playoffs to Green Bay, and in the spring, Plummer retired and took a job as the analyst on the 49ers' game-day radio broadcasts.

The pounding and wear and tear from football did take a toll on Plummer's body, however. Within four years of Plummer's retirement, the ache in his degenerative left hip had become so severe that Plummer decided to undergo surgery to install an artificial hip.

"I can't walk 100 yards without feeling like someone is driving a metal spike in my hip," Plummer said shortly before he underwent the successful hip replacement surgery. "I started to change my gait, and the way I walk now is starting to affect my knee. And then, it's going to affect my ankle and then it's going to affect my other hip. I had to get this done."

The hip surgery performed on Plummer in 2001 was his 18th operation related to football. The previous 17 came over the course of his 15-year career, including four in his four seasons with the 49ers.

He's getting around well now and he's left the painful ordeal behind him.

"There are absolutely no regrets," Plummer said. "The joy, the satisfaction I've garnered from playing football, is immeasurable."

Chapter 21

GARRISON HEARST

Garrison Hearst was in the locker room getting ready for the second training camp practice of the day when he was called into Arizona Cardinals coach Vince Tobin's office. Not for a moment did Hearst think the summons involved anything out of the ordinary. After all, the running back had broken through for his first 1,000-yard season the year before.

The third overall selection by the Cardinals in the 1993 NFL draft, Hearst finally seemed to have his career on track. He had overcome a knee injury that wrecked parts of his first two seasons and finished with 1,070 yards rushing in 1995. He was honored as the NFL's Comeback Player of the Year. He became only the second Cardinals running back in 10 years to hit the 1,000-yard milestone, a hallmark of the NFL's top running backs.

So, getting cut was the last thing Hearst expected to hear from Tobin when he walked into his coach's office. But that's what happened just days before the start of the 1996 season.

Hearst became one of the league's earliest salary-cap casualties. In an outgrowth of the 1993 labor agreement between players and the league, a payroll limit for each NFL team was put in place. But an unwelcome side effect of the new system was that some players were being released not because of their performance but because of economics.

That was the case with the Cardinals and Hearst, who was due a salary of $2 million in 1996. The Cardinals were less than $1 million under the salary cap and they needed more room after agreeing to give top draft pick Simeon Rice, a defensive end, a $5 million signing bonus as part of a four-year contract.

"Sometimes," Tobin told a stunned Hearst, "you got to let players go you don't want to let go."

Tobin said to Hearst that the Cardinals wanted to sign him back, albeit at a lower salary. "No you don't," Hearst shot back.

"I was ticked at the time," Hearst said later. "I was a starter. They were like, 'We're going to try to re-sign you.' And I was like, 'Shoot, as soon as I walk out this door, it's the last time I'm a Cardinal.'"

Hearst left Tobin's office and headed for Phoenix's Sky Harbor Airport. He caught a flight back home but he'd barely rejoined his family in Lincolnton, Georgia, when his agent, Pat Dye Jr., called to let him know he had been claimed off waivers by the Cincinnati Bengals. The Bengals were in need of a running back because of uncertainties over Ki-Jana Carter's return from a severe knee injury. Hearst began as the backup but moved into the starting lineup a month into the season, finishing as the Bengals' leading rusher in 1996 with 847 yards.

One game in particular impacted Hearst's future. He came off the bench to run for 88 yards and make two catches for 25 yards and a touchdown in helping the Bengals to a 21-0 lead over the 49ers. Behind an injured Steve Young, who played through a groin strain, the 49ers rallied for a 28-21 victory. But Hearst's performance—the third-best individual rushing performance of the year against the 49ers—made an impression on Dwight Clark, then a 49ers vice president and the team's director of football operations.

When Hearst became a free agent after the 1996 season and Dye contacted the 49ers to let them know the running back was interested in playing for them, Clark jumped at the chance to sign him. Clark believed Hearst could be the every-down running back the 49ers had lacked since Ricky Watters left as a free agent after helping the 49ers to their fifth Super Bowl championship following the 1994 season.

Both the Bengals and Cardinals made a run at their former player but Hearst decided to sign with the 49ers, opting to take less money for the chance to play with a winning team that was just two years removed from its last Super Bowl title.

"I wanted to win," says Hearst, whose total of 3,232 yards as a college player at Georgia ranked second in school history behind

Garrison Hearst *Photo by Terrell Lloyd*

Herschel Walker. "I was tired of losing—bottom line," Hearst says. "Losing was not accepted here, and that was a change from what I was used to [in Arizona and Cincinnati]."

The change of scenery worked wonders for both Hearst and the 49ers. He ran for 1,019 yards in his first season with the team despite missing the last three regular season games with a broken collarbone suffered at the end of the 45-yard run that put him over the milestone.

After an off-season rehabilitation, Hearst came back to become a dominating offensive force in his second year in San Francisco, putting together the single-most productive rushing season in the team's history—1,570 yards.

"When he first came here, there were maybe some questions about his style, like, 'He's this kind of runner, he's that kind of runner,'" the late 49ers offensive line coach Bobb McKittrick once said. "He can run any kind of play in America's favorite playbook. He can run I-formation plays, sweeps, traps. He's got attitude, toughness, speed, strength, and smarts. There's nothing he can't do."

One day, on one play, in one game in particular, Hearst did it all.

With a broken tackle, a nifty move, and a turn of speed, Hearst broke off a 96-yard touchdown run in overtime, putting an abrupt end to a dramatic passing duel between the 49ers' Steve Young and the Jets' Glenn Foley in a 1998 season opener.

Young had no problem with the sudden change: "From my view, I was seeing a pack of people flying down the field. All I could say, was 'Go! Go!'"

The run that lifted the 49ers past the New York Jets remains the longest from scrimmage in team history. It later was singled out by Steve Sabol of NFL Films as the most exciting run in NFL history, and footage of it pops up regularly nowadays on Internet sites.

"I just wanted to hit the hole quick and get what I could," Hearst says. "Things happened after that."

GAME OF MY LIFE
BY GARRISON HEARST
SEPTEMBER 6, 1998—SAN FRANCISCO, CALIFORNIA

Every time you looked around, it felt like somebody was scoring. It was such a back-and-forth game. In my mind, whoever got the ball last was going to win. The Jets scored with no time left to put it into overtime. We held them and they punted and they had us back at the 4-yard line. We huddled up in our end zone and I'll never forget Steve Young calling the play, a 90-O, and looking me right in the eye: "We need some room here."

It's a trap play right up the middle and I'm thinking, "Oh, shoot! It's going to be hard running up in there." We had run the same play a couple times. One time, it worked pretty well. I busted through for about eight yards. The other time, it didn't go anywhere. I wasn't expecting to get a lot because it's a cloud-of-dust play.

Really, that wasn't the play I wanted. I wanted a play where I had a little more time and opportunity to read the hole. With the 90-O, it happens quick, and you've got one opportunity to hit the hole and that's it. You go right up the middle in the gap between the guard and center and make your cut basically off the center's butt.

But Ray Brown pulled and got the linebacker, and Chris Dalman and Kevin Gogan blocked down on defensive linemen, and the hole opened up in front of me. Going through, I thought, "I'm going to get about 8 yards." A linebacker got his arms around me, but that wasn't going to bring me down. Once I got through him, I just started running.

As a running back, you don't plan on what you do; it just happens. I broke through an arm tackle, and the safety never got his arms on me. I stiff-armed him. From then on, it was me, and I was giving everything I had just to get down field. One thing I do remember was I was running as hard as I could at that point, and Terrell Owens ran by me like I was walking. He and Dave Fiore had gotten downfield and were blocking for me. I was thinking about trying to make a cutback, but just then Dave and T.O. hit somebody a little behind me and I kept running. I carried Mo Lewis on my back the last three yards. He actually helped me. He went for the ball, didn't get it out, and we fell into the end zone together. Jerry Rice was yelling, "You all get off him. He can't breathe."

When I saw we were in the end zone and it was a touchdown, I just said, "Oh, thank you, Jesus, because I couldn't have run any more."

Chad Fann came over and was telling me, "Get up, 'G'! You made it! Get up!" I couldn't quite get up, so everybody lent me a hand and helped me up. I was dog tired, but we had gotten our season started off with a win. Now, I don't have a tape or anything of that run but it will come up and I'll see it on television or someone will show it to me. I'm reminded of it all the time. Once, not too long ago, I was at the gym and

I bumped into a guy wearing a New York Jets cap. He was like, "I know what you did to me. Every step you took on that run, I was crying."

Hearst's game-winning dash not only broke the Jets' heart that day but toppled a 46-year-old team record, eclipsing Hugh McElhenny's 89-yard touchdown against the Dallas Texans on October 5, 1952 as the longest run in 49ers history. It also gave him a career-best 187 yards in the game and foreshadowed a sensational season that reached another crescendo in a December 13, 1998 Monday night game against Detroit.

Though the 49ers were seen as a primarily passing team in the heyday of Steve Young and Jerry Rice and Terrell Owens, they reverted to a smash-mouth style against the Lions that produced a franchise-record 328 yards rushing in the 35-13 victory.

"I've never seen us make that many yards that consistently," said Young, who threw only 18 passes, completing 12 for 82 yards, his lowest total in a full game in 11 years with the 49ers. Hearst accounted for most of the rushing yardage, gaining a team-record 198 yards to surpass Delvin Williams' previous high of 194 yards in a 1976 game against the St. Louis Cardinals.

The record performance came at Candlestick Park after a heart-to-heart talk with his father, Gary, and in front of his favorite running back, Barry Sanders, who was on the opposite sideline.

Hearst, Terry Kirby, and Young all ran for scores and each out-rushed Sanders, the greatest open-field runner of his generation, who was held to 28 yards on 14 carries.

"I always loved watching him run," Hearst said. "But that was a good night for us. It was just a good night for running for us."

It was an even better year for Hearst. He finished with 1,570 yards rushing, the third most in the league that season and surpassing the previous team record of 1,502 by Roger Craig in 1988. He matched Craig's team record by running for at least 100 yards six times and earned his first trip to the Pro Bowl.

"He was a home run hitter," said guard Ray Brown, who helped clear the way for Hearst that season. "Whatever you did, he'd probably be successful, and if we really got on our blocks and stayed on them, he was going to make yards."

Behind Hearst, the 49ers had the top-rated rushing attack in the league and the No. 1 overall-rated offense. They finished with a 12-4 record, two games behind Atlanta for the NFC West title but good enough for a wild-card berth in their 16th trip to the postseason in 18 years.

The next week, Hearst ran for 128 yards in the 49ers' first-round victory over Green Bay, a game punctuated by Terrell Owens' game-winning touchdown catch in the final seconds. Nearly lost in the "Catch II" jubilation was the fact that Hearst had become only the fifth player in 49ers history to rush for 100 or more yards in the playoffs. In one memorable run that captured his rare combination of speed, power, and ferocity, Hearst lowered his shoulder and drove over Packers free safety Darren Sharper. Then he fended off strong safety LeRoy Butler with a stiff-arm before finally getting knocked out of bounds after a 24-yard gain.

The victory over Green Bay ended a string of three consecutive losses to the Packers in the playoffs and infused a sense of confidence and swagger in the 49ers as they advanced to play the Atlanta Falcons in a January 9, 1999, divisional playoff game.

For Hearst, it had all the makings of a triumphant homecoming. Hearst had grown up in the tiny Georgia town of Lincolnton, where he remained a football legend. As a senior, Hearst rushed for 2,397 yards and 47 touchdowns, leading Lincoln County high school to an undefeated season (15-0) and state title.

Now Hearst was returning with the 49ers to play the Falcons in Atlanta's Georgia Dome, a two-and-a-half-hour drive from his hometown. A trip to the NFC championship and return to the Super Bowl for the 49ers were within sight.

But on the first play from scrimmage in the playoff game, the 49ers lost their legs. Steve Young handed the ball off to Hearst and he burst past traffic at the line of scrimmage. Just seven yards downfield, he tried to spin away from Atlanta defensive lineman Chuck Smith but his foot stuck in the artificial turf. With a gruesome twist, his left ankle fractured. Hearst's day was over, the 49ers' running game faltered, and San Francisco lost 20-18 to the Falcons.

For Hearst, the ankle fracture meant dealing with his third major injury in six years in the NFL. But he never envisioned the struggle that would be in store for him before he could walk, before he could run, and before he could play again.

"I said to myself, 'OK, a bone heals in six or seven weeks,'" Hearst says. "Let it play out, start rehabbing, and play next season. The hardest part at the time was that we had come so far to lose to Atlanta. We felt we had the game plan to win. But we didn't win, and other complications came up. That's where the story starts."

Hearst underwent initial surgery to stabilize the break and repair ligament damage but ran into problems when he began working out in the spring to get ready for the upcoming summer training camp. Team physician Dr. Michael Dillingham discovered circulatory complications had choked off the blood supply to his foot, leading to avascular necrosis. The degenerative condition caused Hearst's talus, a primary weight-bearing bone in his ankle, to decay and become brittle. Bo Jackson had also developed avascular necrosis in his hip bone after taking a sideline hit while playing for the Raiders. Jackson eventually had to have hip-replacement surgery. He didn't play football again but did come back to play major league baseball.

Hearst wanted to become the first player to resume his NFL career after suffering from avascular necrosis, but the only certainty about such an effort was that it would be a long, painful process with no guarantee of success. It would take perseverance and determination on the part of Hearst and patience and a willingness to accept risk on the part of the 49ers. The 49ers held up their end by keeping Hearst on the payroll for two years, despite dealing with salary-cap problems and despite being unsure whether he would ever play again.

"I would say some other teams may have cut him because of the slim chance he had," said then 49ers coach Steve Mariucci, who was instrumental in keeping Hearst around. "But it's been a two-way street. He was as good as anybody when he got hurt. So if he was willing to come back, we were willing to give him that chance."

Hearst said he never had any doubts that he would be able to play again and that kept him going. He also felt like he had been there before. Hearst had come back from reconstructive knee surgery and a broken collarbone and played better than ever. He had faith he could do that again.

"You never want a serious injury of course, but it did help me realize that I could come back," Hearst says.

A procedure performed by Seattle orthopedic specialist Dr. Pierce Scranton in May 2000, the third of four operations on Hearst's foot, at last set the course for his comeback. Scranton and Dr. Dillingham removed dead bone and cartilage. Hearst's ankle was basically taken apart and put back together in a bone-grafting operation that Scranton described as the most extensive he had ever performed.

Eight months later, in January 2001, Hearst underwent another surgery to clear out bone chips and other debris in his reconstructed ankle. That spring, he was medically cleared to return to practice. When he stood up to the challenge of daily contact in training camp, Hearst and the 49ers knew he was ready to play again after spending two years on the sideline.

He beat out Kevan Barlow in a training camp competition to reclaim his starting job and showed he was healthy by running for key gains that helped set up a winning field goal in the 2001 season-opening victory over Atlanta.

"I about cried," said defensive tackle Bryant Young, who had come back from a devastating leg fracture of his own. "It was amazing to see a guy come back from an injury like that after having suffered setback after setback."

Hearst went on to run for 1,206 yards in 2001, the first NFL running back to reach such a milestone after an injury-caused absence of two years. He became the first NFL player to win Comeback Player of the Year honors twice.

"I knew it was never going to be as good as it was before I hurt my ankle," Hearst said. "But I knew I could still play. I just never thought about quitting, even when the doctors told me I couldn't play anymore. I was never going to give up."

That same attitude allowed Hearst to become one of the 49ers' best blocking backs in pass protection and to turn a cloud-of-dust play into the longest run from scrimmage in the team's history. Hearst spent seven of his 12 years in the league with the 49ers and ranks fourth in rushing (5,535 yards) on the team's all-time list. He spent his final NFL season as a third-down back for Denver in 2004.

"I miss playing. Everybody misses playing when they first leave," Hearst says. "I'm just staying home with my three kids now." His two boys, Gerard and Gannon, and his daughter, Brooke, range in age from

2 to 7. "It's not bad," he says. "But I get tired, more tired than when I played football."

Chapter 22

JEFF GARCIA

Bill Walsh first came to appreciate the quarterbacking ability of Jeff Garcia while desperately trying to avoid losing to him.

Garcia's running and passing had San Jose State on the brink of upsetting a Walsh-coached Stanford team. Only a couple of late drops by the Spartans, the last coming when the ball slid off the receiver's hands into the arms of a defender, allowed Stanford to escape with the 31-28 victory in September 1993.

Four months later, Garcia caught Walsh's attention again. He came on in the fourth quarter of the East-West Shrine game at Stanford to throw for three touchdowns and earn MVP honors.

But impressing Walsh, who had drafted Joe Montana and traded for Steve Young while winning three Super Bowls in 10 years as the 49ers coach, wasn't initially enough for Garcia to get a shot at the NFL. Most scouts believed that Garcia lacked ideal size and arm strength, so even though he emerged from San Jose State as its all-time leader in total offense and demonstrated leadership and grit in his play, he went undrafted in 1994. Neither was Garcia offered a free agent contract by any NFL team.

A stunned Walsh, who had befriended Garcia, wrote a letter of recommendation on behalf of the aspiring pro to about a dozen of his closest NFL coaching colleagues. Walsh urged them to give Garcia a look, telling them he had the makeup and skills to help them win games. Still, there were no takers.

"When I realized there wasn't going to be a door opening for me, I was fortunate to have another route, and that one was through the Canadian Football League," Garcia says. "I think the disappointment of not going into the NFL really kind of kick-started me into going into the CFL with a positive attitude.

"I was still able to do something I loved to do while being paid a little bit of money doing it. I just thought, 'Let's make the most of this opportunity at this time.' I just really felt that, coming out college, I had the tools to continue to play at a different level."

Garcia spent five years in the CFL with the Calgary Stampeders. Much of the first two years were spent backing up Doug Flutie. When an injury knocked Flutie out of Calgary's lineup, Garcia stepped in and played well. Eventually, Flutie was allowed to leave for the Toronto Argonauts, and Garcia went on to guide Calgary to a championship, winning the Grey Cup in 1998.

With that, the NFL finally came calling. Garcia drew interest from Jacksonville, Oakland, St. Louis, Miami, and the 49ers, who by then were being run by Walsh. The Hall of Fame coach returned in 1999 as the 49ers general manager. He called Garcia and told him the team needed a backup for Steve Young.

Garcia received contract offers from the 49ers and the Miami Dolphins, and he quickly concluded that the 49ers were the best fit, primarily because of the solid relationship that had developed between him and Walsh over the years.

"I think he's the guy who believed in me before anybody else did, and he was willing to go out on a limb and give me that opportunity when so many other people were going, 'Who is this guy?'" Garcia says.

Garcia went into the 1999 season as the 49ers' No. 2 quarterback, beating out Steve Stenstrom and Jim Druckenmiller for the backup job. Druckenmiller, a first-round pick in 1997 who never panned out as a quarterback for the 49ers, was traded away to Miami before the season began.

Less than a month into the season, Young suffered a career-ending concussion on a devastating hit from blitzing Arizona cornerback Aeneas Williams, and Garcia was thrust into the lineup. He led the 49ers past Tennessee in his first career start, but then he and the team went into a tailspin. He hit a low point against Pittsburgh in his fifth start when he

Jeff Garcia *Photo by Terrell Lloyd*

went 7-for-18 for 39 yards. It was the fourth consecutive loss for the 49ers en route to their first losing season (excluding strike-shortened 1982) in 20 years.

Coach Steve Mariucci benched Garcia in favor Steve Stenstrom. But Stenstrom failed to throw a touchdown pass in three consecutive starts, and Mariucci decided to give Garcia another chance.

Before Garica's return to the lineup, his quarterbacks coach, Greg Knapp, collected film of Garcia's 50 best plays as a 49er. He put them together in a highlight reel and played it for him during a meeting at the team facility.

"Look," Knapp told Garcia, "You've shown me and you've shown the coaches you can do this, and here's the proof."

Garcia, his confidence boosted, came back with a startling performance in a 44-30 loss at cold, rainy Cincinnati. Garcia threw for three touchdowns and 437 yards, marking the sixth-highest total and just the 11th 400-yard passing game overall in team history.

"It definitely was a kick-start to get me headed in the right direction," Garcia said. "I really started to believe in myself. That's when I realized I belonged in the NFL."

If there was any more doubt, he erased it in 2000, when in the midst of a 49ers' rebuilding season, Garcia threw for a team-record 4,278 yards passing. He had six 300-yard games in his first full year as starter, the second most in a season in team history. He had 14 overall in five years as a 49er, third most in team history behind Joe Montana (35) and Steve Young (28).

Garcia went on to earn the first of three consecutive berths in the Pro Bowl. His play was at the center of a resurgent offense that helped the 49ers return to the playoffs in back-to-back seasons, including a 10-6 campaign in 2002 that produced the team's first NFC West title in five years.

In the days leading up to their first-round matchup, center Jeremy Newberry boldly guaranteed a 49ers victory over the Giants. The 49ers made good on Newberry's guarantee, but only barely, with Garcia and Terrell Owens delivering key assists. They trailed the Giants by 24 points before rallying for a wild one-point victory. It was the biggest comeback in NFC playoff history and the second biggest in team history. Joe Montana led the 49ers back from a 28-point deficit in a 38-35 overtime win over New Orleans in 1980. The only postseason comeback that was greater came in the AFC in January 1993 when Buffalo beat Houston 41-38 after trailing by 32 points.

Against the Giants in the game's final 17 minutes, Garcia threw for two touchdowns and ran for another, led a drive for a field goal, and passed for two two-point conversions as part of a decisive 25-point closing run by the 49ers. When it was over, Garcia joined John Brodie, Joe Montana, and Steve Young as the only quarterbacks in team history to win an NFL postseason game.

GAME OF MY LIFE
BY JEFF GARCIA
JANUARY 5, 2003—SAN FRANCISCO, CALIFORNIA

Going into the NFC wild-card game against the New York Giants, we felt like we were a team on the cusp. After struggling for a couple years, we had reached the postseason for the second consecutive season, and we were looking to go deep into the playoffs after a first-round exit the year before.

The Giants game started off tremendously well for us. Julian Peterson intercepted a pass by Kerry Collins, and we got the ball at our 24-yard line. I connected on my first pass and Terrell Owens took it the distance. He made a great catch-and-run. As a team, we were thinking this was going to be the start of something really good.

But it turned against us in a hurry. New York began to move the football and they were able to put a lot of points on the board. It got to where things were starting to look bleak. If we didn't make a move soon, we were going miss whatever chance we had.

A missed opportunity by the Giants finally opened the door for us. They were near our goal line, just knocking on the door, and their tight end, Jeremy Shockey, dropped a for-sure touchdown. I think that was a turning point. A touchdown would have given them a 28-point lead with less than five minutes left in the third quarter. Instead, they settled for a field goal and a 24-point lead, which wasn't all that much better for us, but it was something.

While all that was going on, offensive coordinator Greg Knapp came over to me on the sideline and said he and coach Steve Mariucci decided to go with the no-huddle to try to get our offense going.

We went into the hurry-up mode and were able to go down the field and get a touchdown on another scoring pass to T.O. We made the two-point conversion and we felt like at least we were starting to close the gap.

I don't feel there was ever any panic within the team. There was a sense of confidence that slowly grew throughout that third quarter and into the fourth quarter, and it reached a point where we really believed we could win this game. Not only that, but the Giants seemed to be getting tired. When we were running that two-minute offense, they were really starting to wear down, looking frustrated. I think they were starting to turn on each other. There had been all that talk about Michael Strahan and the guys they had up front, but our offensive line had done a good job and those guys hadn't gotten to me all game long, and they wouldn't.

Our defense was able to come up with a stop, and we put together another drive. That one ended with me running into the end zone from 14 yards out as part of a designed play around left end. The line and J.J.

Stokes' downfield blocking created a lane for me and I really wasn't touched. We made our second two-point conversion, and with some 14 minutes left in the fourth quarter, we had pulled to 38-30.

I don't recall every single drive of that game, but I know how critical it was to take advantage of opportunities. And it just seemed the Giants weren't doing the things they had done in the first three quarters of the game that had created such an advantage for them. It breathed new life into us and into our fans—at least, to the ones who'd decided not to leave the game early.

The ones who stayed—and there were plenty of them, too—were treated to some breathtaking football in the final minutes. We made a field goal, and after the Giants missed a field goal (they had major problems in their kicking game), we took over at our 32. There were three minutes left, and we still trailed 38-33.

We just kept putting the ball up throughout the drive. The only run came when I scrambled midway through the drive. Everybody pitched in: the line, the backs. All three receivers, T.O., Tai Streets, and J.J. Stokes, and the tight end, Eric Johnson, had at least one catch during the drive.

With a minute left, Tai ran a corner post. He made a little move to the outside and then broke back inside across the corner's face. I spotted him in a lane and put it where I felt Tai could have a chance to make the play. He made a great catch and fell into the end zone and we were leading by a point. We tried to stretch the lead to three, but this time our two-point conversion didn't work.

Still, when it was all said and done, just that feeling that was in that stadium—the electricity, the excitement—the fans had been on a rollercoaster ride of emotions. I think at the end of the game they were probably more emotionally exhausted than we were on the field.

As a player, you can't get too high and you can't get too low. Hitting that last pass to Tai Streets and then seeing the Giants moving the ball down the field and having a chance to win it: what a swing in emoion. But there was a muffed snap on their last-second field goal attempt, and then there was a desperate throw downfield off the botched field goal. After that, there was chaos. It was a phenomenal finish to a crazy football game, and I was so excited to be part of it.

I wish I could have bottled that moment and experienced it over and over again because there aren't many things that match that feeling. Now, that day is just a piece of history and NFL lore.

With their first playoff victory in four years, the 49ers advanced to a divisional playoff at Tampa Bay. But the Buccaneers' top-ranked defense saw to it that there would be no storybook comeback this time, forcing five turnovers and keeping the 49ers from scoring a touchdown in Tampa's 31-6 victory.

Garcia said he still thinks the course of the game could have been changed if the 49ers hadn't missed two early opportunities for touchdowns. They settled for field goals, unable to convert despite having first downs at the Tampa 4- and 22- yard lines in separate drives.

"Instead of having 14 points we had six, and against a defense like that, especially with the way they were playing, we got put into a position where we were forced into pretty much passing on every down," Garcia said. "It made for a very difficult time."

Three days later, owner John York's firing of Steve Mariucci as coach jolted the 49ers again. York cited philosophical differences in dismissing Mariucci; the coach had taken the 49ers to the playoffs in four of his six seasons, but he had strained relations with York and general manager Terry Donahue, who replaced Bill Walsh in 2001.

After a prolonged search, Donahue hired Dennis Erickson to replace Mariucci, and once again the 49ers were swept in a new direction. Within a year, the 49ers put themselves through another salary-cap purge. Garcia was among eight starters—seven were on offense—traded or released to reduce payroll costs. The exodus of talent resulted in a 2-14 finish in 2004 that matched the team record for losses in a season and cost Donahue and Erickson their jobs.

Garcia's fortunes initially mirrored those of his former team. His first season away from the 49ers, in Cleveland, ended after 10 games because of a knee injury. The next year, he suffered a broken leg in training camp with Detroit and missed the first half of the season. In those two injury-shortened seasons, he threw 13 touchdown passes and 15 interceptions. In his four years as the 49ers starter, Garcia had averaged 25.5 touchdown passes and 11.25 interceptions and twice threw for more than 30 touchdowns in a season.

In 2006 with the Philadelphia Eagles, at age 37, Garcia recaptured the form that had made him a three-time Pro Bowl player with the 49ers. After Donovan McNabb went down with a season-ending knee injury, Garcia came on to go 6-2 in his place. His play fueled a five-game winning streak that carried the Eagles to the NFC East title. He guided them to a first-round win over the New York Giants before New Orleans ended Philadelphia's season in the divisional round. After the season, though, the Eagles passed on re-signing Garcia and he joined the Tampa Bay Bucaneers as a free agent, his fifth team in five years.

Four stops removed from his departure from San Francisco, Garcia says he still wonders what would have happened if the 49ers had avoided the coaching change heading into his last year in San Francisco and put roster continuity ahead of salary-cap savings.

"That 49ers team was just beginning to scratch the surface as to how good they could be," Garcia says. "Not to take anything away from Dennis Erickson and what he had to deal with over the next year, but I just wonder what was the true reason for the firing of Steve Mariucci. Why was this team being forced to go through this transition when we had just gone through back-to-back playoff years? We were a fairly young team experiencing success on the field and we had the ability to continue to grow and get better. I do think back at times, and I wonder why it had to come apart like it did."

Through all the ups and downs, though, Garcia says he remains grateful to the 49ers, but most especially Bill Walsh for going out on a limb to give him his first NFL job.

"It wasn't just the fact that he helped open the door in San Francisco, but he went to bat for me," Garcia said in an interview a month before the 75-year-old Walsh died on July 30, 2007, after a long battle with leukemia. "Nobody wanted to listen, nobody wanted to take his word about this kid who he believed could play the game.

"I've said before that I liked proving people wrong, but I don't just play the game to prove people wrong. It's not necessarily a driving force. And as much as I want to have success for myself and for my family, I wanted to have success for Bill Walsh. I didn't want to let him down. He was someone who was always in my corner . . . I owe Bill so much."

Chapter 23

BRYANT YOUNG

On his first day of practice at Bloom Township High School in Chicago Heights, Bryant Young set his sights on playing in the backfield.

"I had it in my mind that I was going to play fullback," Young says. "Some of my friends were encouraging me, saying, 'Oh yeah, you should play fullback. You'd be a good fullback.' I didn't know what position I wanted to play, but I thought I could be a guy who could catch and run the ball."

So when the coaches signaled to the players that the linemen should go to one part of the practice field, and the quarterbacks, running backs, and receivers to another, Young headed to the section of the field reserved for the backfield contingent. He didn't get very far.

"All of a sudden, I heard one of the coaches say, 'No, Young. You go over there with the linemen," Young says. "I was like, 'Oh, all right.' So, I played offensive tackle and defensive tackle my freshman year."

It proved to be the right move for Young. Combining strength, size, and athleticism with a work ethic that mirrored his parents' blue-collar background—his father worked the graveyard shift at an auto assembly plant and his mom was a homemaker—Young became a dominating defensive lineman and wrestler in high school. He went on to earn All-America honors as a senior at Notre Dame and was the seventh overall selection in the 1994 NFL draft, going to the San Francisco 49ers.

Young became a starter at left defensive tackle as a rookie, and in short order established himself as a relentless, fierce, and disruptive force in the heart of the NFL's trenches. Teammates began calling him "Pink Slip," because he could make offensive linemen look so bad that they'd lose their jobs.

"He's an awesome football talent, and he'll be a Pro Bowler for years," said Dwight Clark, then the coordinator of football operations and player personnel. "You see a lot of guys we call 'Velcro,' players who get locked on blocks and can't get off. Bryant Young just throws blockers off."

Initially, Young was taken aback by the sheer star power of the 49ers' roster, but he also quickly realized he had an important role to fill.

"Being on the same team with Steve Young and Jerry Rice and Tim McDonald and Deion Sanders and some others, I was like 'Wow!'" says Young. "The first mini-camp was a shocker. But gradually, that dissipated because I knew they brought me here for a reason, and that was to make plays and help the team win."

Young played alongside Dana Stubblefield, and despite their relative inexperience—Stubblefield entered the league the year before—the two formed one of the best run-stuffing inside tandems in the league; Stubblefield provided girth and stoutness, while Young brought explosiveness and strength. Both added toughness.

In Young's case, there was one memorable episode in his first year in which the 276-pounder literally tossed aside Minnesota's 331-pound guard, Bernard Dafney.

"How can you expect it from a guy that size?" teammate Derrick Deese said at the time. "But it's more than size. It's leverage. It's intensity. It's heart. B.Y. has a big heart."

Young, who helped the 49ers win their fifth Super Bowl title at the end of his rookie season, would need that big heart to be especially strong in 1998. In a Monday night game against the New York Giants in late November that year, Young and teammate Ken Norton collided while chasing after quarterback Kent Graham. Norton's helmet smashed into Young's shin, snapping both bones in his lower right leg and leaving Young on the field screaming in agony.

"It was a Joe Theismann-type injury," Graham said after the game. "I could tell Bryant was hurting pretty badly. It's something that you just hate to see." Or hear: "It was a pretty loud noise. It was not something that you usually hear out there on the field," defensive tackle Junior Bryant said.

When Young was wheeled off Candlestick Park's field on a gurney that night and taken to the hospital, the only thing that was clear was the

Bryant Young *Photo by Bill Fox Sports Photos*

devastating nature of the injury. His football future was uncertain because the injury was so severe. Young remained hospitalized for 17 days. He had three operations during that span, including having to slit the skin on his lower right leg in two areas to alleviate complications from massive swelling. To this day, Young's leg still contains the titanium rod that doctors installed to stabilize the fracture.

Young, though, was determined not to let that agonizing moment stand as the final one of his football career. Instead, over the course of a grueling and tedious rehabilitation, Young fended off suggestions that the injury had finished him.

He made a new beginning for himself. It was 10 months in the making and commenced with the 1999 regular-season opener against the Jacksonville Jaguars.

GAME OF MY LIFE
BY BRYANT YOUNG
SEPTEMBER 12, 1999—JACKSONVILLE, FLORIDA

For me, this game was a defining moment and a gut check. It really tested my love for the game. Is this what I wanted to do? Would I be able to come back fully from a potentially career-ending injury? In many ways, just by rehabbing and trying to get back, my love for the game had been tested.

The season opener against Jacksonville was my first game since I had broken both bones in my lower right leg against the New York Giants 10 months earlier. It had happened right before my eyes. When their quarterback, Kent Graham, scrambled, I went to chase him. He slid, and one of my teammates was coming toward me and as I began to brace myself to pull up, I just planted my foot in the ground, and that person's helmet plowed right into my leg.

There was no question it was broken. I mean, I could see it was bent and twisted up.

I was like, "What? Did this just happen?" I knew if you played in this league you were going to get some type of injury, but to me that was an injury so overwhelming that I was like, "Wow." I remember coach Steve Mariucci coming out on the field and trying to comfort me and letting me know it was going to be OK and to hang in there. I remember the doctors coming over and putting my leg in the splint, in the air cast, and trying to get me stable. As soon as they were able to get me off the field and into the ambulance, I was given pain meds because I was hurting pretty badly. My wife and Mr. DeBartolo rode in the ambulance with me when they took me away for emergency treatment.

I spent the next 17 days in the hospital. There were some complications that led to heavy swelling in my leg and I had surgery to put in a titanium rod to stabilize the fracture. They tried to take the rod out once, a year and a half later, but it had become calcified and attached itself to the bone. As hard as the doctors tried, they couldn't get it out, so the best thing was to leave it alone.

All along, I was getting a lot of support and encouragement from a lot of different people: my family, the 49ers staff, my dad, my mom, my brothers, my friends, and my teammates. My wife, Kristin, was definitely there for me. The training staff was phenomenal in my approach to the rehab, and just the support I received from people out there—the fans— was phenomenal. I got a ton of letters. I still have a box of stuff. I remember my brother, Tim, coming out to the hospital and he wanted to take some pictures. But I didn't want to remember myself like that, so I didn't let him. Now that I think about it, now that I look back on it, maybe I should have. He had told me our life story is a testimony, and so for me, it's something I wish had done, really for my own sake. But I didn't.

Coming back, Coach Mariucci wanted to bring me along slowly, cautiously. He was listening to the doctors and he wanted to do right by me. He kept me out of all our exhibition games leading up to our season opener.

I had kind of wanted to play a little in the last one, to get a feel for contact in a game again and to get over that psychological hurdle of taking that first hit and seeing that everything was still in one piece. That didn't happen, though. Basically, I was playing the Jacksonville game having had no live contact in almost year, and that was pretty scary. I was questioning my intentions: Am I being honest with myself? Am I doing the right thing? Do I need more time? Am I succumbing to the pressure from not only myself but from others? I had to go through all this doubt, but I didn't want to second-guess myself, and I knew that at some point, I had to bite the bit and go with it.

I was going against Zach Weigert, a hard-nosed, powerful blocker. He was playing guard at that time and I was playing over the center as well. But there I was, about to play a game, my comeback game, after breaking my leg the year before, with really no live contact in practice or training camp. I was starting to think that if it didn't feel right, that maybe I shouldn't put myself in harm's way and possibly hurt some other body part because I was protecting myself or overcompensating. That was a vibe I was getting. So, yes, I was a little tentative at first. But that first hit came and went and I was OK. And then another, and one more from the side and then from both sides at once. I might have gotten 35-40 snaps in that first game back and made two or three tackles. I just missed getting a sack.

My leg was a little tender after the game. I wasn't able to practice the next week, and that's just kind of how it went. I'd have to work through it week by week. I would maybe practice one or two days because if I'd go a couple days in a row, my leg would get really sore and I had to take time off. I could push it hard for a day or two, but on that third day I had to back off.

But for me and for all of us, that first game was a start. It was far from my best game and it sure wasn't one of our better performances as a team. But after what had happened, a start was all I wanted because it meant I could go on. I could go forward. It was a gut check and I'd gotten through it.

It wasn't until maybe five or six games into the season that I truly began playing without being conscious of my leg, but it was from that first game that I gained the confidence and faith that my leg would hold up. It was from that game that I learned I could still dish it out and I could still take it. It was that game that convinced me I could still play at a high level and that I had the chance to play better still. And I think that's what I did from there on out, and I'm thankful, very thankful.

◆   ◆   ◆

As Bryant Young walked off the field following the 49ers' 41-3 season-opening loss in Jacksonville, Jaguars guard Zach Wiegert, who had gone against Young all day, caught up with him.

"Glad to see you made it back," Wiegert told Young.

Wiegert was among those watching the Monday night game the previous November when Young suffered the gruesome double fracture to his lower right leg. And he had wondered, along with so many others, whether he'd be able to return.

"That was such a bad injury," Weigert said. "And to be playing less than a year later, you knew it had to be hurting him, but you couldn't tell. He wouldn't let you. We beat them pretty handily that day, but honestly, it wasn't because of the way he played.

"I was kind of amazed he came back from an injury like that and performed the way he did. He was still their best defensive lineman and he was doing the same things that he had done before the injury. He was always one of those guys who never quit on a play, and was always moving like hell to the ball. He had a motor that didn't stop and that's what made him one of the most difficult players to block."

One of the players who lined up on the field behind Bryant Young in his comeback game, 49ers' teammate Ken Norton, also took heart from his return. It was Norton who had inadvertently smashed, helmet first, into Young's leg while the two closed in from different directions on Giants quarterback Kent Graham.

From the moment of the bone-snapping collision, Norton was overwhelmed with concern, worry, and guilt over his role in the injury, its impact on Young, and the fear that he had ended his friend's career. Norton rarely spoke publicly of his inner torment. On one of the few occasions that he did, in the days before Young's comeback game, it was clear just how much Young's forgiveness and compassion toward

Norton meant to the linebacker. And it paved the way forward for them both.

"He saved me," Norton told *San Jose Mercury News* columnist Bud Geracie. "He and his wife, they saved me." On the night Young was hurt, Norton hurriedly showered and dressed after the game and drove to Stanford Hospital to see Young. Norton already was wracked by guilt over the damaging collision. He feared Young would blame him. But as soon as the shaken Norton arrived, Kristin Young left her husband's bedside to comfort him. And before Norton could even get a word out of his mouth, Young told him he had no hard feelings.

"A guy being in the situation he was in—facing a career-ending injury—this guy should have been hating me," Norton told Geracie. "He should have been trying to get out of that damn bed and whup me."

Years later, recalling the episode, Young says the anguished look on Norton's face told him he had to do something to reassure Norton he didn't blame him.

"He just couldn't believe what had happened, what he had done," Young said. "I tried to tell him, as best I could, that I didn't fault him. I didn't hold a grudge against him. Injuries happened. Accidents happened. But it took a while for him to let that go. I think for the first few weeks [after the collision] he went into the tank. It kind of affected him, the way he played. I remember watching him and you could tell he wasn't the Ken that we all knew. But we kept talking about it. I just had to keep reiterating to him that it was OK. I loved him then, and I love him now. I never hated him for it. It was part of the game."

Young's compassionate words meant a lot, but Norton saw Young's eventual return as his true salvation. He pulled for Young throughout his grueling rehabilitation and the two talked frequently, sharing notes on Young's progress. And when Young got to the point where he was back on the field, pushing the pocket, pressuring quarterbacks and stuffing the run, no one was more thrilled or relieved than Norton.

"To see that guy, after hearing him scream on the field, knowing what he has gone through to come back ... tremendous," Norton said. "Tremendous, tremendous."

As Young gained strength and confidence in his recovery, over a period of weeks his play improved. Young signaled his return to form in a December game against Atlanta, when he had two sacks. One of them went for a safety, the third of his career, tying him for third all-time in NFL history.

The year after suffering the broken leg, Young led the team with 11 sacks and earned his second trip to the Pro Bowl. He also won Comeback Player of the Year honors and became the first three-time winner of the Len Eshmont award, the team's most prestigious award given in recognition of courageous and inspirational play.

Young's comeback season helped him redefine his extraordinary career, restoring the focus on his level of play, and, as he moved beyond the injury, on his longevity, durability, and overall football excellence. Three of his four Pro Bowl berths were post-1998. And he went into 2007 as the only seven-time Eshmont winner in the 50-year history of the award. Five of the seven have been awarded to him since 1998.

Since missing the last four games after suffering his season-ending leg fracture, Young has played in all 16 games in six of eight seasons. He missed one game in 2000. Five years later, he suffered a torn medial collateral ligament in a late November game against Seattle. But he fought back to start the last three games in 2005, when the 49ers finished 4-12 in Mike Nolan's inaugural season as coach.

"It's your job to get back on the field," Young said. "We all go through some type of injury or we're dealing with some kind of pain. But I think it's important that guys understand that; it's almost like you can't cheat the game, because it will eventually catch up to you. That's always been important to me, that I make sure that I do whatever I can not to cheat the game."

It's an approach that has been a constant with Young, whether the 49ers were winning the Super Bowl, as they did when he was a rookie, or suffering through a 2-14 campaign, as they did in 2004.

"Bryant is one of those guys who is a warrior when it comes to working out and wanting to play," Nolan said. "That's why you try to search out as many guys like that as you can get."

After flirting with the notion of retiring, Young, at age 35, signed a one-year deal to return for his 14th season with the 49ers in 2007. Young said he decided he just wasn't ready to retire.

"I feel like I'm still able to go out there and make the plays that are asked of me," said Young. "In terms of my body, it feels a little different than it did five years ago. But with experience, you're able to gain a little wisdom and smarts."

After years of struggle, Young also saw last season's 7-9 finish as a sign of hope that the team could make a run at the playoffs. And he also took heart from a series of major free agency acquisitions highlighted by the $80-million contract that the 49ers gave cornerback Nate Clements. Young likened the 49ers' free-agency spree heading into the 2007 season to the star-studded additions that the 49ers made before their Super Bowl run in 1994.

"I feel like we're on the cusp of being right there," said Young, the only player still on the roster from the 49ers' 1994 Super Bowl team. "I thought we left some on the table last year. With the addition of a few more pieces to the puzzle, we'll be right in the mix. Part of my decision was me wanting to be part of that, and some of it was the unfinished work of leaving the 49ers organization the way I found it. Something special is going to happen here. I believe that."

Chapter 24

FRANK GORE

A couple days after finishing the 2006 season with a team-record 1,695 yards rushing, 49ers running back Frank Gore sat down next to his locker at the club's headquarters and gave thanks to his first football mentor: Neal Colzie.

Colzie, a former safety and punt return specialist, played nine years in the NFL for the Oakland Raiders, the Miami Dolphins, and the Tampa Bay Buccaneers. He's remembered by Raiders fans for helping his team win Super Bowl XI in January 1977 with his defense and punt returns, including a nifty 25-yard return that set up a touchdown against the Minnesota Vikings.

Gore knew Colzie as his godfather, a family friend, and his youth football coach. The first time he put on shoulder pads and a helmet to play organized football, Gore played tight end and nose guard. In his second season, Gore came under Colzie's wing, and his position changed in a hurry.

"When Neal Colzie became my coach, he saw something special about me," Gore says. "He put me at running back. I remember in my first scrimmage against another club, I had maybe seven touchdowns. I played running back from then on."

Colzie went on to coach Gore for several years in the recreational leagues that provided an outlet for youngsters growing up in Miami's rough inner city neighborhoods. But Colzie, who died of a heart attack in 2001 at 47, was more than a coach for Gore. He provided guidance in the absence of Gore's father, who left when Gore was very young and never returned.

"He was my godfather but he was like my dad," says Gore. "He was the one who kind of raised me. He made sure I stayed out of trouble and always had a good pair of shoes. What I remember most is he told me I'd be here one day, in the NFL. He always told me my time would come."

Gore took Colzie's words to heart, but the path he traveled was never easy. Even the game he so readily embraced alternately rewarded him and dealt him punishing blows. Then and now, though, nothing was more important to Gore than family and football, and his mother, Liz, was the link between those two emotional pillars. She was at once his emotional rock and his biggest cheerleader. From the time he was playing Pee Wee football, she would be at his games cheering him on. Now and then, she would even give him advice—sometimes loudly from the sideline—on how to make a move or even break a tackle.

At home, the single mom oversaw a household that at times had up to eight family members living in their one-bedroom apartment, including Frank's younger brother and sister. Through it all, Gore said, his mother found a way to provide for them while struggling through episodes of kidney disease.

"It was tough, all of us in that apartment," Gore said. "But my mom took care of all the people. She was on welfare, couldn't work because she was sick, and she still made sure we had food on the table and clothes on our backs. That's how strong she is."

But when Frank was a junior at Coral Gables High School and coming into his own as a football standout, his mother's kidneys failed, requiring her to undergo dialysis treatments.

"She almost passed," said Gore. "She was in the hospital for a while. It was tough because my mom was there for us all our lives. It's tough to see your momma struggling."

Liz Gore persevered, but more tests and more hardship lay ahead for her oldest son. After setting a Dade County record by rushing for 2,953 and 34 touchdowns as a senior in 2000, the heavily recruited Gore accepted a scholarship to the University of Miami. As a freshman, he ran for 562 yards while backing up Clinton Portis, who would himself go on to star in the NFL. But Gore, pegged as the starter going into his sophomore season, missed 2002 after tearing the anterior cruciate

Frank Gore *Photo © Michael Zagaris*

ligament in his left knee, his first major injury. He came back to start the first five games of the 2003 season before tearing up his right knee, leading to a second reconstructive surgery.

Gore's mother wouldn't let him get too discouraged, telling him over and over again he would work his way back.

"That's the reason I didn't quit. She kept me with a positive mind," Gore said. That's the way it was with the Gores, mother and son, helping each other. Even when Frank went to Miami, he didn't move out of his home. Instead of getting university arranged housing on campus, Gore continued to live in the family's apartment in Miami. He continued to help look after his mother and siblings, and when he got hurt, his family responded by giving him the support he needed to fight back from two devastating knee injuries.

"That's what made me a strong person, because I had to grow up early, since I was the oldest one and my mom was in and out of the hospital," Gore told *SFIllustrated* in a 2006 interview. "That's why I have a strong mind and I'm always trying to keep my head on right and go forward."

That attitude helped him come back from his second knee injury in nine months and regain the starting job in 2004 at Miami, where he ran for 945 yards as a junior.

Wary of risking another injury and anxious to start earning money so he could help his family, Gore decided to forgo his last year of eligibility and declared for the NFL draft. But his stock had fallen sharply because of his injuries. Before the 2005 draft, *Sports Illustrated* referred to him as the most overrated running back in his draft class. Five running backs were taken ahead of him, including three in the top five.

At about the same time, the 49ers were in a full-blown rebuilding mode after going a league-worst 2-14 in 2004. They laid the groundwork for Gore's arrival in San Francisco when newly hired coach Mike Nolan, in consultation with owner John York, brought in Scot McCloughan as the team's vice president of player personnel. McCloughan had been aware of Gore since 2001 when he was Seattle's director of college scouting and Gore was averaging an astonishing 9.1 yards per carry as the freshman backup to Portis.

"You wouldn't have realized how young he was," McCloughan said. "He stepped right in and produced, and you always pay attention to guys like that. You just saw he had natural ability, and it was so evident on tape, so I followed him."

McCloughan took note when Gore missed 2002 with a knee injury. Concerns over Gore's durability were raised anew when he suffered another major injury to the opposite knee. But McCloughan's questions about his health were tempered when Gore came back strong and put together a productive junior campaign. His interest intensified after Gore took the physical at the NFL Scouting Combine and received a solid passing grade from doctors.

Also persuasive to McCloughan was a scouting report on Gore from Alonzo Highsmith, a former NFL running back and a University of Miami standout.

"He was able to tell me things we see even now—Frank lives and dies football," McCloughan said. "If he even misses a practice, it bothers him. It's like taking a part of his life away. All he has is football . . . those are the kinds of guys you're looking for, who are always trying to get better. My decision was easy."

He managed to persuade York and Nolan that Gore was worthy of being taken in the third round with the 65th overall selection. The rest of the teams in the league cooperated by twice passing over the University of Miami running back until the 49ers could grab Gore.

Nolan said that if not for McCloughan, Gore wouldn't even be with the 49ers. "Scot was always big on him," Nolan said. "He was pretty comfortable with the information he had that led him to believe Frank was good not only on the field but the kind of guy we wanted on our team."

One of the first things Gore did with the money from his rookie contract, which included a $600,000 signing bonus, was purchase a four-bedroom home in suburban Kendall outside Miami for his family.

"I feel pretty good about that," says Gore, who shares the home with his mom, his brother, his sister, and his toddler son, Frank Jr. "Now my family will live better. From sharing a room since I was a little boy to having a master bedroom, it feels great."

Gore joined the 49ers in the same draft as No. 1 pick quarterback Alex Smith. Both came to the 49ers with the organization at rock bottom and both have been working since then to try to restore the team's luster.

During his rookie season, Gore shared time with Kevan Barlow. The 49ers had to watch how much they used Gore because he was playing with a torn labrum in each of his shoulders. Still, Gore showed glimpses of the speed, power, and elusiveness that would characterize his breakout season in 2006.

Near the end of a lopsided loss at Washington, Gore broke loose for a 72-yard touchdown run. It was the first career touchdown for Gore and the fifth longest run from scrimmage ever by a 49ers rookie.

In a December game at Jacksonville, Gore started in place of an injured Barlow and turned a screen pass from Smith into a 47-yard advance. He punctuated his rookie campaign with his first 100-yard rushing game in a season-ending win over Houston. He finished the year with a team-high 608 yards, becoming the first rookie to lead the team in rushing since 1990, when Dexter Carter's 460 yards led the club. Gore's total was the most yards rushing by a rookie since Roger Craig ran for 725 yards in 1983.

During the off-season, Gore underwent surgery to repair the damage to both of his shoulders. The successive operations on his shoulders, coupled with reconstructive surgery on both knees, raised concerns anew about Gore's durability. Not so with Gore himself, however. In reality, Gore felt that going into his second season, he was healthier than at any point since high school.

"I can't take back what has happened to me," Gore said. "I don't even think about it. I'm good. I'm all right. I'm just looking forward to going out there and proving I can get the job done."

Before the 49ers played their second exhibition game in 2006, Mike Nolan had seen enough from Gore to be convinced he was his running back. He traded away Barlow and installed Gore as the team's starting tailback.

"Some people come back from injuries pretty good and some guys don't," Nolan said. "Frank, thus far, has come back pretty well from those things. He does run strong and he's still a very physical player."

Despite early fumbling problems that saw him lose the ball four times in each of the first four games, Gore began to shoulder a good portion of the offensive load. In the process, Gore alleviated pressure on the still-developing Alex Smith and put a stamp on an offense that reflected his rugged, physical style.

He was at the center of a strong mid-season run that produced a three-game winning streak, the longest by the team in four years. Held in check by Minnesota's No. 1 rushing defense for most of the game, Gore broke through on sheer desire for an 11-yard run in the late going that allowed the 49ers to seal a win against the Vikings. The next week at Detroit, the 49ers' faced a third-and-16 during their first series. Gore got the handoff from Smith on a draw play, broke several tackles before getting in the clear, and then went 61 yards for a touchdown. His 148 yards in the first two quarters were the most yards ever in a half for a 49ers running back, and he had 159 yards by the end of the third quarter, when he was knocked out of the game with a concussion.

After a 2-5 start that included blowout losses at Kansas City and Chicago, the 49ers had clawed their way back into contention in the NFC West. Next up was division-leading Seattle, and the 49ers suddenly found themselves facing something they hadn't dealt with in years: a meaningful game deep into the season.

By the time it was over, the 49ers were at .500 and the Seahawks defenders were wondering what hit them. Alternately dodging and running over the Seahawks, Gore had the most productive game by a running back in the 61-year history of the 49ers. He had four runs of 20 or more yards, including two of at least 50 yards. In the end, Gore finished with 212 yards rushing, surpassing the previous high of 201 yards by Charlie Garner against Dallas in 2000.

Even his best game, though, included elements of adversity. Gore dealt with the problems the best way he knew how: facing up to them, dealing with them head-on, and then running them into the ground.

GAME OF MY LIFE
BY FRANK GORE
NOVEMBER 19, 2006—SAN FRANCISCO, CALIFORNIA

As a young team trying to establish ourselves, we knew this was a big game. Seattle had gone to the Super Bowl the year before and they were leading our division. They were where we wanted to be.

We hadn't played all that well early in the season but we were coming in on a little bit of a roll. We'd won two straight and my line helped me to have my best game the week before in Detroit, where I ran for 159 yards. But I didn't finish the game because of a concussion. It was the first one I'd ever had and it kind of threw me for a loop. I didn't practice until the Friday before our game against Seattle.

In practice you don't hit, and I was thinking about that going into the game. I felt I was all right, but still, I wondered if when I went out there against Seattle, when I got hit, would I get another concussion? That kind of thinking held me back during my first couple of plays against Seattle. I was initially timid about taking another hit. But after taking hits during our first series, I felt all right. From then on, I just went ahead and played with confidence.

We got the ball back at our 8-yard line after Keith Lewis intercepted a pass by Seattle's Seneca Wallace. The first play we called was a 30 dive. It's designed to lean toward the left side where I can run behind, or between, tackle Jonas Jennings and guard Larry Allen. The fullback, Moran Norris, comes in and leads the way through the hole.

The defensive line kind of slanted toward the play but the right side of our line cut off their backside pursuit pretty well. That opened it up for me when I cut it back toward the middle. One of their safeties came down but he missed the tackle and I got by the other one. I just kept running until they dragged me down. I didn't bother counting at the time, but I saw later I'd gone for 51 yards. We got a field goal out of that drive for the game's first score.

The run was really working that day and we stuck with it. The linemen were hyped up. They were rearing to go, to take it to them. We started mixing it up, running powers, running counters, everything. And our defense was playing great. They were getting us the ball. Walt Harris intercepted Wallace, and that set up a touchdown pass by Alex Smith. Then they forced a Seattle punt, and I broke through for a couple of 20-yard runs before Alex dove in for a score. By halftime we had a 20-0 lead.

But we weren't able to score in the second half, and Seattle scored a couple touchdowns. We were still leading by six points when I thought I might have ruined everything. Seattle had gone for it on a fourth-and-1 play from its own 37, and Bryant Young had stopped Shaun Alexander for no gain and we took over. But on the first play, I fumbled the ball and Seattle got it. We were running a counter, and their guy, Lofa Tatupu, made a good play. I didn't even see him. He hit me from the side and put his helmet right on the ball.

When I went to the sideline, I was pretty upset. There were about two minutes left, and Seattle could win the game with a touchdown and the extra point. My position coach, Bishop Harris, came up and told me to keep my head up. He told me to keep my head in the game, too, that it would be all right and that I was going to get another chance to carry the ball and make something happen.

Walt Harris stepped up and made another play, getting the ball back for us with another interception. The coaches sent me back on the field, and I'll never forget their show of faith. They knew I was going to try my best to make a play happen. When something like that fumble happens, it's easy to get down on yourself and let it affect your game. But with me, at that moment, it didn't, because I grew up. I was able to brush it off and play through it.

On the first play, they gave me the ball and I went for 17 yards. We were able to run down the clock and position ourselves for a field goal try. Even though we missed it, the pressure was on Seattle because there were only about 30 seconds left. The defense forced a fourth-down fumble by Seneca Wallace and with that we secured the win.

It was a relief for me but also a step forward for us as a team. Personally, it let me know that anything can happen and I had to be ready for it. If something bad happens, I had to be ready to fight through it and keep going. When a game is going well, I've just got to keep pushing and not let up. That game also stood out as a signal to the rest of the league. It showed that we, as a team, were moving in the right direction. Yes, we're still learning. But we're out there accomplishing things. We're out there fighting.

Gore's 212-yard performance in Game 10 included four runs of 20 or more yards and put him over 1,000 yards for the season, making him the 49ers' first 1,000-yard rusher since Kevan Barlow had 1,024 in 2003.

After the game, coach Mike Nolan, who sent him back out on the field and gave him the ball again after his costly fumble, presented Gore with a game ball. Gore turned around and gave each one of the offensive linemen a game ball of their own.

Gore's gesture typified why the 49ers offensive linemen loved blocking for him. Center Eric Heitmann said Gore recognizes their work in the trenches and he rewards their efforts with a burst through the line that makes the most of even the smallest opening.

"He's a running back who's not afraid to hit the hole," said Heitmann. "As offensive linemen, we work really hard to get holes open for backs. Even if it's just for a second, Frank will hit it, no matter what. We know that if we block our guys back 2 or 3 yards, Frank's going to turn that into at least 6 or 7 yards. He's always moving forward."

The stunning productivity against the Seahawks was just another example of that. It was his fifth 100-yard game of the season, and his 371 yards in consecutive games (he had 159 the week before at Detroit) was second only in team history to the 374 yards Delvin Williams had in 1976 when he ran for 194 yards at St. Louis before gaining 180 yards the next week against Washington.

After coming into the league under the radar, Gore's accomplishments in his second season were drawing notice from teammates and foes alike.

"That kid's special," said 49ers defensive end Bryant Young.

"He takes advantages of the littlest opportunities, and the next thing you know, he's breaking one for 40 or 50 yards," said Seahawks defensive tackle Russell Davis. "If you don't wrap him up, he'll get away from you."

Gore kept breaking away the rest of the season. In the last six weeks, he went over 100 yards rushing four more times, finishing 2006 with a team-record nine 100-yard games. The previous high was six by Garrison Hearst in 1998. Gore also appeared in each of the 49ers' 16 games, marking his first season in which he hadn't missed time due to an injury since he was a senior in high school.

His 1,695 yards led the NFC in rushing and ranked third in the NFL, behind only San Diego's LaDainian Tomlinson (1,815), who was the league MVP, and Kansas City's Larry Johnson (1,789). Further, Gore's average of 5.4 yards per carry was the seventh-best all time in league history for a running back with at least 300 carries. Gore had a franchise-record 312 carries in 2006. On top of all that, Gore showed his flair as a receiver out of the backfield with a team-high 61 receptions for 485 yards.

"Frank's a very well-rounded runner," quarterback Alex Smith said. "He's not a guy who fits the mold. He's not specifically between the tackles. He's not a slash guy. He breaks a lot of tackles. He makes guys miss. He can catch well. He can run well between the tackles and he can block well. He's a guy who's pretty good in all facets of the game, as far as a running back goes. He does a lot of it, which is pretty special."

The 49ers recognized how special when, with a year left on his rookie contract, they signed him to a four-year extension worth about $28 million. The deal included a $6.5 million signing bonus and $14 million guaranteed and extended the team's commitment to Gore through 2009.

"It was a little early because Frank just finished his second year. But as we said, if you identify somebody you want to have who is a good player, it's good to get it done," said Mike Nolan.

True to past form, one of the first things Gore did upon signing the contract was buy a new car for his mom.

"It feels great. When I was coming up I had to go through a lot. I got a chance to be a starting back and proved to people that I could do it. The hard work paid off," Gore says. Gore added the money wouldn't change his workman-like approach to the game because his hunger to excel and play well remains unchanged.

"It's not about the money with me," he says. "I am happy I have it and that I am secure. But I love the game. No one is going to have to worry about me slacking off. I love competing."

Gore said he believes he has a good chance to have even better seasons in the future and has set some lofty goals, including breaking Eric Dickerson's NFL-record 2,105 yards rushing for the Los Angeles Rams in 1984.

"Every time I step on the field, my goal is to be the best. I want to be the type of back who can be successful year in and year out. I really want to let a lot of people know I can play and get my name out there," Gore says. "God gave me a gift and I'm using it. I've got good feet and I've got great vision.

"I react to what I see," he says. "And when I see something, I go for it."

ACKNOWLEDGMENTS

Five months before he died July 30, 2007, while still in the midst of his personal battle with leukemia, Bill Walsh called me back to say, sure, come on over to his office at Stanford University and we'd talk about what he considered his signature game as coach of the San Francisco 49ers. We met last February, and it struck me then, as it does now, that the first thing he did was thank me for the talks we'd had in the past and the one that lay ahead of us as well. My thought, then and now, was, "I'm the one who should be thanking you." That notion really hit me when he stopped halfway up the stairs to catch his breath before finishing the climb to his Stanford office for our interview. Looking back seemed to be a tonic of sorts, though. Over the next hour, his eyes lit up and he frequently laughed and smiled as he talked (and I listened) about football and the 49ers and the great plays and players involved in a great game.

It was the willingness of Walsh, and Jerry Rice, and Steve Young, and the other 49ers to share their insights, time, and stories with me that made this project possible and even more importantly, worthwhile. I am grateful to each and every one of them.

I would also like to give a special thanks to Brent Jones, who despite short notice graciously agreed to write the introduction for this book.

My colleague at the *San Jose Mercury News*, Daniel Brown, was a helpful sounding board in the course of writing this book, and Rick Eymer provided a huge assist with the research involved in the project.

The 49ers public relations department, headed by Aaron Salkin, helped to put me in touch with players and provided access to archival material. That, along with readings from the archives of the Associated Press, *The Mercury News, The San Francisco Chronicle, Sacramento Bee, Sacramento Union, Oakland Tribune, Santa Rosa Press Democrat,* and *Contra Costa Times,* were crucial to keeping faith with history and lending perspective to the book.

I would like to acknowledge fellow reporters whose work also helped provide depth and texture to the crafting of this book. They include Bud

Geracie, Ann Killion, Tim Kawakami, Mark Purdy, Daniel Brown, Kevin Lynch, Ira Miller, Craig Massei, Greg Beacham, Matt Maiocco, Jim Jenkins, Matt Barrows, Joe Fonzi, Vic Tafur, Roger Phillips, Cam Inman, and Michael Silver.

Thanks to local football historians Donn Sinn and Joe Cronin, who provided me with a complete set of 49ers media guides dating to their inaugural season in 1946. Dan McGuire's book, *San Francisco 49ers*, was also extremely helpful in writing about players from the 49ers' early years. I appreciated the research assistance from Matt Waechter, an information specialist with the Pro Football Hall of Fame, who tracked down newspaper articles about Dave Parks and his move from the 49ers to the New Orleans Saints.

I would also like to thank 49ers' publications manager Katie Lewis for her help in securing photographs and several hard-to-find play-by-play game-books as well as former 49ers director of public relations Kirk Reynolds, who helped to arrange my interview (actually two) with Steve Young. Jason Jenkins, Ryan Moore, Andrew Lutzky and Katherine Madariaga of the 49ers public relations department as well as former staffer Fitz Ollison were also helpful in my pursuit of 49ers history, helping to track down archival material often tucked away in some remote corner of the building.

Thanks also to my editor at Sports Publishing L.L.C., Jennine Crucet, and to John Humenik for bringing this project to my attention.

Finally, a word of thanks for the patience and support of family and friends. You know who you are.

—DENNIS GEORGATOS
PLEASANTON, CALIFORNIA
AUGUST 2007